OUT
of the
ASHES

The Mother's love that healed the scars of the Bali Bombings

Big Sky Publishing Pty Ltd
PO Box 303, Newport, NSW 2106, Australia
Phone: 1300 364 611
Fax: (61 2) 9918 2396
Email: info@bigskypublishing.com.au
Web: www.bigskypublishing.com.au

Cover design and typesetting: Think Productions

 A catalogue record for this book is available from the National Library of Australia

All photographs are from Therese's personal collection and from Cath Byrne and Rada van der Werff's albums.

Author photo: by Paul A Broben Photography.

Cover photo: by Grace Petrou.

OUT
of the
ASHES

The Mother's love that healed the
scars of the Bali Bombings

www.bigskypublishing.com.au

MEGAN NORRIS

Therese remembers the friend who died in a floral tribute
that she arranged to have placed at the site of the bombings
before the first anniversary in October 2003.

In memory of my dear friend Bronwyn Cartwright
and the other 201 innocent people who lost their
lives, or were injured, in the terrorist attacks at Paddy's
Irish Bar and the Sari Club on 12 October 2002.

'For the rest of Australian history, 12 October 2002 will be counted as a day on which evil struck, with indiscriminate and indescribable savagery.'

Australian Prime Minister John Howard in his address to Parliament, on Monday 14 October 2002 – two days after the Bali bombings

CONTENTS

THE STRANGER

In her dreams, he appears out of nowhere. She sees him fleetingly as he passes her on his way towards the dance floor, his smooth latte-coloured face intense and purposeful, his eyes fixed on the crowd.

Eminem is blasting from the loudspeakers, and a machine is pumping smoke over the heads of the party people who laugh beneath the flickering laser lights.

They do not see him coming.

In a split second, the music, the lights and the voices have died. The pub is in darkness. Everything has stopped. The world is on hold.

It starts spinning again and everything around her is moving in slow motion. Hot embers and molten debris rain down from the night sky, and she is hurtling towards it. Then she is gone.

When she opens her eyes, the floor is hot against her back and the heat is choking. Flames are leaping from the walls and the people. The fire dances across her body, but she does not feel the burn against her skin.

These are the flames of hell. And she is dying.

She wakes in another place, where bright white lights bounce off pristine walls and sterile steel. The stranger has followed her here. He is bending over her, his penetrating brown eyes smiling into hers, filling her with dread and panic.

From the brightness a woman appears and gently pulls the stranger away.

'I've got this,' she says.

The woman tells her they are nurses, and she is in the hospital.

'It's okay – you're safe now,' she whispers.

The man leaving the ICU looks shaken. He is not the stranger who surfaces in her dreams – the ghost who slipped silently past her in the bar on the night the world stood still.

The man she sees when she closes her eyes wore a suicide vest attached to an explosive device.

This is not a dream. This is her worst nightmare.

And it is only just beginning.

Chapter 1

A DREAM HOLIDAY

A hot north-easterly wind crept in through the open windows of the tourist bus as it joined the procession of scooters and weather-beaten taxis along the dusty main road through Kuta's vibrant entertainment precinct.

Sweltering in their seats, Australian nurses Therese Fox and Bronwyn Cartwright scanned the teeming street, where horns honked and exhaust fumes competed with the smell of spicy food and hot chips.

On both sides of the road, holidaymakers battled for a seat in one of the cheerful thatch-roofed bars or open-air eateries which draw thousands of visitors every year to this busy Balinese tourist mecca.

The driver pulled over on the side of the road and sat with the engine idling as a few more passengers disappeared out of the door into the blistering midday heat.

'Where are we?' Bronwyn asked him from the seats behind.

The Balinese driver smiled amiably over his shoulder, his perfect white teeth gleaming back at her.

'We are in Legian Jalan, Kuta's club and restaurant district,' he answered politely in broken English. 'Always busy here ... very good!'

The doors closed and the bus driver rejoined the flow of traffic, sounding his horn at the mopeds and the occasional stray dog and weaving his way around the surfers who were drifting back from the beach after another perfect morning riding the waves.

From behind the wheel, the man continued his commentary about the various tourist hotspots lining his route.

'See, over there – Sari Club,' he said, gesturing to a traditional Balinese thatch-roofed property sitting languidly in the sun among the bars and restaurants.

'Tonight, the tourists will come here to drink and dance ... to have a good time.' He flashed his toothpaste smile at the two friends.

'Hey, maybe you come here too ... have some fun!'

Therese leaned over Bronwyn's shoulder for a closer look at the iconic nightclub that was a favourite party haunt for Aussie visitors to this frenetic holiday resort.

In the Sari Club's beer garden, the tourists sipped their lunchtime drinks beneath huts with straw roofs. This place would be packed inside and out after dark, said the driver.

On the other side of Legian Road, a crowd of bronzed Australian surfers in southern cross boardshorts downed cold Bintang beers in a small courtyard outside an Irish pub.

Scattered around them on chairs overlooking the main street sat a larger, noisier group of athletic-looking men in garish matching Hawaiian shirts. Therese suspected they probably belonged to one of the Australian rules football teams, whose players had descended on the bustling party resort for their annual end-of-season celebrations.

'What's the bar called?' asked 28-year-old Bronwyn.

The bus driver said the pub was called Paddy's Irish Bar – another popular watering hole for tourists and backpackers looking for a fun night out.

'October is always busy in Kuta,' he told them. 'Good time to come to Bali.'

The chaos and the crowds confirmed what the friends had already gleaned from the holiday brochures – that the long, lazy days of October were traditionally the busiest during Bali's dry season. At this time of the year, the hot north-easterly winds blew across the Indian Ocean from Australia, bringing the biggest waves and surfers from all around the globe.

Since the 1970s, the lure of Bali's spectacular surf combined with an abundance of budget airfares and the relatively short flights from Australia's east and west coasts had driven the Indonesian island's growing appeal as an affordable holiday destination at the end of the mild Southern Hemisphere winters.

In October, the hotels – like Bali's bars and beaches – were packed to capacity, the tourist trade significantly buoyed by the annual influx of football and rugby teams who arrived for the nightlife in the party epicentre of Kuta.

Although peak party season had not initially appealed to two single nurses wanting a quiet, relaxing holiday, it was the only month that Therese was able to arrange the time off for her first holiday without her two children.

Like her friend Bronwyn, the single mum had never been to Bali before, but her father, Chris – a frequent visitor to its shores – had recommended it as a perfect destination for a girls-only getaway.

They booked their flights to Denpasar for the first Sunday in October – the last month of the dry season – when the weather would be warmer and the crippling humidity lower.

The friends decided to spend the first seven days of their two-week holiday in Kuta, where the beach stretches like a sparkling ribbon along 2.5 kilometres of breathtaking coastline.

According to the brochures, Kuta appealed to visitors of all ages and was as renowned for its white limestone cliffs and ancient temples as it was for its beaches and vibrant nightlife.

So far, the holiday had exceeded their expectations. This picture postcard paradise straddling the equator was perfect for all the things they wanted to do – from the cultural sightseeing tours to the bargain shopping.

They booked what they imagined would be a quiet hotel, away from Kuta's main entertainment strip. From the photos in the brochures, it looked like a safe and peaceful haven for a couple of single girls seeking a leisurely break.

But when they arrived at the Bounty Hotel in Kuta, the lobby was bursting with noisy budget travellers who had clearly come for the nightlife and glitz that Therese and Bronwyn had hoped to avoid.

On the upside, their twin-share room was spacious and clean, and the hotel's staff was warm and welcoming. The Bounty was located a short walk from the shops and Kuta Beach and had an enormous outdoor pool boasting an impressive swim-up bar which served a variety of exotic cocktails –their only criteria when they booked.

The overseas getaway for two had originally been planned as a tropical holiday for four. Sadly, Bronwyn's younger sister, Jess was not able to raise the money in time, and their friend Michelle Larkins had cancelled her booking after securing a new job as a theatre nurse at the University Hospital in Geelong.

'I'm sorry, girls, but I'm not going to be able to make it this time,' she told her nursing mates, looking as disappointed as she sounded.

She made them promise to take lots of photos and have a drink for her in the swim-up bar when they landed.

The friends certainly hit the ground running and their week in Kuta was a whirlwind of early morning starts and even earlier nights as they packed in as much as they could and did everything they had read about in the brochures.

They visited the mountain rainforest, toured the ancient temples and enjoyed an idyllic boat trip to one of the picturesque islands in the Indonesian archipelago. They snorkelled, swam and shopped every day, and had even squeezed in a bus ride to the more upmarket resort of Seminyak, where they had watched the most spectacular sunset over the Indian Ocean.

In between shopping and sightseeing, they topped up their tans beside the hotel pool, and finished their days sipping cocktails in their bikinis at the swim-up bar.

But the outstanding highlight of their week in Kuta was the bungy jump that they had talked one another into at the Bounty's tour desk that morning.

'I'll do it, if you will,' Bronwyn had taunted Therese, waving the brochure under her friend's nose. There was a bar at the bungy jump where they could grab a couple of shots to take the edge off.

To her own amazement, Therese – who was terrified of heights – had accepted her more adventurous friend's challenge. But when they reached the resort, the bar was closed, and what had seemed like a good idea when they booked quickly lost its appeal when they saw the height of the jump, which ended in the pool below.

'I can't go through with it,' shuddered Bronwyn, peering up at the towering platform where other adrenaline junkies were already bungy jumping. Therese had also been having second thoughts. But it was their last morning, and she wasn't about to waste it – or her hard-earned money.

'Bugger it, Bron – this has cost us a fortune,' she said, taking a deep breath. 'We're here now – let's do it!'

And with adrenaline pumping through her veins, she took off up the steps, beckoning to her friend to follow. At the top there was no time to change their minds. The attendant pushed Therese off first and Bronwyn followed, screaming her lungs out. They emerged from the water with their hearts racing, relieved and exhilarated.

Later, Bronwyn confessed that if it hadn't been for her friend's determination, she would have chickened out.

'You never fail to amaze me, Taze,' she said, climbing out of the pool, unaware they had paid for two jumps and were going to have to do it all again.

This time, Bronwyn led the way.

Chapter 1

'If anything goes wrong, tell everyone I died happy,' she said, throwing her head back and laughing out loud.

The thrillseekers caught the bus back into Kuta on a high, happy they'd left the best until last.

For while the party was only just getting started for the newly arrived legion of Australians on 12 October 2002, the girls' week in Kuta was coming to an end.

Saturday was their last day and they were on their way back to their hotel to pack. This time tomorrow they would be in the mountain resort of Ubud, where they had booked themselves into a health spa. As the bus was leaving first thing in the morning, they intended to spend their last afternoon lazing around the hotel. Later, they planned to have a quiet farewell dinner at one of the nearby restaurants ahead of another early night.

But watching the boisterous Aussie 'army' converging on Kuta's 'glitter strip' on Saturday at lunchtime had given Bronwyn a better idea.

'We can't leave without having a drink and a photo,' she said. 'What about we come back to the Sari Club after dinner for a farewell cocktail?'

Therese had cautiously considered Bronwyn's suggestion. They were running out of time, and they still had to pack, she reminded her friend.

Bronwyn shrugged.

'Awww ... come on, Taze,' she wheedled. 'It's only one drink – we don't have to be late.'

And not wishing to be a spoilsport, Therese reluctantly agreed.

The bus dropped them off outside their hotel in Poppies Lane 2, where they hurried to their room to pack. They had left their hotel in such a rush that morning that the floor was strewn with all the bargains they had bought during the week.

They had carrier bags full of clothes, perfume, CDs and knock-off designer clothes, shoes and handbags – not to mention the toys and games Therese had bought for her children: Alex, aged nine and Katie, seven.

They had hidden a few of the more expensive items, like jewellery, under the bed, though their money and passports had been securely locked away in one of the hotel's safety deposit boxes.

Their Aussie dollars had stretched much further than they had ever imagined in this budget retail paradise, and Therese had no idea how they were going to fit everything into their luggage. They agreed to sort it out later.

They spent what was left of Saturday afternoon around the hotel pool and ended their day with a final cocktail in the swim-up bar.

Bronwyn had been in high spirits since the bungy jump and had not noticed that her friend had been unusually quiet since their return from Legian Jalan.

Whether the excitement of their high-octane morning had sapped Therese's energy, or the choking humidity had finally got the better of her she wasn't sure. But on the bus ride along Kuta's glitter strip she had been overcome by a strange feeling of apprehension – as if she was waiting for *something* to happen. She was not sure what that 'something' was, but it was not a comfortable feeling and she had not been able to shake it.

Therese's twin brother, Damien, had experienced the same niggling apprehension a year ago, when she first told him about her plans to go to Bali.

Chapter 1

'Don't go,' he panicked, replaying the haunting images of the terrorist attack on the crumbling World Trade Center in New York on September 11 in 2001.

Like the rest of the world, Damien had watched the destruction unfolding on his TV screen and was shaken by the tragic events.

If a terrorist organisation like al-Qaeda could attack a world power as mighty as the US, on its own soil, he figured no-one was safe anywhere.

'I'm not saying you shouldn't have an overseas holiday,' said Damien uneasily. 'I'm just suggesting you consider somewhere other than Bali.'

But his sister had refused to listen to his gloomy ruminations about the world being a dangerous place. Bali was a million miles away from 'Ground Zero', she told him. The only danger she was likely to be in was spending too much in the shops!

'Don't worry so much,' she said dismissively.

What could possibly happen to them in a health spa?

Damien wasn't sure, but he had left his twin sister's home in Grovedale, Victoria with an overwhelming sense of foreboding about this holiday.

Therese had not given his concerns another thought, and by the time she left Melbourne on 6 October, the conversation was long forgotten.

The holiday in Kuta *had* been the low-key escape she had assured Damien it would be, and apart from their sunset trip, they had been tucked up in bed early every night.

Their last night would be no different, promised Bronwyn. They would have an early dinner – and a quick drink and photo at the Sari Club – and be back at their hotel at a reasonable time, ahead of their early check-out the following morning.

Still, it *was* their last night, and they had decided to get dressed for the occasion. They might as well – there would be no dressing up in Ubud, where they anticipated they would spend most of their time at the spa in bath robes and slippers.

While Bronwyn rummaged through the carrier bags looking for something suitable to wear, Therese slipped into a casual white cotton skirt and a simple purple singlet. Around her wrist she sported the cheery Balinese shell and coconut bracelet she had bought from one of the local street traders, which captured the holiday mood in paradise.

It was still hot and humid when they wandered out of the hotel down Poppies Lane 2 to find the Indonesian seafood restaurant where they had eaten during the week. Bronwyn, a vegetarian, had enjoyed the Asian salad there and planned to have it again.

Over dinner they reflected on the idyllic holiday that had almost been over before it had begun.

'I can't believe you didn't think you would need your passport, you bloody goose,' said Therese, recalling the oversight that had almost cost them their flight.

Bronwyn laughed. She couldn't believe that she had been so flaky either and had not realised that Bali was a foreign country with a currency and language of its own.

Fortunately, they had been the first passengers to front up at the Garuda check-in desk that Sunday morning, and had arrived so early, that there had been enough time for Bronwyn to race home to get it.

Chapter 1

A friend had driven out to the airport to pick her up for the round trip to inner city Hawthorn and back, leaving Therese anxiously waiting on the footpath with their luggage.

Therese had watched the car tearing off towards city freeway, hoping Bronwyn would make it in time for the plane. It had been a challenge, on a single parent's income, to scrape the money together for this dream holiday and Therese had no contingency funds for another plane ticket if they missed their flight.

But the passport had not been the only thing Bronwyn had overlooked that morning. When they arrived at her unit, she realised she had forgotten her keys too and had had to break in through a window to dig out the passport.

Therese, unaware of the unfolding drama, had spent an anxious hour smoking and pacing the footpath outside the terminal, with one eye on the time and the other on the dwindling queue at the Garuda desk inside.

The first passengers to arrive at the airport that Sunday morning became the last to check in, making it to the departure gates just as the last travellers were boarding.

Seven days later, the holiday that had felt doomed at Melbourne Airport was now something they could laugh about, though it hadn't been funny at the time. On the flight over, Therese had dug out the inflight magazine and pointed to Bali on the map.

'See … it's not another Australian state,' she had chuckled. Bali was further away than they'd realised too.

At 10.35pm they settled the bill for their final meal and headed out into the street.

Although Therese was reluctant to say so, she had wanted to go back to the hotel. She felt uneasy walking down these narrow laneways after dark.

A few nights earlier they had got lost and ended up in a deserted car park where they had been involved in an unsettling encounter with a group of young Indonesian men.

The group were engaged in an animated discussions beside a stationary car that had ended abruptly when they noticed the Australian friends approaching them from the side street.

There were around half a dozen men, and while they had not said anything to the women, they had watched them so intently that it had stopped Therese in her tracks. There was something insidiously 'off' about the scene that had made her feel vulnerable and uneasy. She immediately suggested going back to the hotel, though she had not been able to explain why.

On their last night, the same ominous feeling crept over her again.

Her gut was telling her to go back to the hotel, but Bronwyn was on a mission, and Therese had kept her reservations to herself, because she had not wanted to disappoint her.

'Come on … just one photo,' she said, urging Therese to follow.

At approximately 10.50pm they wandered along Kuta's nightclub strip, which was even livelier after dark than it had been at lunch time. The place was lit up like fairyland, and the main thoroughfare, like the surrounding laneways and streets, was teeming with pedestrians, taxis, and beaten-up scooters.

They scanned both sides of the street but could not find the Sari Club anywhere. Therese was ready to call it a day when Bronwyn spotted Paddy's Irish Bar. The pub was heaving with people, and she decided they would have a drink and a photo there instead – unaware the club they had been searching for was a few metres away, on the opposite side of the road.

The friends followed the sound of pounding techno music into the pub, which had nothing remotely Irish about it apart from the green T-shirts the bar staff were wearing. The place was packed with backpackers and young holidaymakers who were gearing up for another big night on the town. From the accents around them, they could see that the Aussies were out in force tonight.

They made their way to the bar and joined the queue of tourists who were waiting to be served. The music continued to blast across the dance floor and the party was just getting started.

Trying not to spill their tropical pineapple cocktails, the two friends made their way through the crowd towards the back of the pub where young suntanned men and girls in skimpy outfits were dancing under the flashing laser lights.

Groups of tourists milled around the edges of the room trying to make themselves heard over the noise. Smoke was pumping from a machine behind them, and everywhere, happy, relaxed holidaymakers were laughing and drinking. The atmosphere was infectious, and Therese could see why the place was such a popular nightclub haunt among the foreign visitors.

The friends had just wandered onto the dance floor when a handful of young Australian guys burst into the pub carrying ironing boards under their arms. The larrikins were staying at a nearby hotel and cut a comical sight with their impromptu 'surfboards'. The group's high jinks sent a ripple of laughter around the crowd, who cheered as they made their way to the bar and ordered a round of drinks.

Therese suspected the jokers were on a footy trip and had probably borrowed their 'surfboards' from their hotel rooms. By now Eminem was booming across the bar and a few of the larrikins had abandoned their surfboards to join the girls on the dance floor.

At 11.08pm, Therese left Bronwyn dancing with the ironing board 'surfies' and made her way back towards the bar to grab two last drinks.

As she reached the bar, she was vaguely aware of an Indonesian man walking purposefully behind her in the direction of the dance floor.

And in a single shattering split second everything stopped – and the world fell eerily silent and still.

From somewhere outside her own body, Therese felt a powerful, invisible force propelling her through the air into an impenetrable void of darkness.

And thousands of miles away, watching a violent thunderstorm sweeping across the skies over Melbourne, her twin brother, Damien, felt it too.

And he *knew.*

Chapter 2

COUNTDOWN
TO TERROR

While Therese and Bronwyn were finishing their evening meal on their last night in Kuta, Australian soldier Rodney Cocks was making his way towards Paddy's Irish Bar to join his army mates for happy hour drinks.

Saturday night had also been Cocks' final night in Bali, and he intended to end his 10-day holiday the way he had started it – with another big night out on the town.

For the past five months, Cocks, 26 had been stationed in East Timor as part of the multinational UN peacekeeping forces posted there to quell militia violence against the East Timorese people, who had recently achieved their independence from Indonesia – one of the biggest Islamic states in the world.

In May 2002, more than 450 members of the Australian and New Zealand Defence Forces had joined the UN's Mission of Support in East Timor (UNMSET) to assist the fledgling nation of Timor-Leste during the handover to its new authorities.

In recent weeks, Cocks, a captain, had been dispatched to patrol the mountainous border of East Timor in response to intelligence reports that three members of an extreme Islamic fundamentalist terrorist group had illegally entered the new independent nation. The authorities believed the trio were on a reconnaissance mission to identify targets for a possible attack on the UN peacekeeping forces and Australian assets, including the Australian Embassy in Dili.

At the time, several fundamentalist groups were believed to be covertly operating across Southeast Asia and had been under close surveillance by the US Government and its Western allies. One of them was the violent militant network Jemaah Islamiyah (JL). The group was suspected of having an affiliation with al-Qaeda, the terrorist organisation responsible for the devastating attacks on the US mainland the previous September.

New intelligence in September 2002 had revealed that the group might be planning another terrorist attack to mark the first anniversary of the strike on the twin towers of the World Trade Centre in New York and the botched plot to crash a hijacked commercial airline into the Pentagon.

The threat of a possible terrorist attack in East Timor had prompted the Australian Department of Foreign Affairs and Trade (DFAT) to issue a warning the day before the anniversary, advising its citizens to avoid all travel to Aceh West Timor, West Maluku and Maluku. The warning had not extended to Bali or other parts of Indonesia, where tourist services continued to operate normally.

Chapter 2

In East Timor, the grim anniversary had passed without incident, though the intelligence had been partly correct. A terrorist strike *had* been planned for 9 September – but Jemaah Islamiyah had their sights set on a different location.

In early 2002, covert operatives from the terrorist cell had been called to a secret meeting at a hotel in southern Thailand to discuss a plan that would unleash mass destruction on innocent Western civilians. Attending the talks was the terrorist organisation's military figurehead – Riduan Isamuddin – also known as 'Hambali', who was believed to be the main contact in Southeast Asia for Osama Bin Laden's feared al-Qaeda terrorist network.

With Bin Laden now in hiding following the devastating terrorist attacks on the US the previous September, the extremists had been called together to hear about a new strategy to strike 'soft' civilian targets like bars and nightclubs instead of the usual political targets such as foreign consulates and embassies.

As the hunt for Bin Laden – the mastermind behind the 9/11 attacks – intensified, the terrorist cell had declared a jihad, or holy war, in retaliation for the US 'war on terror' in Afghanistan and Australia's involvement in East Timor.

Striking 'softer' civilian targets frequented by Western civilians outside their US homeland would inflict a new kind of suffering and claim more casualties. It would also send a chilling message to the US Government and its Western allies that the jihadis were only just beginning.

By August 2002, the peaceful Indonesian island of Bali was on Jemaah Islamiyah's radar.

The plot to attack Bali had first been unveiled at another secret meeting in Solo, Central Java. At the meeting, the terrorist cell's 'field commander', Imam Samudra, identified the island as a popular destination for US and Australian citizens. He was partly right. Bali was certainly a popular destination for Australians.

While Cocks was patrolling the border of East Timor, one of the militants, an Islamic teacher called Ali Ghufron – also known as 'Mukhlas' – had begun to identify possible targets for the attack.

Mukhlas had already secured the finance for the bomb plot from his al-Qaeda network in Afghanistan and had enlisted two of his younger brothers, Ali Imron and Amrozi bin Haji Nurhasyim – known as Amrozi – to play key roles in the terrorist strike.

On the orders of Hambali, the attack on Bali was scheduled to take place on 11 September to mark the first anniversary of al-Qaeda's attacks on the US. The attack had claimed the lives of 3000 innocent civilians and injured 6000 more. It was the biggest loss of American lives since World War II.

The new strike would unleash more suffering and send the message to the US and its allies that the holy war was far from over. But the bombs had not been ready in time for the anniversary and JL was forced to postpone the attacks until October.

Although DFAT's warning on 10 September about the risks of a potential terrorist attack in Southeast Asia had not specifically included Bali, the Australian Government had warned citizens travelling to Indonesia to remain vigilant about possible terrorism activity in the region.

On 26 September, the United States Federal Bureau of Investigation had also issued a warning to American citizens and other Westerners travelling to Indonesia, advising them to avoid crowded tourist hotspots – particularly places like bars and restaurants which were known to be frequented by Western visitors.

Indonesia's bloody history of terrorist attacks had given the authorities every reason to be nervous. In the past decade alone there had been a string of bombings by the various arms of known terrorist groups operating in Southeast Asia. These had included strikes on a mosque, a major shopping centre in Central Jakarta, and a car bomb in the basement of the Jakarta Stock Exchange which had triggered a chain of explosions in which multiple cars were set on fire. Most of those who were killed were drivers who were waiting by their employers' cars.

In May 2000, Christian militants had stormed the Walisongo school in Central Sulewesi, sparking a two-day massacre during which the militants reportedly raped and slaughtered 165 villagers using guns and machetes.

Three months later, a bomb was detonated by another terrorist group in Jakarta outside the official residence of the Philippine Ambassador to Indonesia. Two people had died and another 22 were injured in the attacks.

The bloody millennium bombing campaign concluded on Christmas Eve 2000 with a large-scale coordinated attack by al-Qaeda and JL on churches in eight different locations across Indonesia that left 18 people dead and injured many more.

Despite this reign of terror, no alarm bells had been specifically raised in relation to Bali, and in October 2002, thousands of tourists had flocked to the island for the peak holiday season. Many of the holidaymakers, like Therese Fox, Bronwyn Cartwright and ADF soldier Rodney Cocks, were Australians.

Cocks had flown into Bali on 2 October from East Timor on 10 days leave. He had booked a ground floor room at a budget hotel in Kuta with three of his army mates, who had arrived on an earlier flight and were waiting for him by the pool.

The Masa Inn was full of young backpackers, budget travellers and other ADF personnel from East Timor who were making the most of their annual leave. After his tense few weeks as an observer on East Timor's mountainous border, Cocks was ready for some downtime and a chance to party.

The army lads' holiday had quickly fallen into a routine of sleeping in late, followed by a spot of surfing and parasailing, or lounging around the hotel's pool

At 8pm the soldiers gathered for dinner at one of the restaurants near their hotel on Poppies Lane 1, and by 10pm had commandeered the long wooden bench in front of the bar at Paddy's for the happy hour that appeared to last all night.

Over the past 10 days Cocks, and his mates Nick, 'Cisco' and Mike had become familiar faces at Paddy's, where they knocked back Bintang Beers or bad locally brewed Germany lager and socialised with the Aussie footy players and the pretty foreign tourists. At midnight each night they found their way across the road to the Sari Club, where the party continued until well after dawn.

At 6am, as the staff at the Masa Inn were clocking on for their morning shift, the army rascals were staggering into their rooms to sleep off their boozy all-nighter so they could do it all again the following evening.

While Cocks and his mates were checking out the bikini girls around their hotel pool, and Therese and Bronwyn were checking out the bargains in the shops, the terrorists had arrived in Bali and were finalising plans for the chilling bomb attack that was set to take place at the end of the week.

They had come prepared. In early September Amrozi and another Islamic extremist called Idris had purchased a 1983 Mitsubishi L300 van from a trader in East Java.

Amrozi, a mechanic, had then driven the van to his home in the small East Javanese village of Teggulum where he stripped out the seats and air conditioning unit, and ground off the engine's chassis number. Afterwards, he installed a false floor in the back of the van, strong enough to fix a bomb to it.

On 18 September Amrozi visited a chemical shop in Surubaya where he bought a tonne of chemicals which would be mixed by the cell's bomb makers into a deadly bomb that was to be fitted into the back of the van.

In late September Samudra and Amrozi's younger brother, Ali Imron aged 22, travelled to Bali to conduct covert surveillance on locations frequented by foreign holidaymakers. In Kuta's Legian Road they quietly observed the tourists coming and going from the various pubs and restaurants. Samudra determined that Paddy's Irish Bar and the Sari Club were particularly popular among Western visitors and would be ideal targets for the suicide bombings.

The day before Therese and Bronwyn arrived in Kuta, Samudra texted Amrozi informing him that the chemicals for the bombs had arrived in Bali and instructing him to take the Mitsubishi van from East Java to Denpasar with Ali Imron and other members of the terrorist cell. The group arrived in Denpasar on Monday 6 October to find Samudra waiting at their hotel.

While the Australian friends were sight-seeing, the terrorists had been finalising their plans with JL's bomb makers - Malaysian-born Dr Azahari bin Husin and 'Dulmatin' – also known as Abdul Matin – who was a senior Indonesian figurehead known in the militant organisation as 'the genius.'

In the coming days, Samudra was introduced to the two young suicide bombers who were ready to deliver the terrorist organisation's grim message to the Western world and sacrifice their lives in the jihad.

During his discussions with the bombers, Samudra instructed that a third bomb was to be planted outside the US Consulate in Denpasar. The three bombs were to explode simultaneously, leaving the authorities in no doubt that the nightclub bombings were part of a broader message to the US about its war on terror in Afghanistan.

Two days before the bombings, Amrozi, Ali Imron and Idris wandered into a motorcycle dealership where they purchased a new Yamaha motorcycle to use in the bomb attack outside the US Consulate. While other members of the terrorist cell returned home to provide themselves with alibis for the night of the bombings, Samudra, Ali Imron and Idris remained in Bali with the suicide bombers ready to activate the heinous plot.

On Friday 11 October, Imron ran through the plan one last time and showed the suicide bombers how to detonate the switches on their respective bombs. He would be responsible for exploding the third device outside the US Consulate.

On Saturday night as the army lads were gearing up to celebrate 'Cocksy's' last night in Bali, Ali Imron rode the new Yamaha motorcycle 12kms into Denpasar. There he planted a small bomb packed with human faeces outside the US Consulate. The 5kgm bomb bore a device which would enable the terrorists to activate it remotely by one of their mobile phones.

Imron then rode the motorbike to a rental house in Denpasar where the van and the suicide bombers were waiting.

The vehicle had been carefully fitted with a larger, deadlier 2250-pound bomb, comprising 12 plastic filing cabinets loaded with explosives. Each contained potassium chlorate, aluminium powder and a sulphur mixture with a TNT booster that was connected by 150 metres of PETN-filled detonating cord.

Ninety-four RDX electronic detonators were fitted to the TNT. The lethal combination of explosives and chemicals was designed to create a powerful high-temperature blast similar to the destruction caused by a thermobaric explosion.

Idris then rode the motorbike back to Kuta while Ali Imron followed in the van with the two suicide bombers in the back.

It was a typically busy Saturday night in Legian Jalan and the streets were teeming with people. The taxis were working around the clock as they made the dash in and out of the entertainment precinct, dropping off passengers at one of the assorted pubs and restaurants along the glitter strip.

Amidst the procession of taxis, mopeds, honking horns and spruikers peddling their wares, nobody noticed the unremarkable white Mitsubishi van cruising along the main drag. At 10.55 pm, the driver pulled over on the side of Legian Road a short distance from the Sari Club, which at that time on a Saturday night was bursting with people.

Across the street, the Sari Club was buzzing inside and out. Its outside beer garden with its thatch-roofed structures was full of tourists and the loud techno music coming from the dance floor had attracted a steady stream of young holidaymakers into the club to party.

On both sides of the road, unsuspecting pedestrians milled innocently around the stationary white van, unaware that inside the vehicle, the countdown to terror had begun.

While people continued innocently past into Paddy's and the Sari, one of the bombers had slipped on a customised vest filled with deadly explosives. Ali Imron then instructed the other terrorist – a man called Jimi who could barely drive – to arm the more powerful car bomb.

Across the road at Paddy's Irish Bar, Therese and Bronwyn were on the dance floor. On the bench in front of the bar, Cocks' buddies had just ordered another round of drinks to toast his last night in Bali.

Cocks was late joining his mates that night because of some last-minute internet banking. He was leaving Dili first thing in the morning and had packed his bags and settled his bill in advance. He intended to swing past his hotel to collect his things early in the morning, after his final all-nighter at the Sari Club.

From the Masa Inn, he would get a cab straight to Denpasar Airport and catch up on some sleep on the two-hour flight back to East Timor before he resumed his peacekeeping duties.

His mates, who were staying on for another week, had headed off to Paddy's without him, while he wandered up to the other Poppies Lane to the Bounty hotel's internet café to sort out his online banking. But the hotel internet connection was playing up, and not wanting to waste precious time on his last night in Kuta, he had decided to join his friends for a quick beer and come back again later before he'd had too much to drink.

Cocks had found the army lads on their usual seat in front of the bar with a couple of English girls they had met at the Sari Club during the week. The place was packed that Saturday night, and he had chatted with some of the Aussie footy players who were on their end of season trips.

Among the crowd at the bar was AFL football star, Jason McCartney, who was enjoying a drink with his North Melbourne team-mate Mick Martyn.

After his big week of all-night partying, Cocks was struggling to finish his beer and his friend Mike had remarked on it.

'It's your last night, mate – you gotta go out with a bang!' said the strapping Kiwi, slapping him on the back.

Minutes later, Cocks left the group and wandered past the dance floor to check out the beer garden. When he returned, Mike was getting another round of drinks. Cocks gestured to him that he was off to sort out his internet banking. If he was quick he would be back in time for the next round before they went over the road to the Sari Club to continue the party. When he left the bar, Therese and Bronwyn were dancing with the surfboard jokers behind them.

At 11.05pm, as Cocks made his way out of the door, into the street, the suicide bomber was crossing the road towards Paddy's, strapped into his lethal explosive vest. In the van up the street, his associate turned on the ignition and slowly drove the vehicle with its deadly cargo down Legian Road and parked it outside the Sari Club.

Their terrorist associate, Ali Imron, watched them go before disappearing into the crowds for his motorbike ride back to Denpasar, where the third bomb was waiting to be detonated outside the US Consulate.

Inside Paddy's, Therese had just left Bronwyn dancing to Eminem. She was on her way to order two last drinks when the suicide bomber entered the pub.

As she approached the bar where the soldiers sat, she caught a fleeting glimpse of the Indonesian man walking slowly behind her towards the dance floor.

And in a single horrifying split second, the bomb went off. And everything stopped.

From outside her body, Therese felt herself hurtling towards the ceiling. She sluggishly wondered whether the shadowy figure behind her had been one of the 'ironing board surfies' who had crept up behind her and thrown her into the air for a joke. She was wrong.

The intense heat generated by the massive explosion had ignited the alcohol behind the bar, turning it into a powerful fireball that had sent dozens of bystanders flying across the room.

During the sudden impact, the force of the blast propelled Therese into the ceiling, her head slamming against a beam in the collapsing roof, knocking her unconscious.

While she lay lifelessly among the burning debris, injured people were beginning to pull themselves from the rubble, their shock giving way to mass panic.

Among them were the two North Melbourne footballers, Cocks' army friends and the two British girls who had been sitting with them.

Chapter 2

From 30 metres along the street, the sound of the explosion had stopped Cocks in his tracks. When he turned to see what the noise was about, he was stunned to see clouds of smoke and giant flames leaping from Paddy's. The force of the impact had knocked the power out and plunged the street into darkness.

Suspecting a gas bottle may have exploded inside the pub, Cocks raced back towards the bar to look for his friends. But as he ran, there was a deafening noise and a blinding flash as the second, larger car bomb went off outside the Sari Club.

The force of the impact threw him backwards onto the footpath, knocking him out. When he came around a few seconds later, he could see that the club where he and his mates had partied every night was ablaze, and screaming people were trying to escape from the flames.

The grass-roofed huts in the Sari Club's beer garden, which moments earlier had been packed with tourists, were also on fire and in the darkness, burning people were running for their lives.

On both sides of the street, shocked observers raced towards the flaming nightspots to help the casualties and rescue the survivors who were screaming for help inside.

Just a year earlier, the seasoned soldier had completed the army's demolition and mine warfare course, so he was familiar with the sound and smell of explosives. From the terrifying scenes around him, he was convinced he was looking at a bomb attack.

Like Paddy's Irish Bar, the Sari Club was a raging inferno, with flames as high as 50 feet leaping from the carnage. Everywhere, screaming people fled the destruction, many of them on fire or critically injured by shrapnel, flying glass and debris. Nobody knew what had hit them.

In 20 chilling seconds, the two simultaneous, carefully orchestrated terrorist strikes had transformed Kuta's formerly vibrant entertainment strip into a scene from a terrifying apocalyptic movie. Cocks had no doubt that there would be many fatalities from this horrific tragedy.

In the smouldering wreckage of Paddy's, Therese's eyes weakly fluttered open, struggling to comprehend the horror unfolding around her.

She felt hopelessly disorientated and disconnected, yet vaguely present. Amidst the chaos, she could feel herself floating out of her body, her mind quietly disengaging from the devastation in the bar.

Through her shock, Therese registered the intense heat of the floor tiles against her back. When she looked up, she could see a gaping hole in the roof where the ceiling had been and molten debris and hot embers raining down on her. Through the hole, the blackest sky peered sorrowfully down on the carnage, willing her to move, urging her to get out.

The extent of the destruction emerged in slow motion. It appeared before her eyes one horrific image at a time, like a surreal and hideous movie slideshow. The images appeared bloody and blurred at first – clouded by falling ash and choking smoke. But they grew sharper and clearer as they slowly came into focus and a more confronting and terrifying scene began to emerge.

Therese stared blankly out across the darkness, her eyes struggling to take in the charred and broken bodies trapped among the burning rubble.

All around her people were hauling themselves out of the burning wreckage. Others lay trapped where they had fallen, beside the living dead whose contorted mouths uttered muffled screams she could not hear.

In the force of the blast, Therese's eardrums had burst and she could hear little more beyond the faint repetitive popping of exploding bottles of alcohol, which had been launched across the bar like deadly missiles during the impact.

From her prone position on the ground, she was suddenly aware of the giant flames leaping from across the bar and racing over her body. The terrifying realisation dragged her back into the moment and a raw primal survival instinct immediately kicked in.

Mustering all the strength she had, she rolled weakly over on the hot tiles, trying to extinguish the flames her body was too shocked to feel. The air around her was incredibly hot and her eyes and throat were burning.

Somehow in her shocked state, she recalled the fire safety lessons her children had learnt at their primary school in Grovedale when a visiting fire officer from the local brigade told them what they should do if their house ever caught fire.

Drop. Stay low. Close your eyes and mouth. And get out!

Closing her eyes and her scorched lips, Therese shakily began to crawl across the debris on all fours, unaware that her skin was still burning and that her long brown shoulder-length hair was alight.

On autopilot, she negotiated her way through the rubble towards the street, where the agonised screams of the injured and dying filled the air on Bali's darkest night.

Outside, the strip, which only 15 minutes earlier had sparkled like fairyland, now smouldered under a blanket of fire and smoke.

Therese crawled into a nearby doorway and rolled in the dirt to extinguish the remaining flames. Slumped in an upright position with her back against the wall, she numbly observed the mayhem.

Everywhere, people with smoke-covered faces were attempting to help the injured. One of them was Jason McCartney, who had managed to flee into the street with his friend, but returned to the blazing building to help other injured people

Another was a young Victorian called Natalie Goold, 24, who had hauled herself out of the rubble and escaped into the street. Realising her girlfriend was missing, she had dashed back into the flames and had dug her out from under the smoking rubble with her bare hands and dragged her out to safety.

Goold's friend was fellow Victorian Nicole McLean, also 24, whose right arm had been crushed in the blast and was in deep shock. The quick-thinking Goold had begged two men in the street to give her their shirts, which she turned into tourniquets and bound around her screaming friend's injured arm. One of the men helped her to carry the injured woman 50 metres to a nearby ute whose driver was ferrying the injured to hospital.

Up and down the street, bleeding tourists screamed out the names of missing friends and relatives. Others, injured by flying shrapnel, sat on ash-covered footpaths covered in soot and blood, howling in agony. Many wandered the streets lost and confused, or mute with shock. Mangled cars, many of them still on fire with passengers trapped inside, lay upended in the road. Nobody was sure what had happened.

Watching from the doorway, Therese felt strangely comforted. From the darkness, a surreal sense of peace had descended on her and gently wrapped itself around her like a warm, comforting doona. Out of the chaos, a soft white light crept slowly towards her, growing bigger and brighter as it approached the doorway.

'Come closer,' it whispered. 'It's OK – you can leave now.'

From the centre of the light, the pale faces of Therese's children appeared, peering out at her from the brightness like frightened little ghosts.

'Please don't leave us, Mum,' they croaked.

The sound of their voices hauled Therese back to reality and the light shrank away, leaving her alone and injured in the dark. Over the confusion, a strangled voice cried out for help. The voice belonged to her.

From the street the tall silhouette of a man emerged from the smoke. The stranger was Cocks' English army mate 'Big Nick', a strapping soldier from Liverpool UK, who was part of the UN peacekeeping forces in East Timor.

Nick had pulled himself from the debris and had discovered the place was on fire. He had called out his friends' names and was relieved to find them covered in soot but alive.

Amidst the confusion and panic, they had observed their Kiwi friend Mike running across the road towards the Sari Club. Everywhere had been so chaotic in Paddy's that they had not heard the second bomb exploding across the road. They had been focussed on finding the English girls and getting them out of the blazing building.

Cocks' mates had found the two friends among the debris. One had suffered shrapnel wounds to her legs, the other had more serious injuries and had suffered severe burns to her body. They were covered with soot and blood and were crying.

Unaware of their own injuries, the soldiers had limped away from the carnage, pulling the girls along with them.

The scenes in the street were even more harrowing, as injured casualties from both explosions fled screaming into Legian Road, which was now in complete darkness.

The force of the two explosions was so powerful that it had destroyed nearby commercial businesses and homes and shattered the windows in neighbouring hotels, bringing staff and guests outside to find out what had happened.

One French tourist, who had only arrived in Kuta that day, was convinced there had been a plane crash. Others thought it had been a gas explosion. Bodies and severed limbs lay scattered across the roofs of neighbouring restaurants and the remaining shops that were still standing. Many of the properties were now unstable. The blasts were heard and felt by people more than 2 kilometres away.

By now, the destruction had cut off the power to the surrounding streets and laneways, and droves of panicking locals joined the exodus of panicking tourists making their way down to Kuta Beach.

From the smoke, the injured soldiers had heard a woman's voice crying out for help. Nick had followed the anguished cries to a nearby doorway, where he had found Therese slumped against a wall, her eyes wide with shock.

Kneeling beside her, Nick silently studied the extensive burns covering her body and knew it was bad. Every scrap of clothing had been scorched from her body apart from her cotton underpants, and bra which were as black as charcoal. Without saying a word, he took off his T-shirt and handed it to her. Therese weakly held it in front of her body, too shocked to appreciate how critically injured she was.

'We've got to get out of here,' he told her gently. 'It's not safe!'

But Therese was too weak to answer.

'You're coming with me,' said the burly soldier, lifting her into his arms and carrying her back to his friends.

Thirty metres away up the road, Rodney Cocks brushed the splinters of shattered glass from his body and checked himself for injuries. To his relief, he had suffered a few minor cuts and scrapes, though the muffled sounds around him told him his eardrums had probably burst during the deafening blast.

His shock had begun to wear off and adrenaline had kicked in. Where the hell were his mates?

He had begun to run towards Paddy's when he saw Nick's bulky frame limping out of the smoke towards him with Cisco, and the British girls.

Nick had blood streaming down his face from a shrapnel wound to his forehead and had suffered an injury to his foot. When Cocks looked closely, he could see that the bone in his mate's big toe was exposed and part of it was missing. Cisco also had a wound to his head and had been badly burnt too, and both of the girls were injured.

'Where's Mike?' asked Cocks, suddenly aware that his Kiwi mate was missing. His friends explained they had last seen him racing across the street towards the Sari Club.

Rodney Cocks' heart sunk. He had witnessed the more powerful blast outside the Sari Club and had no doubt there would be many fatalities from the explosion. He hoped to God that Mike had not been in it.

It was a few seconds before Cocks had registered the injured woman lying limply in his friend's arms. She was naked except for her blackened undies and was holding a T-shirt over her breasts.

Nick set Therese down on the road, where she wobbled unsteadily on her feet. Cocks was shocked by her horrific burns and suspected she was about to pass out.

'My name's Rodney, what's your name?' he asked her, calmly introducing himself and telling her he was from Melbourne.

She made no reply.

The stench of her burnt flesh made the seasoned soldier dry retch.

'What's your name?' he ventured again, struggling to compose himself.

'Therese,' she answered weakly.

Her entire face was black, and her eyes were wide with shock. Cocks could see that her skin was falling off and suspected she was about to die.

'Where's my friend Bronwyn?' she asked, looking vaguely around her.

Cocks scanned the flames and chaos at Paddy's Bar, thinking the worst.

'Come on, let's get out of here,' he shouted, over the noise.

He led the group away from Legian Jalan, pushing a path through the procession of locals who were sprinting past them in the opposite direction to see the destruction for themselves.

Around them, groups of Balinese people gathered on the footpath, gaping in disbelief as the soldier led the injured group back towards his hotel two blocks away.

Chapter 2

By now, his mates had noticed the giant flames leaping from the Sari Club and had guessed that this had been a terrorist attack. Two simultaneous explosions within a matter of seconds was neither an accident nor a coincidence, they concluded. The powerful explosion at the Sari Club had been a secondary blast designed to target the first responders who had rushed to help the survivors of the initial attack on Paddy's Irish Bar. The secondary bomb is generally a larger, more powerful explosive than the first, aimed at inflicting maximum suffering on those fortunate enough to have survived the first strike and the people who are trying to help them. This was a tactic commonly used by the IRA during the troubles in Northern Ireland.

Given the brief time lapse between the two explosions, the soldiers wondered if the secondary bomb had exploded prematurely. If it had gone off 10 minutes later, more survivors may have sought refuge at the Sari Club and the bomb would have claimed more lives.

An hour later, Cocks and his friends would have been in the Sari Club partying and might not have survived at all! He was afraid this is what had happened to Mike.

The irony of a terrorist attack on the tourist island of Bali was not lost on the experienced soldier. After patrolling the border of East Timor on the look-out for terrorist activity, he had not expected to be fleeing a new 'ground zero' on his holiday in Kuta.

Cocks continued to lead his friends away from the danger zone, offering words of gentle encouragement to Therese, who limped compliantly beside him. Her feet were hurting, and through her shock, she wondered why he didn't just sweep her up in his arms and spare her this agonising ordeal.

But her skin was already oozing blood and her burns were so severe that her skin was falling off. Cocks was too afraid to touch her.

He could see that her condition was deteriorating and when she stumbled over the stormwater grates in the darkness he stopped and lifted her over them. As he placed her down again, chunks of her charred skin clung to his shirt.

'Please don't let me die,' she begged.

Cocks held his breath.

'Stay with me, Therese,' he yelled, pushing her the last 500 metres back towards his hotel.

It was 11.25pm when they reached the Masa Inn, where a crowd had begun to gather outside.

By a miracle, Therese had hobbled 1.5 kilometres with the most shocking burns Cocks had ever seen. He was amazed she was still standing and was desperate to get her to the nearest hospital, though he thought it would be a miracle if she survived long enough to make it there.

Less than 30 minutes ago, Mike had slapped him on the back and told him he needed to end his holiday with a bang.

Now his mate was missing, and his innocent remark had taken on a whole new meaning.

Chapter 3

OVERWHELMED

At around the time that the suicide bombers were making their way into Paddy's, two blocks away, Australian teachers Rada van der Werff and Cath Byrne were settling into bed on the first night of their holiday in Bali.

It was less than three hours since Cath had arrived in Kuta to join her long-time friend Rada, who was waiting for her at the Masa Inn, where Cocks and his defence force colleagues were staying.

Like Therese and Bronwyn, they had come to Bali for a relaxing holiday and had also planned to start their getaway with a few days shopping and sightseeing in Kuta.

Cath had also booked them into a health resort in Ubud to do yoga and indulge in the sort of therapeutic pampering the nurses had planned for the final week of their holiday.

It had not been the holiday that Rada had initially had in mind, but she was looking forward to it.

In 2001, Rada had given up the job she loved as a special needs primary school teacher on Queensland's Sunshine Coast and was planning to travel to Afghanistan with her Afghan friend, Mahboba Rawi, who had been raising money in Sydney for orphans in her former homeland.

The women had met after Rada saw a story about Rawi's charity – Mahboba's Promise – on the ABC's *7.30 Report*. She was so inspired by the philanthropist's work that she had called the network for her contact details.

The two had met in Sydney and had forged an instant bond that extended beyond a mutual desire to help refugee children. Both women had lost their sons in freak accidents. Rawi had been mourning the death of her six-year-old son, Arash, who had drowned after being swept away to sea with other six other relatives and friends during a visit to the Kiama Blowhole, south of Sydney, in 1992.

Rada had also lost her only son, Matthew, 24, in an accident in June 2001 after a mine collapsed in Tasmania.

The tragic accident had taken a heavy toll on Rada, who had given up the job she loved after being diagnosed with post-traumatic stress. She had been embroiled in a legal battle with the mining company whose negligence she believed had caused the mine collapse, burying her son - a mining engineer - and another young colleague under 300 tons of rock.

Rada's family had been horrified when she mentioned her plans to visit orphanages in Afghanistan to observe Rawi's charitable work in action. They had urged her not to go, saying it was far too dangerous.

Since the terrorist attacks on the US in 2001, the US had escalated its war on terror and had drafted more troops into

Chapter 3

Rawi's native homeland. It had also stepped up the hunt to find al-Qaeda figurehead Osama Bin Laden – now the world's most wanted fugitive.

Rada had reluctantly abandoned her plans to go to Afghanistan. She had shared her disappointment about the aborted trip with her good friend Cath, who was teaching at an international school in Brunei.

Aware that Rada had been struggling with the death of her son, 35-year-old Cath had suggested they go to Bali for a relaxing holiday instead.

'It will do us both good,' she said brightly. They had never been to Bali before, and it would be much safer than Afghanistan.

Cath's colleagues in Brunei regularly spent their school holidays there and had recommended it as an idea place for a relaxing getaway. The 90-minute flight from Brunei to Denpasar made it a convenient destination for a quick overseas getaway, and would give Cath an opportunity to enjoy the nightlife away from the strict Sharia laws that prevailed in the Islamic nation where she was a primary school teacher.

'Why not come and stay with me for a few days first?' Cath had suggested to her friend. 'You'll be here for your birthday.'

At Cath's suggestion, Rada flew from Brisbane to Brunei and spent a few relaxing days at the tropical villa Cath shared with some of her school colleagues.

On Friday 11 October, Rada turned 52 and the two friends had celebrated her birthday with a swanky lunch at the upmarket Brunei Country Club. Despite Brunei's strict no-alcohol laws, they boldly sneaked a bottle of bubbles into the restaurant and hidden it under the table. Fortunately, the restaurant was empty, and they sipped their illicit grog behind the waiters' backs like a couple of naughty teenagers. Cath promised Rada that when they arrived in Kuta they would celebrate her birthday properly – without breaking the law.

Because Cath was working on Saturday morning, Rada had decided to go ahead on the early morning flight to Denpasar, saying she would spend the day exploring the shops in Kuta. Cath would join her after work on the afternoon flight from Brunei.

Unfortunately, the later flight had meant a short stopover in Singapore, which had delayed Cath's arrival in Denpasar. She had spent two hours in the transit lounge at Changi Airport browsing the shops, where she had found a book that appealed to her. *Love, Greg and Lauren* was penned by New York father, Greg Manning, whose wife, Lauren, had survived the terrorist attack on the World Trade Center the previous September. The book recounted Manning's inspirational battle to reclaim her life after the horrific injuries she had suffered when the planes struck the twin towers where she had worked. Cath enjoyed stories with an inspirational message and decided she would read the new book on her holiday.

When Cath's plane finally touched down in Denpasar it was around 8pm and she had developed a thumping headache. She had arrived in Kuta 20 minutes later to find Rada waiting for her in their twin-share suite on the ground floor, close to the room Rodney Cocks was sharing with his friends.

Their room had not been ready when Rada arrived that morning and she had spent a lazy two hours in the garden with her crossword puzzle watching the young guests horsing around in the pool. When her room was ready, she had taken a shower and gone for a walk around the neighbouring streets browsing the local shops. Rada loved shopping and promised herself she would return with Cath and splash out on some new holiday clothes.

But after her hectic day, Cath had felt too tired, and they had settled for a quiet meal at a restaurant near their hotel. After dinner she was feeling better and they had walked down Poppies Lane 2 towards Legian Jalan for a drink in one of the bars on the busy main strip.

It was dark in the unfamiliar side street, and they had changed their minds and decided they would grab a cocktail in the Hard Rock Café instead, which was in the opposite direction.

At 10pm they made their way back to the Masa Inn. In the other Poppies Lane, Rodney Cocks had just left the Bounty Hotel's internet cafe after struggling to access his online banking. It is possible they passed him as he made his way towards Paddy's bar to join his army friends.

At the hotel the women's plans for an early night had taken a U-turn when the friendly Australians in the room next door asked them to join them on the terrace for a welcome drink.

It was 11pm when they finally returned to their room. The air conditioner was not working. It was a hot and sultry night and Cath had spent the next few minutes lying in bed trying to adjust the temperature on the remote control.

At 11.08pm – the exact moment that the first bomb exploded at Paddy's bar – Cath pressed a button and was stunned to hear a huge explosion.

'What did I do?' she yelled to Rada as the lights went off and the building trembled. All around them, they could hear smashing glass, as the blast two blocks away shattered the hotel's windows and knocked the power out.

Cath was convinced her random pressing may had blown up the hotel's transformer. Large shards of glass continued to fall from the hotel windows as the impact of the second more powerful car bomb outside the Sari Club shook Kuta to its core. But to the shocked women it had sounded like a single enormous explosion.

The friends had immediately leapt out of bed and rushed outside onto the balcony where other guests had begun to emerge from their rooms.

Nobody knew what had happened. Had someone on the upper level of their two-storey building accidentally fallen through one of the windows causing the glass to shatter? Rada seriously doubted it; the explosion had felt too powerful for a fall.

The friends followed the other guests outside, where a crowd was staring up at an enormous mushroom-shaped cloud of fiery orange smoke hanging in the skies over Kuta.

'What the fuck's that?' asked one young guest, turning to his friends in alarm.

Nobody knew. Some of the guests wondered if a gas cylinder may have exploded in one of the nearby restaurants, or a generator had blown up at one of the bigger hotels. Given the size of the explosion and thick fiery smoke, others thought it was possible that a plane had crashed over Kuta Beach.

Among the crowd were members of the Australian Federal Police (AFP), who were on annual leave from their peacekeeping duties in Dili. The giant mushroom-shaped cloud in the sky confirmed what some of them had immediately suspected.

'It's a bomb,' observed one of the officers turning to his mates.

Chapter 3

Rada and Cath were stunned. A bomb? It sounded inconceivable.

'Surely not,' whispered Cath, certain the explosion must have been an accident.

Whatever the cause the blast sounded serious, and the friends rushed back to their room to grab some clothes.

They rummaged in their bags in the dark and grabbed whatever they could find. Cath slipped a bright yellow polo-shirt on over her nightie and Rada dug out a clean top which she pulled down over her pyjama bottoms.

When they rejoined the other guests at the front of the hotel, two young tourists were sitting on the steps near the entrance covered in blood.

One of the pair, a young European man, was trying to pull large shards of glass from his arms. Beside him, his girlfriend sat in a daze, soaked in blood. From the blank expressions on their faces, it was clear they were in a state of shock. A few minutes later AFP officer Tim Fisher came rushing into the hotel and Rada could see his hands were badly burnt.

People were running up and down the street, screaming that there had been an explosion. Suspecting there might be more injured casualties, one of the more practical guests urged everyone to return to their rooms to see if they could find any first aid supplies.

As teachers, Cath and Rada had undertaken basic first aid training, though it had not occurred to them that they might require medical supplies on their quiet, relaxing holiday. They returned empty-handed.

Inside the Masa Inn and out in the street, the scenes were utterly surreal. People were running on adrenaline and the atmosphere was now one of panic and fear.

A member of staff came into the garden and instructed everyone to strip the sheets and blankets off their beds and bring them down to the pool. From the nature of the injuries suffered by the two tourists on the hotel steps, she imagined there would be more casualties with similar wounds, or even worse.

They could help by setting up a makeshift triage area to prioritise the injured, while arrangements were made to transport those in need of medical attention to one of the nearby hospitals.

By now the power had gone down across Kuta and the few remaining streets with lights were also plunged into darkness. It was a black night in Bali which those who were there will never forget.

The hotel management quickly organised some emergency lights and placed them around the lawn by the pool.

The Australian teachers were spreading sheets and blankets across the lawn when Rodney Cocks arrived at the Masa Inn with his injured friends and the burnt woman Nick had found dying in the doorway.

A silence descended on the gathered crowd as the group limped into the lobby covered in blood and soot. Therese's burns were so confronting that a few of the young female guests were reduced to tears. The two English tourists now clung to one another, sobbing in other's arms.

Blood continued to pour from the shrapnel wound on Nick's forehead, and Cisco was trying to control the bleeding from his wounded toe. His own arms and hands appeared to be badly burnt.

'I need help over here,' shouted Cocks, calling out for someone to bring him a blanket. 'Hurry, she's dying.'

Cath stepped forward, trying to hide her own shock as she studied Therese's dreadful burns. Every piece of her clothing – apart from her cotton bra and underpants – had been scorched from her body. Her skin was completely black, and she was horrifically burned.

One of Therese's breasts was partially exposed, and her face was completely charcoaled. What appeared to be a burnt scarf or T-shirt, hung limply around her neck, which resembled rare, cooked meat. Cath would later discover that the charred 'scarf' was the burnt skin from Therese's face which had melted off in the intense heat.

Her long hair was still smouldering, and large areas of melted skin hung from every party of her body. Around her wrist was what appeared to be a bracelet, which apart from looking charcoaled was miraculously intact.

Rada was so traumatised by Therese's appearance that she had not been able to see beyond the soot. All she had registered was the reeking smell of burnt flesh and smoke that had followed the group in from the street. But her mind had not allowed her to process the severity of the burns beneath the black debris.

Trying to contain their horror, Cath and Rada gently introduced themselves and asked the woman her name.

'Therese Fox,' answered Therese, sounding surprisingly lucid.

They helped her over to the garden and encouraged her to lie down on one of the blankets on the grass. Therese meekly followed their instructions and cautiously lowered herself onto the blanket. They had been mortified to see the melted soles of her feet falling off in front of their eyes.

Cath and Rada exchanged alarmed glances, desperately hoping their patient had not witnessed this horrific spectacle. But despite her own shock, Therese *had* observed them peeling away, and knew immediately that she was in serious trouble.

The women wondered how this critically injured survivor had been able to walk at all, with burns as devastating as these and were not sure how their basic first aid knowledge could possibly relieve this kind of suffering.

At the reception desk, Rodney Cocks, scribbled Therese's name, age and address on a piece of paper and handed it to the shocked staff. It would help them to identify her at the hospital if she lost consciousness, which he anticipated she would.

From the talk on the street, it appeared that other burnt casualties had been seen jumping into the pools of nearby hotels to ease their suffering.

But Cath, who was accustomed to living in a hot, tropical climate, knew that the pool water would be loaded with chlorine and bacteria, which would do more harm than good to burns as serious as these.

When one of the guests suggested lowering Therese into the pool, Cath immediately discounted the idea. Even the local tap water would carry bugs capable of introducing a potentially lethal infection.

Leaving Rada with the patient, she disappeared to find the hotel's kitchen, where she gathered up all the bottles of chilled purified water from the fridges. Cath returned with her supplies and she and Rada took turns pouring the bottled water over their critical patient.

Chapter 3

Therese's flesh sizzled as the cold water splashed over her burns. Cath asked a couple of observers if they would mind helping the hotel staff to collect more bottles from the fridge behind the hotel bar and bring it to her.

She knew it was important to keep the patient conscious until they could get her to hospital and endeavoured to keep her talking.

Cath asked Therese to confirm her name again, and she repeated what she had already told them. In a lucid voice she told them her age and that she came from Grovedale, outside Geelong in Victoria.

She went on to tell the teachers that she was on holiday in Bali with her friend Bronwyn Cartwright who was 28. They had been staying in Room 318 at the Bounty Hotel in Kuta.

'Oh, my God ... Oh, God,' gasped Therese, her shock suddenly giving way to panic.

'W...w...where's Bronwyn?'

Cath tried to calm her down, but she was inconsolable.

'Where's my friend ... where is she?' she gabbled, the enormity of the situation overwhelming her.

Rada calmly told her that they were not sure where her friend was, but it was possible she had been taken somewhere else and was being cared for too.

Therese stared despairingly into Cath's eyes.

'Please help me,' she begged weakly.

Throughout the conversation, Therese's speech remained surprisingly clear and her answers lucid. Cath continued to maintain eye contact, hoping her questions might distract Therese from her own suffering. Cath did not want her looking too closely at her injuries and panicking again. It was clear to everyone that she was in an extremely critical condition and Cath wanted her to remain conscious and focussed until they could get her to a hospital for proper medical attention.

'My children … I want my children,' Therese suddenly blurted out, her thoughts now about Alex and Katie.

The teachers looked at one another with new alarm. Where *were* her children? they wondered. Had they been involved in the explosion that had left their mother so badly injured? At this early juncture they still believed that the blast must be a dreadful accident. It had not occurred to anyone – apart from the AFP officers and the defence force soldiers – that it might have been caused by a terrorist bomb, or that there had been multiple strikes on two of the busiest tourist haunts in Kuta's popular entertainment precinct.

'Where are your children?' asked Cath, desperately trying to retain her own composure.

Calming down, Therese remembered that Alex and Katie were at home in Grovedale with her mother.

The teachers tried to distract her by keeping her talking. It had now been 15 minutes since she had arrived at the Masa Inn and the shock was replaced by paralysing pain.

'Is there anyone you want us to call?' asked Rada, kneeling beside her.

'You mentioned your mother lives in Victoria. Would you like us to contact her?'

Therese began to panic. Her parents had been separated for years, and her elderly mother would not cope with this news.

'No. Not my mum,' she told them decisively. 'Call my dad.'

Therese told Rada her father's mobile number and explained that he lived in Tewantin on Queensland's Sunshine Coast.

'I'm from Tewantin too,' said Rada, eager to keep the conversation going.

'What's your dad's name? Maybe I know him.'

Therese told her that her dad was Chris Fox, a local accountant who had an office in Tewantin's main street. The teachers were amazed by the coincidence.

'I know where his office is,' said Rada.

Therese went on to explain that she and her children had also lived in Queensland. She had separated from her children's father before her daughter, Katie, was born. They had lived in Noosa for 18 months, near her dad. They had returned to Victoria because the kids had missed their own father and their grandmothers.

Keeping her engaged, Cath remarked on this new coincidence. She told Therese that before she had accepted her teaching position in Brunei, she had lived outside Noosa in the neighbouring suburb of Sunshine Beach and had taught at the same school as Rada.

The teachers continued to make small talk about this pretty pocket of the Sunshine Coast that they all knew so well.

Rada told her it was possible they may have passed one another on the streets of Tewantin or Noosa. She had certainly passed Therese's father's office. She assured her she would call him and let him know what had happened.

But what *had* happened? wondered Therese, beginning to panic about Bronwyn again. She remembered they had been drinking and dancing in Paddy's Irish Bar. Then something had happened – she could not recall what it had been.

Her eyes began to close.

'I'm so thirsty,' she choked, telling them her throat was burning.

Cath and Rada were not sure whether they should be giving her water and decided to err on the side of caution. They filled the small blue plastic cap from one of the bottles with a tiny amount of water, and gently wet Therese's lips to keep her mouth moist.

By now, the guests had returned with more bottled water from the hotel bar and Cath and Rada began to pour it over her, and over one of the blankets. They placed the wet blanket over their injured casualty to keep her cool. By now Therese was wracked with pain.

While the teachers were tending to Therese, Cocks and a few of the other army guys from the hotel were out on the street trying to organise transport to take the casualties to hospital. His friends also needed urgent medical attention, but Therese would die if they didn't get her to hospital quickly.

Cocks had spotted a taxi outside the hotel foyer and another pulling up behind him. The soldier addressed the drivers in Bahasa, the official language of Indonesia.

'Do you speak English?' he asked.

One of the drivers said he did.

Cocks had explained that he needed to get his injured friends to hospital and was prepared to pay them in advance. One of the women was so badly hurt that unless she got help right away, she was not going to make it.

The first driver had refused. He did not want blood in his taxi.

The frustrated soldier offered him more money. It made no difference. The driver drove off leaving Cocks on the footpath hurling abuse at him.

Chapter 3

Over the past 10 minutes, more casualties had continued to arrive at the triage by the pool. Many were screaming in pain. Everywhere on the hotel's floor pools of sticky blood mingled with soot and broken glass.

A foul smell of burnt flesh hung in the air outside and guests and staff were taking it in turns to pour cold water on burnt bodies or wrapping tourniquets made from clean cotton sheets around shrapnel wounds.

The casualties were not just tourists but included several locals – mainly hospitality workers who had suffered burns. Some were passing pedestrians who had been injured by flying shrapnel or debris.

Everyone wondered how many more people were hurt. From the horrors that Cocks had already glimpsed from the street outside the Sari Club, he imagined there might be hundreds.

By now Cocks and another guest – Australian Federal Police officer Frank Morgan – had spoken to the hotel manager, who had been woken by the commotion. He was out in the street in his shorts and sandals helping his injured guests. And Cocks and Morgan had explained that they urgently needed transport to ferry the injured to hospital and the manager disappeared to see what he could find. He returned a few minutes later telling them he had managed to organise two trucks and had instructed the drivers to take the casualties to the Bali International Medical Centre, which was the closest clinic to the hotel.

The locals referred to the small private ex-pat clinic as 'beemak', which was its acronym, BIMC. He explained that 'beemak' was closer than the big Sanglah General Hospital in Denpasar, which would already be overrun with people.

The two men returned to the garden where Cath was comforting Therese, and Rada was helping the burnt AFP officer, Tim Fisher, who was lying on a blanket on the grass.

In the 18 minutes since Therese had arrived, their makeshift triage had been filling with other casualties, and a few other guests had begun taking turns to pour cold bottled water over Cocks' burnt friends and helping to dress their injuries.

Near Therese, on another blanket, lay the young European tourist they had found on the hotel steps with glass in his arms. The most they could do was comfort him and wrap clean sheets around his wounds until they could get him to hospital. All the while, Therese lay trembling with shock under her wet blanket. Cath endeavoured to keep her talking.

Cocks helped Morgan to transfer her onto a dry blanket, then with the help of half a dozen strapping army colleagues, they carried her out to one of the open trucks and gently placed her into the back. Rodney Cocks was amazed that Therese was still conscious, though her paralysing pain had escalated, and she was screaming in agony.

'Please don't leave me,' she said, turning to Cath and Rada with fearful eyes.

'Don't worry,' said Cath, climbing into the back of the truck with her. 'We're coming with you.'

Frank Morgan climbed into the front of the truck with the driver, making room on the seat for Fisher, whose hands needed urgent attention. The driver sped off towards BIMC and Cocks helped his two friends into the second truck with one of the more seriously injured English girls. The second driver headed off after the others.

Cocks was intending to walk back to Legian Road to look for his missing Kiwi friend when he spotted a figure running towards him wearing only his shorts and shoes. He was overcome with relief to see that it was Mike. In the chaos and confusion after the blast at Paddy's, Mike had been found wandering the street in the dark by a couple who had taken him back to their hotel.

The soldier's back, neck and arms had been badly burnt in the inferno at Paddy's, and his ears were also burnt. The kindly couple had helped him into their shower and hoped the cool running water would help to soothe his injuries.

Cocks could see that the skin on Mike's back was black and sticky and that some of his burns were bleeding. He was thankful his friend had not made it to the Sari Club as he likely would not have survived.

Cocks explained that the trucks would be back soon for another hospital run and led him towards the triage area, where the remaining English girl was still being attended to. He took turns pouring cold water over his mates' back, reassuring him that the transport would not be far away.

While they waited, Mike – a squadron leader and engineer with the Royal NZ Airforce – called his wife, and Cocks contacted his own parents in Melbourne to tell them what had just happened and assure them that they were OK.

Afterwards, Cocks called one of his senior officers in East Timor and told him about the bombings in Bali. Within minutes, a more senior officer from the UN Peacekeeping Mission had called back. He instructed Cocks to collect information about how many armed forces personnel were among the injured or dead, and how many active soldiers were still on the ground. He also needed to know how many overall casualties there were. He made Cocks the official liaison between the UN forces and the Australian Federal Police.

While Cocks was updating the UN authorities about the attacks in Bali, Therese was on her way to the Bali International Medical Centre. It had been touch-and-go in the back of the truck and Cath and Rada had been doing their best to keep the deteriorating patient conscious.

In the distance, the inferno at the Sari Club continued to rage and all roads in and out of the area were being cordoned off by the Indonesian authorities.

Fortunately, the local truck driver knew the area well and had avoided the chaos by taking the back routes down Kuta's narrow lanes and side streets, aware that the patient in the back desperately needed urgent medical attention.

From the back of the truck, Therese weakly asked again about her missing friend. Cath tried to allay her rising anxiety. It was clear that she was growing weaker by the minute, and it was important to preserve her energy by keeping her as calm as possible.

'She may have been taken somewhere else,' Cath explained again, reassuring her that wherever Bronwyn was, they would find her.

The roads around Kuta were more chaotic than ever in the aftermath of the explosions. With the power out, driving was even more hazardous in the dark. The back streets of Kuta were riddled with potholes and bumps, which made the journey more painful for Therese, who was screaming out in the back.

Cath had continued to offer her small capfuls of water to sip and had kept her talking. She had asked Therese what she did in Geelong and discovered that she was a nurse at an aged care facility in Grovedale. Bronwyn was a nurse, too, she told them.

'A lot of people were hurt,' Therese remembered, her eyes clouding with pain as she tried to fathom again what had happened.

The teachers quickly changed the subject to her holiday, and Therese told them that this had been their last day. They were due to leave in the morning for Ubud, where they had booked into a health spa. She had also told them how about the bungy jumping.

'I won't be doing it again,' she told them.

The women looked at one other, shaken by the irony of this tragic situation.

Under different circumstances, they may have crossed paths with Therese and her friend at the health retreat in Ubud. But from the look of her devastating injuries, they were not sure she was going to survive the night.

Trying to keep her voice positive and calm, Rada told her that they were on their way to hospital, where she would receive the medical help she needed.

'We'll be there very soon,' she assured Therese, who was drifting in and out of consciousness.

Cath hoped it would be sooner than later. Therese's pain was now out of control and her cries had grown more anguished with every bump in the road.

It was midnight when the truck driver finally pulled up outside the emergency doors of BIMC, where a large crowd of locals had gathered on the footpath outside.

Two Balinese nurses rushed out of the sliding doors, frantically waving their arms at the truck.

'No … no … so sorry, we can't take any more patients,' gabbled one of the stricken nurses in broken English. From her sitting position in the back of the open truck, Cath thought the poor woman looked distraught and overwhelmed.

Frank Morgan's expression was dour. He had no idea what was going on inside the clinic, but he *did* know that this woman was close to death and needed treatment urgently.

"Get her out now,' he instructed the two teachers, climbing out of the truck. 'We can't go anywhere else – she *has* to come here.'

Cath looked at Therese, writhing in pain, and doubted she would survive a trip to another location if they were turned away from here.

The nurses looked agitated as Morgan and the driver proceeded to open the truck. But after observing the injured woman's shocking burns, they offered no further resistance and led the group towards the entrance doors.

Hundreds of locals had congregated around the entry to the medical centre's emergency department. Cath and Rada asked some of the stronger men in the crowd if they would help them carry Therese into the clinic. Nobody stepped forward or uttered a word. The locals continued to watch in silence as the two Australian teachers struggled to help Morgan and the driver lift her out of the truck in her blanket and carry her in through the doors.

The ghastly scene that greeted them inside the medical centre took everyone's breath away. Like the floor, the sterile steel sinks were covered in blood and everywhere they looked there were critically injured people screaming out for help.

Chapter 3

Lifeless half-conscious bodies littered the floor, many with faces as black as charcoal. Around the room, more casualties were propped against the walls, with shards of glass and debris or exposed bones protruding from their skin. All around them injured people shrieked in agony. Others were so traumatised their words had dried up completely.

From the surreal images around them, the friends were filled with the ghastly realisation that the explosion at Paddy's bar must have been enormous to have injured so many people so badly.

Rada imagined that on a normal Saturday night, the staff at this tiny clinic would probably have been treating the occasional heart attack or car crash victim, or maybe the odd surfer with a cut or fracture.

But it had been less than an hour since the explosion, and the medical centre and its staff were drowning under the deluge of casualties that continued to arrive on an unprecedented scale.

Apart from the British nurse, on the front desk, most of the staff were Indonesian and spoke Bahasa, though a couple of Western nurses also spoke English. They were rushed off their feet as they dashed around taking people's blood pressure, hooking patients to IV drips and taking blood samples for possible transfusions. It appeared to Cath and Rada that everyone was critical and that it would be a challenge for the staff to prioritise which patients needed their help the most.

The scope of injuries appeared to be as complex as they were critical, and the medical centre was ill equipped to deal with them. Rada heard one of the English-speaking nurses reminding her colleagues to make sure all the used syringes were placed in the plastic containers, which were rapidly filling up.

There were only three beds in the treatment room which were already full when they arrived. Rada and Cath had helped Frank Morgan to lower Therese onto the floor near the entrance doors. They tried not to stare at the man in the bed nearest to them, who lay clutching his leg, and screaming and twisting in agony. Beside him lay another young patient with a serious head injury and bones protruding from his arm.

Slumped against the wall at the back of the room was another young woman with what appeared to be a serious head injury. She sat in silence, obviously traumatised, staring vacantly into space.

They would later discover that the patient was a Sydney tourist, Carren Smith, aged 32, who had come to Bali with the intention of taking her life following the suicide of her fiancé a year earlier.

She had chosen the first anniversary of his death on 14 October for her own suicide. But she had not shared her tragic intentions with the two girlfriends who had travelled from Sydney to Bali with her that morning.

In a cruel twist of fate, Smith – and her friends Charmaine Whitton, 29, and Jodi Wallace, 30 – were at the Sari Club when the second bomb went off. Now Smith's friends were missing, and she was seriously burnt and battling what looked like a life-threatening head injury.

But Cath and Rada, unaware of the second explosion or the tragic motivation behind Carren's trip to Bali – or her missing friends – wrongly assumed that everyone at the clinic had been the unfortunate victims of a single explosion in Paddy's bar. At the time, Cath still believed the blast had been accidental. But from the grave nature of the injuries around them, Rada now believed the AFP officer at the hotel may have been right when he said the mushroom-shaped cloud in the sky had been caused by a bomb explosion.

While they comforted Therese, another Australian tourist called Brendan Barry was brought into the medical centre suffering extensive burns and injuries to his arms. He had been in the garden at the Sari Club less than 10 minutes when the car bomb exploded 5 metres away from him. Now his friend Jodie Cearns was among those missing and he was seriously injured. With no beds to spare, he was placed on the floor close to Therese who continued to scream in pain.

'Where am I?' she asked Cath, drifting in and out of consciousness.

'You are in hospital, Therese,' the teacher gently reminded her.

Cath glanced anxiously around the room; it seemed everyone was calling out for pain relief. If Therese was to receive the morphine she obviously needed, she had to get it now before it ran out. She leant forward and whispered to Therese to scream as loud as she could.

'If you don't, they will run out of morphine and there will be nothing left for you,' she said.

Therese took Cath's advice and screamed louder. Her throat burned as her cries for help reverberated around the clinic. Two nurses immediately rushed over to her and handed Cath a large bottle of saline solution.

'Pour this over her,' they instructed, checking Therese's arms for a suitable access vein where they could insert a line for an intravenous morphine drip.

'Stop … stop it … stop it! You're hurting me!' Therese shrieked, writhing in agony as the salty solution stung her deep burns.

She looked at Cath in horror, her eyes like saucers.

'Why are you doing this to me? Please … please don't,' she begged.

Cath took a deep breath, and trying not to burst into tears herself, continued to pour the cool saline solution all over Therese.

'I'm so sorry, Therese,' she whispered, her heart breaking for her.

The nurses handed her another bottle, and she continued to pour.

They looked frantic. They had not been able to find a suitable vein beneath the burnt skin on her arms, which both resembled chargrilled meat.

They scoured her legs instead, hoping to find another vein where they might be able to insert an intravenous line. The patient's injuries were so extensive that they eventually gave up and one of the nurses rushed off to find help. Rada noticed Therese's sticky black skin was stuck like glue to the blanket.

The nurse returned with a male nurse who managed to insert an access line into a vein in Therese's neck. The procedure was difficult and painful, with the patient writhing and screaming in pain as the IV line pierced through layers of scorched skin.

The entire time, Cath and Rada maintained a calm and positive front, though their hearts wept for the young mother. Her anguished cries were unbearable, but the last thing they wanted was for their distress to add to her trauma and fear.

With the IV line now safely attached to Therese's neck, one of the nurses handed the friends a couple of bags, one containing fluid, another filled with morphine. She gestured to them to hold the IV bags over the patient, who continued to writhe in pain on the floor.

As the morphine finally started to kick in, the gut-wrenching cries slowly subsided, and Therese began to lose consciousness. It was becoming difficult to keep her talking, though she repeatedly continued to ask through the haze of opiates if there had been any news about her missing friend.

The survivors continued to arrive. Rada, observing the overwhelmed staff, asked one of the doctors how they could help.

'Just be here,' he said, wiping the perspiration from his brow.

Amid the chaos the Balinese receptionist began calling some of the clinic's off-duty staff, beginning with the head charge nurse, Stefanie Breen.

'There's been some sort of explosion – everyone is burnt,' the receptionist told Breen, sounding frantic.

Breen, who had just returned from a night out, said she would come into work as fast as she could.

'Call in as many staff as you can,' she instructed, rushing off to grab her car keys.

On the drive into Kuta from Sanur, Breen collected US trauma specialist, Dr Art Sorrel, who had been in Bali training some of their doctor's in trauma and critical care medicine. He had only been there three days.

In the distance they could see towers of flames and thick smoke filling the Kuta skyline. Breen wondered if one of the local petrol stations had exploded. She had frequently observed motorists dragging on lit cigarettes while filling their cars and scooters with petrol and had always thought it was a catastrophe waiting to happen.

But nothing could have prepared them for the scenes at the small private medical centre where around 1000 locals had gathered in front of the entrance watching. All around them, taxis and mopeds continued to arrive with more injured casualties who were being turned away by distraught orderlies.

The scenes inside resembled a war zone. Breen was shocked to find the reception area flooded with blood and water as badly burnt patients fought to get to the 20-litre filtered water machine for cool water to pour over their injuries.

'Everyone stop!' she shouted, immediately taking charge.

'Someone's going to slip and hurt themselves.'

She called someone over to mop up the mess, and took over the triage system with Dr Sorrel, prioritising patients according to their injuries.

Breen knelt beside Therese, who was now writhing in agony on the floor.

'You're going to be okay,' said the New Zealand-trained nurse, giving her another shot of morphine for the pain.

She carried out a preliminary assessment of the patient and determined that Therese had suffered burns to 90% of her body - most of them third degree burns.

'Oh my God,' she thought, convinced she had to be mistaken. How could anyone still be alive and conscious with such severe injuries.

Breen asked Dr Sorrel to examine her again.

'No, you're right,' he concurred, his face serious.

Studying the severe burns to Therese's face and neck they determined she needed to be on a ventilator before her breathing became a problem.

Chapter 3

'We don't have any ventilators here,' said Breen, shouting to the receptionist to ring around the other hospitals to find out who had a spare ventilator so they could organise the patient's immediate transfer.

While Therese was screaming for morphine, Cocks arrived at BMIC with Mike and their injured English friend. The crowd outside was bigger than ever and the car park was mayhem as trucks, taxis and motorbikes unloaded more injured people.

Inside the clinic the British nurse on the desk advised Cocks to take his injured friends to the Sanglah General Hospital in Denpasar. But as they left, an orderly suggested a medical clinic in Kuta called SOS. Hopefully it would not be as busy as the big general hospital would be and his friends might be seen faster.

Cocks watched the truck leaving with his friends and returned to the desk to show the nurse his army ID. He explained that he had been told to account for any UN and service personnel and ascertain the number of casualties so that medical support could be sent to help the local doctors and nurses.

The nurse handed him a list of all the hospitals and medical centres in Kuta and Denpasar. She predicted that most of the casualties would be at Sanglah.

Cocks hailed a taxi, but the driver refused to take him. He had only come to watch, he said. Later, another driver picked up him and apologised for what had happened that night. The people behind these attacks must be from Java, he insisted. The peaceful Balinese would never do such a terrible thing.

He handed the driver the list of hospitals and medical centres and they began at the nearest – the Wisma Kuta Medical Centre. He discovered that the emergency room there was even worse than the one at BIMC. The treatment room was a warzone and he had slipped in the blood covering the floor.

Cocks had still been there when a more senior UN commanding officer rang from East Timor for an update. The soldier described the nightmare. They needed urgent medical back-up immediately, he said. Tragically, the scenes would grow worse at every hospital he visited and all night, the death toll and numbers of casualties continued to climb.

At BIMC a fleet of ambulances had arrived to transfer some of the more critical casualties to specialist units at the bigger hospitals in Denpasar that were better equipped to deal with their injuries.

To Cath's relief, one of the first to go was the man who had been writhing and screaming with pain when they first arrived.

'Please don't leave me,' pleaded Therese, watching him go. She was given another dose of morphine for the pain and continued to float in and out of consciousness. Cath reassured her that she was not going to leave her, and anticipated she would soon be transferred too, hopefully to an intensive care burns unit where she would get the care she badly needed.

At 2am, the doctors informed the Australian friends that Therese was being transferred to the Prima Medika Private Hospital in Denpasar where they had a ventilator for her.

'Will you stay with her?' the doctor asked Cath, concerned for his dangerously ill patient. Over the past two hours, Therese's body had begun to swell from her injuries, and she had grown weaker. Cath assured him she would stay with Therese for as long as it took.

'Should I go with them?' asked Rada. The doctor shook his head.

Chapter 3

'No – we need you to stay here and help us,' he replied.

Rada watched Cath accompanying Therese outside where she climbed into the front seat of the ambulance beside the paramedics. Cath explained to Therese that only the nurse was permitted in the back with her, but she would be in the front and would stay with her when they reached the hospital in Denpasar.

The ambulance sped off across Kuta in the darkness with its sirens blasting and lights flashing. In the back, Therese continued to deteriorate.

Not long after they left, a different doctor asked Rada if she would help them with another young foreign casualty who had just been brought into the clinic.

French tourist, Marie-Antoinette Le Clerc was 23 and had also been severely burnt. She had arrived, alone and wracked with pain. She looked terrified and Rada immediately approached her to offer her some comfort and support.

Marie-Antoinette had grabbed Rada's hands looking desperate but grateful. She spoke very limited English and Rada's high school French was rusty, but the injured girl appeared to take comfort from the reassurance of a calm mother figure, who did her best to convey to her that she was in safe hands.

For Rada who was still grieving for her son, it was her chance to offer support to another young person whose own mother could not be here to support her in this life-threatening situation.

When paramedics arrived to transfer the French patient to another bigger hospital, the doctor asked Rada if she would go in the ambulance with her.

'Of course,' she said, reassuring the frightened young woman that she would not leave her.

She had climbed into the front of the ambulance, where the Balinese paramedic behind the wheel immediately apologised to her. He had been called into work at such short notice that he had not had time for a shower.

Rada, touched by his humility, told him not to worry. The smell of smoke and burnt flesh clung to her nostrils and she couldn't smell anything else anyway.

The journey to Denpasar was hair-raising and when a motorist came careening across the road in front of them, Rada had closed her eyes expecting to hear a terrible crash. But the ambulance had managed to swerve out of its path, and after some shouting and horn-honking, it had continued along the road with its lights flashing.

At the Dharma Usadha Public Hospital, a doctor watched his new patient being stretchered into the emergency department with tears in his eyes.

'I am very sorry about your accident,' he said compassionately. At this stage, he was so rushed off his feet with patients that most of his hospital shift believed the casualties had been involved in a single accidental explosion.

A short drive away at the Prima Medika Private Hospital, Therese was admitted to a private emergency room; her pain was off the scale. She was shrieking and writhing, and Cath was relieved when the doctors increased her morphine.

Other casualties from the bomb blasts had begun to arrive in the waiting room from the smaller hospitals and clinics in Kuta, though most had already been taken to Sanglah.

One of the new admissions was a young Australian woman who was struggling to make herself understood among the Indonesian speaking staff.

Chapter 3

Twenty-five-year-old Melinda Kemp was from Western Australia and had been staying with her parents and her older sister, Tracey Ball, 31, in a hotel in Kuta.

'I don't know where my sister is,' she kept repeating, sounding utterly distraught.

Cath went over to offer her help and try to calm her down.

In tears, Melinda explained that she was worried about her sister, who had been separated from her after the explosion at the Sari Club. Melinda had been knocked unconscious in the blast and had been carried out of the burning building by a young footballer from the Kingsley Football Club in WA and another survivor. She had woken in the street and was rescued by a Balinese woman who led her out of the destruction and took her back to her village.

Although she was burned herself, Melinda caught a taxi and trailed around various medical centres looking for her sister. At the BIMC she was treated for her burns and transferred to Prima Medika by ambulance where she joined Therese in the emergency room.

'I need to find my sister,' she told Cath, panicking again.

Cath asked for the name of the hotel where her family was staying, and their room number. Cath reassured her that she was in good hands and asked for a phone so she could call the hotel and speak to Melinda's parents.

At first, the phone at the hotel had rung out. When Cath called back she was put through to the family's room and Melinda's father, Ron Kemp, took the call.

The relief in his voice was tangible as Cath explained that his daughter was in hospital in Denpasar where she was being treated for burns to her arms and back. She explained that Melinda had been asking about her sister, and he told her that Tracey was currently lying in a bath of cool water for the burns she had also sustained in the explosion. Cath gave him the name of the Prima Medika Hospital and explained that his daughter was in the private emergency waiting room.

'Don't worry,' she reassured him. 'Melinda is in good hands.'

By 3am on Sunday morning, Carren Smith, the woman who had come to Bali to take her own life, was now fighting for it. Cath had watched her being stretchered into the hospital and recognised her as the patient who had been slumped against the wall at BIMC.

It seemed to Cath that everyone – from the medical staff to the patients – was running on adrenaline. The doctors and nurses were doing a stellar job dealing with so many casualties with injuries so serious and complex; she doubted they had treated anything like this before.

Most of the patients appeared to be in a state of shock and almost everyone was asking about missing friends and relatives.

Despite her increased morphine, Therese had still been in agonising pain. It had now been four hours since the blast and her eyes had become so swollen that they were beginning to close. Her badly burnt face was black and bloated and she looked nothing like the fragile young woman who had limped into the Masa Inn with Rodney Cocks.

Cath had noticed that Therese's badly burnt body appeared to be bloating with excess fluid. The doctors explained that fluid retention is common in seriously burnt patients and is caused by fluid leakage from the blood vessels which collect around the damaged area.

Chapter 3

The swelling generally occurs during the first hour after a burn injury, with a gradual build-up of fluid in the burnt skin and soft tissue around 24 hours after the injury has occurred. In the case of deep full-thickness burns such as these – particularly where shrapnel and debris has penetrated the layers of skin – infections set in. This was a major concern as most burns victims die of infections rather than the injuries themselves.

The air in the private waiting room hung thick and heavy with the reeking smell of burnt flesh, smoke and singed hair, and Cath had begun to feel physically ill. As much as she did not want to leave Therese, she desperately needed to go outside to get some fresh air.

At 4am, the doctors who had been constantly in and out of the waiting room checking on their deteriorating patient approached Cath with some paperwork.

Since no next of kin was available, they required her consent to take Therese into surgery to remove the debris from her skin and prevent an infection from setting in.

'Without the surgery she will die,' advised the Balinese specialist bluntly. His face was deadly serious as he explained the risks of an infection turning to life-threatening sepsis.

Cath was in a dreadful quandary. The doctor was asking her to make a life and death decision about a woman who, until a few hours ago, was a stranger to her.

Whatever her decision, this poor young mum might die. Cath was not a doctor, but even she could see that Therese might be too seriously injured to survive the surgery. But to withhold her consent would mean a certain death sentence.

The doctor understood her dilemma. But he needed a decision – and he needed it now.

Cath reluctantly signed the paperwork, hoping her decision was the right one.

The doctor disappeared with the paperwork to prepare for the surgery. After he had gone, Cath sat beside Therese's bed, trying to make eye contact and explain what was about to happen. By now one of Therese's eyes was completely closed.

'Am I going to die?' she asked, sounding terrified.

'No,' replied Cath, praying she was right. 'But you might need a good haircut when this is all over,' she said, desperately trying to lighten the mood and reassure the patient that it was all going to be okay.

Cath explained that while she would not be permitted inside the operating room, she would be waiting for her when she returned from the surgery.

With Therese now slipping out of consciousness, Cath ducked out of the hospital for more fresh air. The repugnant odour of burnt flesh clung to her clothes and hair, and she had begun to feel nauseas again.

As Cath passed through the hospital's reception area, she noticed a handful of tourists at the main desk, anxiously inquiring about missing friends and relatives.

They looked stressed and exhausted after hours spent trawling various hospital emergency departments and local clinics, looking for friends and relatives who had been missing since the explosions on Kuta's nightclub strip.

The Balinese receptionist on the desk also looked drained and distressed as she struggled to make herself understood. In broken

English, she politely tried to explain that not all the patients'
names were available yet as the staff had been too busy dealing
with critical people to provide them with that information. Some
of the names had not filtered down yet and more casualties were
arriving from other places.

Among the crowd at the reception desk were three young
holidaymakers from Brisbane. The girls were looking for some
friends who had been missing since the blasts in Kuta. One of
the trio had become very upset and complained about the way
she perceived the staff were treating them.

Cath empathised with the young woman's anguish, but had
felt desperately sorry for the hospital staff too. The Indonesian-
speaking receptionist looked as overwhelmed and weary as the
dedicated nurses and doctors who had been dealing with the
injured all night.

For hours, Cath had watched them doing the best they could in
the most unimaginable circumstances. She approached the girls
and introduced herself, explaining that she was also Australian
and asking how she could help them.

Cath told them she had spent hours at another smaller clinic
and was likely to be at the Prima Medika Private Hospital for a
while yet. She would ask around and try to find out where their
friends had been taken.

She also explained that a number of Australian casualties were
being treated in the hospital's ICU, and at other hospitals around
Denpasar.

'I'm sure you will find them,' she said.

Cath sat down with the girls and held their hands while
she said a prayer for their missing friends. Saying a prayer

seemed like the only thing she could do for them on this hideous night.

She was still in reception when Ron Kemp arrived looking for his daughter. When she heard an Australian voice asking for Melinda, she approached him and introduced herself. Kemp expressed his gratitude for her earlier phone call and revealed that he had spent hours frantically walking around the streets of Kuta, praying that his daughter had survived the destruction. By now, his older daughter, Tracey, was on her way to Hospital and by the time he arrived back at the hotel, nobody knew where she had been taken.

When Cath returned to the private emergency room it was slowly beginning to clear. Patients with less severe injuries had been transferred to other general wards.

She sat beside Therese's bed, quietly studying the yellow polo-shirt she had pulled on over her nightdress a few hours earlier. Like her hair and skin, her clothes reeked of burnt flesh too.

Cath checked the time on the clock on the wall outside. It was after 4.30am; with the two-hour time difference it would be 6.30am in Australia. Her thoughts raced to her own family in Queensland. Soon her parents would be waking to the news about the overnight explosion in Bali. Cath did not want them to see the headlines and panic that something terrible had happened to her and Rada.

It was too early to call them yet. Instead, she rang one of her brothers and left a message on his answering machine.

'Hi, John, it's Cath,' she said, her forced chirpiness belying her trauma. 'There's been a big thing in Bali – but I'm safe. Tell Mum and Dad I'm OK.'

Chapter 3

Unfortunately, John would not check his messages until later that morning. By then, Cath's elderly grandmother had seen the news and knew all about the bombings in Bali, where she was aware her granddaughter and her friend were on holiday. She immediately called Cath's parents to ask if they had heard from her. Cath's mum, who had not yet seen the news, was beside herself with worry.

When Cath's brother had finally checked his answering machine at 9.30am on Sunday morning, he struggled to make any sense of her cryptic message. He immediately called his mum saying he'd just had a 'weird' message from Cath in Bali, wanting them to know that she was safe. What was she talking about, he wondered?

'Why didn't you tell us this earlier?' gasped Cath's mother, slumping into the chair in relief. She explained about the terrorist attacks and hung up the phone to ring Cath's grandmother and put her mind at rest.

Cath's nan would later tell her granddaughter how relieved she was to know that she always took her small travel Bible with her whenever she travelled overseas.

Her elderly nan hailed from Irish stock and was a good Catholic. She had given her well-travelled granddaughter many holy medals of the Blessed Mother and St Christopher and other religious memorabilia to ensure her personal protection. God had obviously been watching over her in Bali, she concluded.

At 5am in Bali, Therese was taken to theatre for the agonising six-hour procedure to scrape the debris from her burnt body.

After cleaning the soot and rubbish from her injuries the doctors had been able to determine that Therese had sustained burns to 85 per cent of her body – 65 per cent of them third-degree burns. This was extremely serious. Third-degree – or full-thickness – burns cause injury to the surface of the skin and the deeper layers below, sometimes right down to the fatty tissue. This damage has the potential to affect the skin's ability to recover and can affect nerve endings, causing severe pain. Complications in burns as widespread and deep as third-degree burns increase the likelihood of serious infection setting in.

The Balinese doctors chose their words carefully but emphasised to Cath that even with the surgery, Therese may not survive.

Cath watched Therese being wheeled away, feeling sick to the stomach, and tormenting herself about her impossible choice.

She had now been up a full day and night and after the traumatic events during the night, she felt emotionally, physically and mentally drained. With Therese now in theatre for at least the next six hours, there was no more she could do. She decided she would take Dr Dina Hadiningsih's advice and go back to her hotel to try to get a few hours' sleep. She promised to be back before Therese returned from her procedure.

Outside the hospital, a new day was beginning to dawn over Bali. Cath prayed Therese would live to see it.

Chapter 4

AN OMEN

On Sunday 13 October, while Therese had been undergoing life-saving surgery in Denpasar, Australia was waking to the devastating news of the overnight terrorist attacks on the tropical island of Bali.

The world's media had reported that two popular nightspots had been the targets of simultaneous terrorist attacks which were believed to have claimed the lives of dozens of innocent holidaymakers and seriously injured hundreds more.

It was revealed that the dual bomb blasts had taken place late on Saturday night in the popular holiday resort of Kuta and that the two busy tourist haunts had been packed with foreign tourists at the time of the attacks.

The reports from eyewitnesses at the scene suggested that an unspecified number of Australians were among the dead and injured.

The media had also revealed that while no-one had claimed responsibility for these callous attacks on innocent civilians, there was speculation that the bomb blasts may have been linked to al-Qaeda.

At her comfortable suburban home in Grovedale, Victoria, Therese's mum, Dawn, had just put on the kettle for her Sunday morning cup of tea when the story flashed up on her TV screen.

The elderly grandmother slumped into her armchair, shocked as the horrific images of the destruction at Paddy's Irish Bar and the Sari Club flooded her screen.

In her panic, all she could think about was Damien's chilling premonition about Therese and Bronwyn's holiday and his unshakeable belief that the trip to Bali spelled danger.

Dawn recalled a private conversation that she had had with her son when he had begged her to try to persuade Therese to cancel her travel plans.

'I'll try talking to her,' promised Dawn, holding out no hope at all that anything she said would make any difference. She was right. When she tried to raise the subject, Therese had shrugged off Damien's concerns, saying her holiday was booked and nothing was going to spoil it.

But Damien's bad feeling about the trip to Bali had persisted. Although Therese was not aware of it, the week before she was due to leave, he had been woken by a bad dream about something terrible befalling her.

It was one of those vague dreams which leave you gasping for air, but whose details are lost the second you wake – your fear and panic subsiding when you realise that it had not been real.

Still, while Damien could not remember the details of his frightening dream, the fear he felt was as real to him as his premonition of danger.

Chapter 4

It had felt like a dreadful omen, he told his mum, who hadn't known what to think.

A few days after Damien's bad dream, Dawn was watching the news on TV when she heard the Australian Government's warning, advising people to be cautious about travelling to Indonesia. The bulletin, on top of Damien's bad dream – had unsettled the 65-year-old grandmother, though she saw little point in troubling her daughter with it. It was too late anyway. The holiday was already booked, and as Therese had said, nothing was going to spoil it.

All the same, before Therese left for the airport on 6 October, Damien had made her promise to stay away from crowded tourist hotspots – particularly places like clubs and pubs. She had assured him she would.

Watching the morning headlines, a shaken Dawn Fox recalled the worrying conversation, but remained optimistic that Therese and Bronwyn would have been nowhere near the scene of the destruction. The girls had been due to leave for Ubud this morning, so the chances of them being in a busy pub or club on a Saturday night seemed highly unlikely.

But unknown to Dawn, in the early hours of the morning – at the exact time that the first bomb went off in Paddy's Irish Bar in Kuta – Damien had been standing outside his house in Lara watching a massive thunderstorm building in the skies over Melbourne.

It was a wild storm and as Damien watched the lightning zigzagging across the sky, he had immediately known his dark premonition had been right all along. Something had happened to his twin sister in Bali. He didn't know what it was – he just knew it was bad.

The thunder brought a downpour of rain, and Damien had retreated back into the house where his wife and child were sleeping. He had watched the rain beating against his lounge-room window. It was as if God was weeping that Sunday morning and by daybreak he would understand why.

The call that Damien had been expecting came before 7am on Sunday morning.

'Have you seen the news?' gabbled his mother, pausing while he rushed to turn on the TV for the morning's headlines. Watching the footage of the apocalyptic destruction in Kuta, Damien had known immediately that this was the danger he had foreseen in his dream.

Despite his mother's tangible anxiety, her words were ones of complete denial.

'Therese wouldn't have been anywhere like this,' she insisted. Therese had promised him she would stay away from crowded tourist places like pubs and nightclubs.

To put her own mind at rest, she was going to call the hotel in Kuta where Therese and Bronwyn were staying – just in case.

'I'd better go now,' croaked Dawn, hanging up the phone.

Damien sat in the chair in front of the TV, his heart twisting in his chest. He had heard the incredible stories about the mysterious telepathic bond that twins supposedly share which allows them to know instinctively if the other is in trouble.

It is a special bond apparently formed at a cellular level in the womb, and one that continues to grow after birth. It is believed to foster an inexplicable sixth sense that enables twin siblings to sense – and even to feel – one another's pain.

Chapter 4

Damien had never experienced it before and had not been convinced it even existed. But watching the storm in the early hours of the morning, he had been gripped with such an overwhelming sense of foreboding that he had felt the danger his sister was in from thousands of miles away.

After observing the sickening images of mass destruction on the TV, he did not share his mother's optimism that Therese had escaped the carnage. He *knew* she had been caught up in this atrocity, though the same sixth sense also told him she was still alive.

From her home in Grovedale, Dawn telephoned the phone number Therese had given her for the Bounty Hotel in Kuta.

'Just in case there's an emergency,' she had told her mum, who assumed she had been referring to something happening to one of her children.

'Don't worry,' Dawn had reassured her. 'The children will be fine with me ... it's only two weeks, enjoy yourself. Nothing is going to happen.'

Nothing is going to happen. Dawn's words had returned to haunt her. Nothing *had* happened to Alex and Katie. But if Damien was right, something terrible had befallen their mother.

The phone rang out on the Bounty Hotel's reception desk, where the scenes were as chaotic and distressing as the ones that Cath and Rada had witnessed at their hotel on the other Poppies Lane.

Like the Masa Inn, the Bounty's clientele were mostly young people including footy players, backpackers and budget travellers. Many had fled the mayhem and found their way back to their hotel with dreadful burns and other serious injuries. Others had returned covered in ash and debris, deeply traumatised, and panicking about missing friends and relatives.

All night, the phones across Bali had run hot. The lines had been jammed with incoming calls from desperate families and outgoing calls from shaken tourists wanting relatives to know they were alive. By the morning, the telecommunications network was buckling under the deluge of phone calls and people were having trouble getting through to anyone in Kuta.

Dawn's panic had manifested itself in more denial. It must be the middle of the night in Bali, she told herself, checking the two-hour time difference, which revealed it must be 5am in Kuta.

She decided to ring again and leave a message, asking Therese to call her back. The girls would be off to Ubud today, so she imagined they would be up bright and early. Hearing her daughter's voice would put her mind at rest.

Dawn rang the hotel again, and this time the receptionist answered. She asked to be put through to Therese's room, her panic increasing when the phone rang out and nobody answered. The call was transferred back to reception. Dawn asked if Therese had returned to her room that night. Nobody appeared to know the answer. She left a message with the reception desk asking Therese to call her as soon as possible. Just in case, she left the number of her landline in Australia.

Feeling increasingly anxious, Dawn telephoned her ex-husband in Queensland to ask if he had seen the news. Chris Fox immediately turned on the TV, stunned by the devastating scenes emerging from his favourite holiday destination.

During their conversation, an emergency hotline had begun to flash across the screen appealing to anyone with friends or family in Kuta who might be involved in the bombings to contact them with names.

Dawn saw the appeal from the Australian Department of Foreign Affairs on her own TV and hastily jotted the number down. She told Chris she intended to call and register her concerns for Therese and Bronwyn. But when she rang, the line was busy and despite repeated attempts, it would be hours before she managed to speak to anyone.

* * *

More than 5000 miles away in Bali, good Samaritan Cath Byrne had been on her way back to her hotel, where the evidence of Saturday night's destruction was everywhere.

Stepping out of the taxi, she made her way towards the lobby of the Masa Inn, avoiding the pools of sticky blood on the steps where the two injured tourists had sat bleeding the night before. Broken bottles were strewn around the hotel and the floors were still covered in shattered glass.

Cath found Rada resting on her bed in their hotel room, her face ashen with exhaustion. Like Cath, she was dressed in the same bloodstained top and pyjamas she had been wearing when they had left one another at BIMC a few hours earlier.

While Cath had been at the hospital in Denpasar with Therese, Rada had spent an equally harrowing night with the burnt French woman at the Dharma Usadha Hospital. The doctors had also asked her if she would give her consent for them to perform the same dermabrasion procedure that Therese was currently undergoing at the private hospital, a short distance away.

'B...b...but I'm not Marie-Antoinette's next of kin,' faltered Rada, not knowing what to do. She had only met the patient two hours ago and was a stranger to her.

Fortunately, despite her critical condition and escalating pain, the young French patient had been lucid enough to decide for herself.

'I will do it,' she said in her heavy French accent, understanding what the discussion had been about. Her hands shook with pain as she scribbled her signature on the consent form. Later a thoracic specialist had come to see them to determine whether she was strong enough to undergo the general anaesthesia for the painful procedure.

'Do you want me to stay with you?' Rada had asked.

'What about your husband?' replied the injured girl thoughtfully.

Rada explained she was separated from her husband and on holiday with her friend, who was at a different hospital supporting another patient.

'Yes, please,' said Marie-Antoinette gratefully.

With the patient in theatre for the next two hours, Rada had returned to the hotel to rest. The roads around Kuta had been more chaotic than they had been on the trip in the ute to BIMC, and she had been forced to take two separate taxis back to Kuta. There, the last driver had dropped her two blocks from the hotel; she had walked the rest of the way.

When she arrived at the Masa Inn the power was still down, and she looked as worn out as Cath, though she was too wired to sleep.

'We'll have to contact the Australian Consulate,' said Cath, flopping back on her bed, her mind in overdrive. With so many people missing in the chaos, she thought it might help if the authorities were given a list of all the casualties they had encountered during the night and a rundown of the hospitals where they were being treated.

From Cath's brief discussions with Melinda's father and the young Queenslanders at the hospital in Denpasar, it was clear that nobody really knew which medical centre the casualties had been taken to. If the Australian Consulate had a full list of names and places, it would make it easier for friends and families here in Kuta – and back in Australia – to locate people who were missing.

After the catastrophic events last night, there would be many more Australians trailing around the various hospitals and clinics today, looking for people they loved. Most of the survivors were now at Sanglah, but others, like Therese and Marie-Antoinette, remained scattered around other smaller hospitals and clinics in the region.

Cath thought it might bring families some peace of mind if they knew that the people they loved had survived the blast and were being treated in hospital. At that time, she was still under the impression that all the injuries she had seen had been caused by a single explosion.

Things had been so stressful during the night that there had been no opportunity for Rada to call Therese's father, and she did not have a mobile phone to contact him on. She had decided to wait until Cath returned from the hospital when they would have more news for him. She hoped it would not be bad news.

'Therese is in surgery,' said Cath, explaining that the doctors were not optimistic about her chances of surviving the procedure or her extensive injuries.

It had been such a surreal and traumatic night that the friends had eventually dozed off in the clothes they were wearing.

They had woken at 7am on Sunday morning to an eerie silence they had never known before. The foul smell of burnt flesh and smouldering hair still clung to their hair and skin. Cath could smell it on her clothes too. The stench appeared to have permeated the fibres of her yellow polo-shirt and filtered into every pore on her skin. The smell had made her nauseas again and she disappeared into the bathroom and pulled off all her clothes.

Cath turned on the shower and stood under the running water, replaying the macabre scenes she had witnessed in her head. While the doctors in Denpasar had been dermabrasing the debris from Therese and Marie-Claire's bodies, Cath began to scrub her own. Sadly, no amount of sweet-smelling soap was enough to purge the odious smell of death that had wrapped itself like a ghastly shroud around the hospital and the Bali International Medical Centre that night.

After a shower and a quick change of clothes, the friends made their way down to the hotel pool, where evidence of the mayhem was everywhere. The lawn was strewn with plastic bottles and broken glass. Bloodstained sheets lay scattered around, and the wet blankets and soot-covered towels were still on the lawn where Cath and Rada had left them.

They were standing beside the pool silently processing everything that had happened when Frank Morgan wandered over with some updates.

There had been two separate explosions, he revealed. The first had been at Paddy's followed by another bigger explosion a few seconds later outside the Sari Club across the room.

Chapter 4

'It was a car bomb,' added Morgan.

Just as the defence force guys had originally suspected, it appeared a larger 'secondary' device had been deliberately planted to inflict more suffering on the survivors who had fled the blaze at Paddy's towards the Sari Club.

'Who would do such a thing?' asked Rada.

Morgan suspected that a callous and premeditated attack on innocent civilians at two of Kuta's most popular tourist haunts on a busy Saturday night could only be the work of terrorists.

He revealed that another smaller bomb had also been detonated outside the Australian Consulate in Denpasar at around the same time. From the initial reports, it had apparently caused only minor damage and there had been no casualties.

But the fact that it had been strategically placed outside the US Consulate suggested that the US Government may have been the true target all along.

They wondered if the attacks had been some sort of payback attack for the US involvement in the war against terror in Afghanistan – and possibly retribution against the Australian Government for their involvement in East Timor.

Like the doctor who had apologised to Marie-Antoinette about the 'accident', Cath and Rada had also assumed that all the casualties they had encountered had been the victims of a single event. Now it occurred to them that some of the people they had seen during the night may well have been injured in the second explosion at the Sari Club.

Until now, Cath had also believed the blast was accidental. But recalling the ominous mushroom-shaped cloud over Kuta, and the devastating burns suffered by all the casualties, a bomb attack made more sense.

According to Morgan, the media were speculating that the bomb blasts might be al-Qaeda–related, though they were yet to claim responsibility. Like Cocks, the seasoned AFP officer had received instructions from the brass to stay on in Bali, where he was about to be joined by other members of the AFP.

The Australian and Indonesian authorities were currently involved in diplomatic negotiations, and it appeared likely that the AFP would be permitted to lead the investigation into the terrorist attacks. The masterminds behind the atrocity would be apprehended and brought to justice. Under Indonesian jurisdiction, the likely penalty would be the death sentence.

At 7.30am Cath and Rada wandered down the narrow laneways towards the site of the terrorist attacks, trying to make sense of the violence inflicted on so many innocent people.

Signs of the devastation lay everywhere that Sunday morning – from the mangled burnt-out cars to the collapsed businesses and the crumbling homes and restaurants of the local Balinese people, whose exposed structures now looked unstable. The explosions were so powerful that they had been felt across the island and had shattered the windows in the surrounding properties closest to the blasts. The local people looked at the two Australian tourists with a new sadness in their eyes, also unable to fathom how this atrocity had occurred in their peaceful island home.

While Rada and Cath were at the hospital, the Indonesian police had been out all night and had sectioned off the road into Legian Jalan. Overnight, a recovery effort had been underway to rescue any survivors still buried beneath the rubble and to remove the bodies of the dead. Rodney Cocks had been down there helping. A number of foreign doctors and nurses had joined rescuers at the site and had been tending to the injured.

On Sunday morning, the area around Paddy's Irish Bar and the Sari Club – which had now been reduced to a smouldering crater of ash and rubble – was completely blocked off.

As they approached the bomb site, the teachers could see that a crowd of locals had gathered at the barrier and were surveying the aftermath of the bomb blasts that had claimed so many lives. Many were in mourning for their own relatives and friends, who had been working in the busy tourist precinct when the suicide bombers struck on Saturday night. Some had been innocent pedestrians or taxi drivers who happened to be passing by, going about their business, when the bombs went off.

Nine hours ago, this vibrant area was the epicentre of Kuta's pulsing party scene. In the cold light of day, it resembled an apocalyptic war zone.

Rada and Cath surveyed the devastation. But for their own last-minute change of plan, they may have been here too when the terrorist's struck.

By good fortune, they had decided to turn back – away from the hustle and bustle – and head to the Hard Rock Café for their cocktails. If they had continued into the beating heart of Kuta, they may have been one of the unfortunate souls whose bodies had been recovered from the wreckage, or fighting for their own lives in one of the ICUs in Denpasar.

The friends had been reflecting on their fortunate escape when they noticed a small white van negotiating a path through the crowds of people. The vehicle was coming from behind the barrier and at first glance, looked like an ambulance. But it was not like the large well-equipped modern ambulances the friends were used to seeing on Australian freeways. The small innocuous vehicle was more like a 'tradies' work van, with doors at the back, and clear windows.

Rada could see what was inside the van, and immediately looked away.

'Don't look Cathy,' she advised her friend, as the vehicle headed through the crowd towards them.

As it passed them, Cath had a clear view through the windows into the van's interior. To her horror, she realised that it was not an ambulance at all – neither was it transporting more rescued casualties to hospital. It was piled high with bodies!

Although efforts had been made to cover the dead with sheets, Cath could see that exposed limbs, bones and hands protruded from the van's grim cargo.

Her stomach twisted as she wondered what horrors these poor souls had endured, and who the skeletal hands had belonged to. Who had they held and who had they comforted? Had they slipped wedding rings onto the fingers of people who loved them, or nursed newborn babies? Tragically, they appeared to be reaching out from beneath the sheets, as if they had left this world pleading to be saved from the fires of hell.

'Can we go back now?' said Cath, utterly traumatised by the scale and futility of the carnage.

Sadly, these tragic and gruesome images of the deadliest day in Bali's modern history would return to haunt them both in the years ahead. They would surface in Cath's dreams, or creep up on her unexpectedly during waking hours, bringing sudden haunting flashbacks of a ghastly moment that would remained forever imprinted on her consciousness.

The walk back to the Masa Inn seemed further than the 1.5 kilometres they had covered on the way down. The women considered the impossible ordeal that Therese had endured as she hobbled to their hotel on feet so burnt that her soles had melted away before their eyes.

In their hotel room they had turned on the television; the harrowing footage of the terrorist attacks dominated the Sunday morning news. The sound on their television was muted. But no words were necessary. The macabre images of pain and suffering said it all.

The friends had not eaten since Cath's arrival the previous evening, not that they had any appetite for food. But they had no idea what the new day held for them and forced themselves into the hotel's restaurant for breakfast, which they swallowed without tasting a morsel.

It was 8.30am in Bali, and Cath wanted to get back to the hospital before Therese returned from surgery. Rada also wanted to visit Marie-Antoinette, who should be back from her own surgery by now.

Rada had been so overwhelmed that she had forgotten the name of the hospital where doctors had been performing the same painful procedure on Marie-Antoinette's burns. She would have to do a ring-around later to find it.

The teachers decided to visit Therese first and figure out where the French girl was later. Perhaps someone at the Prima Medika might know, suggested Cath.

But first they wanted to call around at the Bounty Hotel to see if anyone had any news about Bronwyn. The roads were so busy on Sunday morning they decided it might be quicker to walk.

At the Bounty Hotel, the management had set up a registration area at the bar beside the pool. The manager, Kossi Halemai, had been compiling a list of guests who were missing or injured. They had been encouraging people to register the names of injured friends or family beside the hospitals where they were being treated.

From the length of the list, it was apparent that many of the guests at the Bounty had been young holidaymakers, which Rada had noticed was the case at the Masa Inn, where she had observed lots of young people splashing around in the pool the previous morning.

Like the staff at their own hotel, the workers at the Bounty had spent a stressful night too, tending to the injured, handling concerned phone calls from overseas, and trying to locate foreign guests who were missing.

Rada and Cath went to reception to let the management know that Therese Fox was being treated at the Prima Medika Private Hospital for serious burns and asked if anyone had heard from her friend. Their hearts sunk when the staff confirmed they had not seen her since the friends left the hotel at around 8pm the previous evening.

The hotel had not heard anything from Bronwyn, but they had received a call from Therese's mother in Australia. The manager said she had called at around 5am and had left a message with reception asking her daughter to call back as soon as possible. He handed Cath Dawn's phone number in Australia.

Chapter 4

'Perhaps you could call her,' he said, gesturing to the phone on the reception desk.

Trying to remain calm and reassuring, Cath introduced herself and explained that Therese had been burnt in the explosion at Paddy's bar and was being treated in hospital in Denpasar for serious burns. She had chosen her words carefully because she had not wanted to frighten Therese's mother by telling her how critical her daughter's condition was.

'Praise God, she's okay,' choked Dawn, sobbing softly on the other end of the phone. Her anguish was tangible, and Cath kept the call brief, but explained there had been no news yet from Bronwyn. She gave the distraught mum the name of the hospital in Denpasar where her daughter was being treated and assured her that Therese was in good hands. Cath explained they were on the way to the hospital now and promised she would be in touch when they had more news.

Cath and Rada caught a taxi back to the private hospital, where they were told by the receptionist that Therese's father, Chris Fox, had been calling about his daughter. Rada guessed he had been given the number by Therese's mum who had just spoken to Cath. She said she would call him back once they had spoken to the doctors.

They were relieved to hear that Therese had survived the surgery and had just returned to the ICU. One of the nurses escorted them into the small intensive care unit which had three beds and was air conditioned, though it was nothing like spacious well-equipped special care units seen in most major Australian hospitals.

They found her heavily sedated on a bed beside two young Japanese women, who had also suffered horrific burns in the terrorist attacks. All three patients were naked and bloated, and in the cold light of day appeared almost skinless – their red, raw flesh resembling that of skinned animals.

Every inch of Therese's body was covered with a thick, gooey cream and her lips were more swollen than ever. Her hair was shorn close to her head, and her ears had been so burnt they had lost their formation entirely. Rada, who had not seen her since her transfer in the early hours of Sunday morning, was shocked and had not recognised her at all.

In the garden of the Masa Inn in the aftermath of the bombings, she had been too traumatised to see beyond the soot and debris that concealed Therese's ghastly injuries. Now that the grime had been scrubbed away, the extent and severity of her life-threatening burns was immediately apparent, and Rada felt shaken. Her heart went out to this poor young mother. How could anyone possibly survive injuries like these?

Dr Hadiningsih arrived in the ICU to check on her patient and update the friends.

She explained that apart from the burns, an X-ray had confirmed that Therese had suffered a fractured skull and that her eardrums had also been perforated in the deafening explosion.

By a miracle, the delicate skin on her breasts had remained untouched by the flames, probably protected by the cotton underwear which had clung to her body like charred scraps of burnt tissue paper the previous evening.

The cheap shell bracelet she had bought from a local trader had also survived the intense heat of the explosion and had left a strip of untouched skin around her wrist.

Chapter 4

Like the Japanese tourists who lay unconscious in the beds beside her, a plain cotton sheet had been suspended over Therese's body and an oxygen mask had been attached to her face. All three patients looked like the living dead.

The sound of voices filtered through Therese's subconscious and her eyes flickered open with vague recognition.

'It's Cath and Rada,' Cath gently reminded her.

'Am I in trouble?' she asked groggily.

Picking her answer carefully – but not wishing to lie – Rada told her she was being well looked after.

Therese smiled weakly back at them.

'Am I going to be alright?' she asked.

The teachers looked at one another, not knowing how to answer. Cath hoped Therese had not noticed their shock as they processed her confronting injuries.

As a mother who had lost her own child, Rada's heart broke for Therese's mum in Melbourne, who she felt certain would give anything to be with her daughter right now. She wondered how the poor woman would cope when she finally saw her – or whether Therese would survive long enough for her mother to say goodbye.

Like Cath, she hid her concerns behind a warm smile and told Therese in a positive voice that belied her distress that she was in safe hands.

Glancing at the two Indonesian nurses who sat quietly monitoring the three critically injured patients, they doubted the staff had ever dealt with burns of such a serious nature before.

Through the haze of morphine and anaesthetic, Therese's thoughts were still on her missing friend.

'Have you found Bronwyn yet?' she asked again, her swollen lips struggling to form words that were further muffled by the oxygen mask covering her face.

Her swollen eyes closed before they could answer her.

'I have to go home,' she told them weakly.

Despite Therese's life-threatening condition, she suddenly remembered their suitcases were packed and waiting at the hotel. She was orientated enough to realise it was Sunday. They should have left the Bounty Hotel by now and would have been arriving at the health resort in Ubud.

'I need my things,' she panicked. 'Do you think you could collect them for me?'

Despite her surgery and the effects of the anaesthetic, she gave the name of the hotel in Kuta, and her room number. She sounded so anxious about her belongings that the women agreed they would.

'The room's a mess,' said Therese apologetically. 'We did a lot of shopping.'

Slurring her words, she described the carrier bags and all the things they had not been able to fit in their suitcases. She also mentioned the hiding places they had found for some of the more special items like jewellery. Some of the expensive items she had bought were under the bed, she said.

'Our passports are still in the hotel's safety deposit box,' explained Therese, remembering again about Bronwyn.

'Do you know where she is?' she mumbled. Cath told her again they would find her.

Therese was drifting off to sleep when the friends left ICU. They made their way upstairs to check on the other

Australian casualties who had been transferred to lower dependency wards.

After her father's visit, Melinda was in better spirits, particularly now that she had been told that her sister was safe. They had both suffered burns and would require hospital treatment on their return to Australia, but on Sunday morning, Melinda appeared relieved to be alive

'Thanks for contacting my dad,' she told Cath gratefully.

Melinda said her sister had been taken to Sanglah but arrangements were being made to transfer her to Prima Medika Private Hospital so they could be together. Tracey was also burnt, and while the doctors wanted to perform surgery on Melinda, they changed their minds when her more seriously injured sister arrived and operated on her instead.

Carren Smith, the woman Cath had watched being brought in from BMIC in the early hours of the morning, now lay quietly on a bed in the same ward where a Balinese nurse was carefully picking glass and debris from a large wound in her head. An X-ray had revealed that her skull had suffered a depressed fracture during the explosion at the Sari Club.

Cath and Rada did not know it, but the woman who had gone to Bali to die had run for her life with the stampede of injured holidaymakers Cocks had observed fleeing the inferno at the Sari Club.

The impact from the car bomb had thrown her across the dance floor fracturing her skull. By a miracle, she had managed to haul herself out of the rubble and escape through a small hole in a wall.

An Australian man had been helping injured women through the hole and Smith had fled through the flames – climbing a wall three times her size – and had run for her life. At the time, she had been too pumped on adrenaline to hear the screams of other victims, all she could hear was the sizzling of skin on her back.

The good Samaritan who had been helping women escape had been policeman Senior Constable Timothy Britten from Western Australia who was on leave from East Timor. His heroic actions saved many lives at the Sari Club that night.

On the street, Smith had had the good fortune to be spotted by a passing Australian tourist on a moped. His name was Jeff, and after observing her shocking injuries he had immediately stopped and pulled over.

'Darl, get on the back … you're in need of attention,' he said in a strong Aussie accent.

The moped sped off with Smith on the back. As they rode, she noticed pedestrians beside the road gaping at them, though she had no idea why.

Her left eye had begun to feel heavy and when she put her hand up to her head, she realised there was a large piece of her skull protruding from it. This was what the locals had been staring at. She had no idea it was bone until she plucked it out.

The moped rider had taken her directly to the BIMC, where Cath and Rada had noticed her slumped against a wall.

There, Carren Smith had waited hours to be seen. Finally, the US trauma specialist, Dr Art Sorrel had performed temporary surgery to stem the bleeding from her head wound. It was now held together by 38 staples.

After her transfer to Prima Medika, Smith had been told that she needed emergency surgery to insert a plate in her fractured skull. But the medical supplies were running low and after watching an overwhelmed nurse struggling to sterilise and reuse the same syringe on six different patients requiring Tetanus shots, she flatly refused to let the Balinese doctors operate on her because of the risk of possible cross infection.

Instead, Carren contacted her doctor in Sydney, who told her she needed specialist treatment for her head injury, and for her burns, in a more sterile environment. He urged her to get herself back to Australia as soon as possible.

'They can't deal with complex surgeries in here,' she told the teachers. She telephoned her brother on the hospital phone, and he was trying to organise a flight back to Sydney. Despite the staples holding the wound together, she said she intended to leave as soon as she could get her things from her hotel.

Cath and Rada had offered to collect her bag and her passport too and bring them back to the hospital. Carren told them the name of her hotel and her room number.

It had been less than 24 hours since Carren and her two friends had arrived in Bali, and they had not had time to put their passports and money into the hotel's safety deposit box.

'Where can we find them?' asked Rada.

Carren said they had hidden the passports under the bathroom sink.

Since her hotel was on the way to the Bounty, Cath and Rada decided to call there first, and left the hospital to call a taxi.

Unknown to the friends, the taxi's route back to Kuta took them past the Sanglah Central General Hospital in Denpasar, where most of the other casualties were being treated. As they drove past the grounds of the building – unaware it was a hospital – Cath had noticed a crowd of local people standing beside a tall fence. Scores of people had climbed up the fence and were hanging over it. They appeared to be watching something on the other side of the fence.

'What are they doing?' asked Cath, curiously watching them from the cab window.

The driver inhaled.

'I think it's a football match or volleyball game,' he lied.

The Balinese driver knew full well that behind the fence lay a makeshift open-air morgue, where the bodies of the victims of the terrorist attacks now lay in the blistering sun, awaiting forensic examination by the Australian investigators.

But the man was thoughtful, and not wanting to distress his Australian passengers, he told the white lie to protect them from the ghastly truth.

At the Hotel Jayacarta, a security guard showed the friends to Carren Smith's room and watched them gathering up her things. In normal circumstances, Cath imagined they would never have allowed strangers into someone else's hotel room. But nothing was normal in Bali right now, and nobody objected.

The security guard waited while the friends collected Carren's things and retrieved her passport from its hiding place under the sink. In the bathroom, Rada was in the process of wrapping some of the injured woman's toiletries in a towel when the security guard gruffly confronted her.

'You can't take that,' he said, scowling at her. 'It's the hotel's property!'

The two women glanced at one another in disbelief. Who cared about a towel at a time like this? thought Cath crossly.

Rada politely apologised and returned the towel to its rack.

Chapter 4

Everything felt wrong and emotions were running high on this sad, sunny Sunday in Kuta.

They had one last look around the room and realised there was a door leading into an adjoining bedroom. There were more bags and belongings scattered around and it was clear to them that Carren had been staying here with friends.

The beds in the adjoining room had not been slept in, and the friends turned to one another in alarm. Where were the occupants of this other room? they wondered. Had they been caught up in this terrible atrocity too? And if they had, where were they? They went downstairs into the hotel lobby where the management had posted a register with the names of the missing and the injured, like the one at the Bounty Hotel. Jodi Wallace and Charmaine Whitton's names were on the list. They added Carren Smith's name to the list of survivors and noted the name of the hospital that she was trying to check out of.

The friends loaded her suitcase into the back of the taxi and the driver took them on to the Bounty to collect Therese's suitcases. They desperately hoped they would find Bronwyn there.

At the Bounty Hotel, the receptionist on the desk organised one of the staff to escort the women to room 318, where Therese and her friend had been staying.

Cath and Rada sadly surveyed the assortment of carrier bags containing all the bargains the friends had bought. Therese had mentioned that she had two young children, and they guessed the bag of toys, computer games and other gifts must be for them.

These girls certainly knew how to shop, thought Rada – a keen shopper herself. And Therese had been right – their room really was a mess. Rada and Cath were struck by the tragedy of it all. Therese and her friend had obviously been having a fabulous time before this dreadful atrocity.

Rada's heart broke as she looked at the bags of pretty summer sandals. So many shoes, she thought, sadly reliving the harrowing spectacle of the soles of Therese's melted feet falling onto the blanket in front of their eyes. Rada wondered if she would ever wear the beautiful shoes she had bought. Would she even survive to see them?

The toys, the clothes and the shoes were a poignant reminder of the senselessness of an attack that had injured and killed so many innocent people. Rada felt like bursting to tears, but was afraid if she started, she might not stop. Without exchanging a word, the friends quickly began to pack everything away.

It had become clear from the untouched beds and the state of the room that Bronwyn had not been back that night, though Cath had still been hoping she might walk in on them and demand to know why they were rifling through her things.

Still, if Bronwyn *had* been admitted to one of the other hospitals, she was going to need her things. Unsure whose things belonged to who, they stuffed everything they could into the suitcases.

Before they left, Cath scribbled a note for Bronwyn, explaining that they had taken Therese's suitcase to the hospital in Denpasar where she was being treated for burns. They left Bronwyn's bag in the room, certain that the hotel's management would store it away in their secure luggage room for her.

If by a miracle Bronwyn returned to the hotel, she would know where to find her things and would know what had happened to Therese. Cath was still hoping that someone had rescued her from the wreckage of Paddy's bar and taken her to hospital. But watching the hotel staff adding Bronwyn's name to the list of missing guests, she knew things were not looking promising.

Chapter 5

WHERE IS
BRONWYN?

In Australia, Cath's conversation with Dawn Fox on Sunday morning had prompted a flurry of distressing phone calls between family and friends.

Dawn's first call had been to Therese's father in Tewantin to tell him about the call she had received from an Australian holidaymaker in Bali telling her that their daughter had been hurt in the terrorist attacks, and that Bronwyn was missing.

'Apparently she has been seriously burnt, and no-one knows where Bronwyn is,' gulped Dawn, relaying the brief information Cath had given her on the phone.

'She's on her way to the hospital to see and is going to call me back as soon as she has more news.'

Dawn told her ex-husband the name of the hospital that Cath had mentioned and hurried off the phone to call Damien. The news confirmed what Therese's twin brother's sixth sense had already been telling him – that her life had been in danger, but she was still alive.

Chris Fox had begun to panic and had immediately called the Prima Medika Private Hospital where he had struggled to make himself understood to the receptionist who spoke Bahasa. Desperate for news he had called around at his next-door neighbour's house in Barkley Avenue, Tewantin to tell her what had happened. His neighbour had a son who lived in Bali, and Chris wondered if he might be able to find out more information than Dawn had been given by the stranger on the phone. Chris' neighbour had contacted her son, asking him if he could go to the hospital to find out how Therese was.

After the call from his mother, Damien had telephoned Therese's nursing friend, Michelle, whose new job had saved her from the nightmare that his own family and Bronwyn's were now grappling with.

Michelle was partway through her morning shift when the call came through to the ward. She had been up most of the night with one of her three girls, whose asthma had kept them awake. She had seen the breaking news bulletins about the explosions at the nightclubs in Bali, but it had not occurred to her that Therese and Bronwyn might have been involved. The authorities were already speculating that the two bomb blasts may have been a terrorist attack.

'It's an urgent call for you,' shouted one of Michelle's nursing colleagues, gesturing her over to the phone on the ward reception desk.

Michelle, 34, was stunned to hear Therese's twin brother on the end of the line.

'What's wrong' she asked, afraid Damien might be calling to tell her something had happened to one of Therese's children.

'Have you heard the news?' he asked, his voice sounding serious.

Michelle could feel his anguish from the other end of the phone line as he explained about Therese and Bronwyn being caught up in the terrorist attacks in Kuta.

'Therese is in hospital with serious burns and Bronwyn is missing,' he explained, breaking down in tears. 'We don't know any more yet.'

Michelle felt as though she had been kicked in the stomach.

She listened as he went on to tell her about the call from Cath in Bali.

Damien had felt too upset to continue the conversation. Michelle put down the phone and burst into tears too.

Her nursing colleagues, observing her ashen face, gathered around, wanting to know what had happened. But she was crying so hard she could barely breathe.

'I'm sorry, I...I...I have to go home,' she said, her entire body shaking with shock.

Michelle drove straight home, trying to process the shattering news.

If these terrorists had been targeting a nightclub filled with Australian holidaymakers, and the girls really had been there, Bronwyn would almost certainly have been on the dance floor, she concluded, weeping again.

Her heart began to race as she considered another unthinkable scenario. If she had been there with the girls, she would have been dancing with Bronwyn and might be missing too. She couldn't bear to think about it.

Her thoughts turned to Therese, who Damien had said was badly burnt. Michelle knew the heartache that a fire could cause to families. Four years earlier, on 2 December 1998, her younger brother, Christopher – a 27-year-old voluntary firefighter with the CFA – had perished with four members of his brigade after being trapped in a firestorm in a bushfire at Lynton, in Victoria. His body had been found slumped behind the truck. He had been trying to turn on the water and had died trying to save his crew.

The loss of five volunteer 'firies' from West Geelong had been an unimaginable tragedy for their family and their small community. But a terrorist attack? It was beyond Michelle's comprehension.

As a nurse, Michelle had some insight into the suffering of burns patients, but this was a bomb blast. She could not begin to imagine how devastating her friend's injuries might be. Her heart went out to Therese and her family. Her twin brother had sounded completely shattered by the news.

Michelle's husband, Michael, had been watching the news on the TV when his wife burst in through the door and broke down in his arms.

'Thank God you didn't go with them,' he said, looking visibly shaken.

Michelle continued to sob.

'If it hadn't been for my new job, I *would* have been there too,' she said, inconsolable.

Michael held his distraught wife in his arms.

'You were not supposed to be there,' he soothed.

He recalled how his dad, Bob Larkins, had tried to talk her out of the holiday, echoing the same sentiments Damien Fox had shared with Therese about Bali being a dangerous place.

'It's not safe,' the straight-shooting Bob had warned his daughter-in-law, urging her to reconsider the holiday. In the end, fate had intervened, and Michelle's new job had prevented her from going.

After hearing the news on Sunday morning, Bob had called around at his son's home to comfort Michelle, who was now tormenting herself with guilt.

He repeated what Michael had already told her – that she was not supposed to be there. She had a husband and three daughters who needed her more.

'It wasn't your time,' said Bob, wrapping his daughter-in-law in a giant bear hug.

Michelle had held her husband and children a little closer that Sunday, her thoughts with Therese and Bronwyn's families, who must be out of their minds with anxiety.

Her dream job had saved her life and she felt so guilty it was paralysing.

Twenty minutes away in Grovedale, Dawn called the 1800 hotline number again. It had been an hour since Cath's call from Bali and she was consumed with anxiety. She had decided to call Bronwyn's mum to see if she had had any news about their daughters.

Bronwyn's family had heard about the terrorist attacks on the two nightclubs in Kuta and had gathered at house of their mother, Jenny Hobbs, in Geelong. Jenny, and Bronwyn's younger sister,

Chapter 5

Jess, had spent the past two hours ringing the emergency hotline and trying to get through to the Department of Foreign Affairs.

Jenny – a critical care nurse at the Royal Melbourne Hospital – had heard about the bombings from two of her sons. Anthony and Jason were both bakers and had been working on Saturday night when the first bulletins came through on the radio. They knew their eldest sister, Bronwyn, was on holiday in Bali but they had no idea where she was staying, or if she was even in Kuta. But they knew she loved to party and were concerned she might have spent Saturday night at one of the tourist haunts that were now all over the Australian news.

At 8am they had called their mum's mobile phone to ask if she had seen the news about the terrorist attacks in Kuta. Jenny, who was out with a friend, was so alarmed by the call that she had driven straight home, where Jess was already waiting for her.

Twenty-one-year-old Jess had also seen the headlines about the bombings at the Sari Club and Paddy's Irish Bar and had driven down from her home in Melbourne, an hour's drive away, to tell her mum what had happened before she saw it on the news.

'It happened last night and both places were apparently packed with tourists,' said Jess, who would have been with them if she had saved the money in time.

'Has Bronnie got her mobile with her?' asked her mum, looking worried.

Jess thought she had, but suspected Bronwyn had not bothered to organise international roaming on her phone. She had tried calling her sister during the week to see how the holiday was going, but her phone had rung out.

'She's probably too busy to answer – you know what she's like,' said her mum, her reassuring words belying her anxiety.

They rushed into the house and turned on the TV. The terrorist attacks were on the news and the hotline number was scrolling across the bottom of the screen. But when Jess rang the emergency number, it was engaged. She rang repeatedly over the next couple of hours, but it was busy every time. She imagined that thousands of worried families must be calling the number to register their concerns about injured or missing relatives and friends. Jess was right. Over the course of 36 hours, DFAT would handle more than 15,000 calls from concerned Australian family and friends.

By now, Anthony and Jason and their other brother Phil had all arrived at their mum's place to wait for news about Bronwyn, the eldest of Jenny's five children.

'The girls are both nurses,' said Jenny, trying to remain calm. 'They're probably out there helping people who have been injured.'

She had last seen Bronwyn a few days before the trip and knew how excited she was about her holiday. But she realised now that she had known nothing about the girls' plans, except that they were spending a week in Kuta and going to a mountain health spa for a week on the Sunday morning.

'That's today – they're probably there by now,' said Jenny, trying to figure out the time difference.

Bronwyn loved a drink and a party, but Jenny doubted she and Therese would have been partying the night before their trip to the mountains, particularly since they were leaving early in the morning. But if they *had* been in Kuta when the bombs went off, her daughter would certainly have wanted to help.

Jess was about to try the hotline number again when Dawn rang on Jenny's landline number. The phone had not rung all morning and a hush fell on the room as she rushed into the lounge to answer it.

'It's Dawn, Therese's mum,' said Dawn, hurriedly telling her about the phone call from an Australian woman in Bali called Cath.

Jess watched her mother's shoulders sag as she listened to the story about Therese being in hospital with serious burns and nobody knowing where Bronwyn was.

Until that moment, Jess was expecting a phone call from her sister to say she had spent the night helping to care for the casualties who had been hurt in this atrocity. But watching her mother's crestfallen expression as she listened in silence to Therese's mum, she immediately knew the news was not good.

Jenny hung up looking visibly shaken.

'They *were* there,' she told her kids, her face white with panic. 'Bron's missing and Therese is in hospital, critically burnt.'

In the background the TV was replaying the horrific scenes of the two blazing nightclubs with eyewitness accounts of the carnage, and chilling shots of the crowds outside the hospitals where the injured had been taken.

Jenny was gripped by fear. She did not want to think that her beautiful daughter might be lying among the smouldering wreckage of these bombed-out buildings – trapped, frightened and horribly burnt. The thought of it left her feeling physically sick.

Of her five children, Bronwyn had always been such a whirlwind. From an early age she had been continually on the go – always rushing around and doing a million things at once – never afraid to try something new. There had been an urgency to her daughter's life that she had not glimpsed in her four younger children. Jenny had always felt that a light as bright as Bronwyn's was not destined to shine for a long time. Perhaps that was what this was all about. Perhaps she had to dazzle the world while she had the chance. Maybe this was why Bronwyn was always so busy – as if she sensed that her time on this earth was too precious to waste and she had to pack in as much as she could, while she could.

But the idea of her beautiful daughter suffering a horrible, lonely death in a foreign country, without her loving family around her, was too awful for Jenny to bear.

During her call, Dawn had given Jenny the name of the hospital in Denpasar where Therese was being treated. Steadying her hands, Jenny handed the number to Jess and asked her to call it.

The Balinese nurse who took the call at the Prima Medikia Private Hospital was friendly and helpful, but her English was limited, and Jess was struggling to make herself understood. The nurse gestured Rada over and handed her the phone.

'I'm Jess, Bronwyn Cartwright's sister in Melbourne,' explained Jess, sounding stressed. 'Does anyone know where she is?'

Rada explained that they had been to the hotel where the two girls had been staying but no-one had heard from her yet. Jess sounded so stricken that Rada tried to reassure her.

'The casualties have been taken to a number of different hospitals so it's possible she's somewhere else,' explained Rada. She assured Jess they would continue to look for her sister and would call back as soon as they knew anything.'

Chapter 5

'It sounded chaotic,' said Jess, putting the phone down in tears.

She googled the numbers of a few more hospitals in Denpasar and continued the search for her sister. By now their close-knit extended family of aunts and uncles had arrived at the house to support Bronwyn's distraught mother.

Jess' brother Phil decided to call the hotel to see if his sister had turned up yet. The call had been put through to the girls' room where Cath and Rada had returned to collect Therese's bags and were already busy packing.

Cath answered the call and told Phil what Rada had already told Jess about the possibility of Bronwyn being in another hospital.

'We are going to try and find her,' said Cath. Phil said his family were planning to book flights to Bali to join the search for his sister.

While Jess continued to ring a few more hospitals, Bronwyn's Uncle Michael began to check out flights from Melbourne to Bali. They couldn't just sit here waiting helplessly for news – they needed to do *something*.

Chapter 6

A BEAUTIFUL
NOISE

I t was 3pm in Bali when Cath and Rada returned to the ICU with Therese's suitcase.

In the time it had taken them to collect Carren Smith's suitcase and passport, and pack up Therese's belongings at the Bounty Hotel, her condition had markedly deteriorated. Her body had become dangerously bloated with fluid and she appeared to be growing weaker by the minute.

'We've got all your things,' they said, trying to reassure her. She had been so anxious about her belongings; they hoped that knowing all her things were packed and ready to go would bring her a little comfort.

On the way into the hospital, one of the doctors told them that the Australian authorities were planning to evacuate all their injured citizens back to Darwin, and possibly to Perth. The talk around the hospital was that the Australian Government was in the process of formalising permission from the Indonesian Government to allow the Royal Australian Airforce to land a convoy of Hercules planes in Denpasar. Apparently, a taskforce was being set up to provide medical relief to the Balinese doctors and nurses on the ground and coordinate the evacuation effort.

'Does that mean I'm going home?' asked Therese weakly.

The friends certainly hoped so.

Cath and Rada disappeared into the hospital's reception area to find out when the evacuation was likely to begin. While they were there, they had encountered a well-dressed French couple who had come to the hospital looking for someone. Cath overheard them speaking to the receptionist and asked if they could help.

The couple introduced themselves to Cath and Rada and explained that they lived in Bali and were next-door neighbours.

Philippe was a well-groomed man with a strong French accent. His neighbour, who was also French, introduced herself as Danielle. They explained that they had been asked to come to the hospital to look for an Australian patient.

Phillipe told them his mother had called him earlier that morning from Tewantin in Queensland. She had just spoken with her next-door neighbour, Chris Fox, whose daughter had suffered burns in the bomb blast and was currently in hospital. They had been told she was on holiday in Kuta with her friend who was now missing.

'My mother asked me to let the family know how she is, so I am here trying to find her,' explained Phillipe. He said they had driven around lots of hospitals in Denpasar and Kuta trying to track her down.

'You are talking about Therese?' said Rada, amazed at the astonishing coincidence. 'We are here with Therese – she's in the ICU.'

Rada told the pair about Therese's critical situation and explained that she was in Paddy's Irish Bar when the bomb went off and that her friend Bronwyn was still missing.

Phillipe and Danielle spoke French and Indonesian and said they might have better luck finding Bronwyn. Looking greatly relieved, Rada asked if they would mind speaking with Marie-Antoinette, the injured French girl she had supported during the night.

Speaking to someone from her own country, in her own French language, would be reassuring for her and might lift her spirits, explained Rada.

'Where is she?' asked Philippe.

Rada felt terrible. She had still not been able to remember the name of the hospital where she had left Marie-Antoinette and had no idea where it was. She went over to the receptionist who gave her the names of a few other hospitals in Denpasar. She did not recognise any of them, but scribbled them down with their respective phone numbers.

'Don't worry,' said Danielle. 'We will find Marie-Antoinette for you.'

The teachers told them about the army evacuation, which they hoped would begin that night.

'Hopefully, they will take the most critically injured casualties first,' said Rada.

When they heard how grave Therese's condition was, Philippe said he would go directly to the Australian Consulate and plead with them to evacuate her as a matter of urgency. Cath said she would ring them and do the same.

Afterwards, Philippe said he would find Marie-Antoinette.

'Why don't you join us for drinks tonight?' he offered, studying their weary faces and handing them his business card. They agreed to call later, depending on the situation with Therese.

After the neighbours had left the hospital, Cath and Rada returned to the hospital to deliver the suitcase that Carren Smith was waiting for. While they had been gone Carren had spoken to her sister in Australia who had told her that Qantas were putting on a specialist medical flight to transport some of the bombing casualties back to Sydney.

'It leaves at 10.30pm – you need to get yourself to the airport and be on it,' she told Carren, unaware of her critical condition.

The doctors at Prima Medika Private Hospital were shocked when she announced she was leaving, and urged her to stay, warning that the flight home could be a death sentence for her. But despite the advice of the Balinese doctors, Carren was still determined to discharge herself and catch the next flight back to Australia.

'I have to,' she told Cath and Rada. 'I can't get the treatment I need here.'

They asked her about the friends whose belongings they had glimpsed at her hotel.

Carren explained that Charmaine and Jodi were her friends from Sydney who had joined her at the Sari Club. She had lost them in the mayhem after the blast and had hoped they might have found their way back to the hotel.

But there was no sign of the young women; Cath and Rada added their names to the growing list of Australians they needed to find.

The friends were leaving the hospital when Phillipe called to tell Rada he had driven around various hospitals and found the French girl at the Dharma Usadah Hospital. He had also had a face-to-face meeting with an official at the Australian Consulate and told them that evacuation was Therese's only chance.

'Where are you staying?' he asked, changing the subject.

Rada explained they were staying in a hotel in Kuta.

'No – you can't stay there!' said Phillipe, sounding alarmed. 'It's not safe in Kuta right now.'

After the terrorist attacks, the atmosphere on the streets of Bali was tense and people were afraid there might be further terrorist attacks.

Danielle took over the call and insisted they pack their things immediately and come to stay with her in Seminyak, where Therese and Bronwyn had watched the sunset a few days earlier. When Marie-Antoinette was better, she would stay too, she said.

Danielle owned a large property next door to Philippe's place, which had guest bungalows in the grounds which she regularly rented out to tourists. They were empty and the accommodation was theirs for as long as they needed it.

Philippe told them to call him later to make the arrangements.

The women had still been at the hospital when a volunteer from the Australian Consulate arrived to determine how many patients needed to be evacuated.

The official's name was John Wilkinson, and he had already spoken to Philippe about Therese. The friends immediately approached him and introduced themselves. They wanted to brief him on the Australian patients being treated at the hospital, as well as the casualties they had seen at Bali International Medical Centre who may have been transferred elsewhere.

'Therese Fox is the most critical patient here,' said Cath, pulling no punches. 'She has to be one of the first to go.'

Wilkinson shook his head, clearly overwhelmed by the scale of the injuries.

He had been to all the hospitals in Denpasar and Kuta and was shocked by the number of critically wounded Australian casualties who needed to be airlifted home.

'There are many more seriously injured people at Sanglah too,' he said.

But Cath and Rada were determined to make sure Therese was evacuated as a priority. Cath was convinced she would have a better chance of survival if she could make it back to Australia.

'You have to see this woman,' persisted Cath, gesturing to the official to follow her into the ICU.

The friends stood quietly beside him, watching the shock that swept across his face as he studied the young Australian mother fighting for her life on the hospital bed in front of him. Wilkinson quickly composed himself and moved closer to the bed, clearly touched by Therese's dire situation. Her eyes flickered open at the sound of another Australian voice.

'We will do our best to get you home,' he promised, his voice choking with emotion.

While they were in the ICU, one of the surgeons, Dr Kubera, came to speak to them. He told Wilkinson that Therese's full-thickness burns were by far the worst he had seen in his entire medical career.

'I've treated patients with 15 to 20 per cent burns before,' he said. 'And some of those did not survive.'

Dr Kubera went on to say that the hospital did not have the facilities or the expertise to treat such severe burns. The doctor was frank with the official, and said he was not convinced Therese would even survive the flight back to Darwin, but unless she was airlifted immediately, she would die.

The positive news was that the patient's urine output was still good, which meant the build-up of fluid in her body had not yet reached a critical stage and her kidneys were still working. This was another reason for her to be evacuated immediately, before organ shutdown became a problem. By then it would be too late to save her.

Wilkinson had left the ICU, promising the friends he would do his best to ensure Therese had a place on the plane. From what he had seen he had to agree – she was one of the most seriously burnt patients he had seen.

The friends were still in ICU when Chris Fox called again and Rada was called to the phone in reception to speak to him. She briefly updated him on what the doctors had said and told him that the authorities were planning to airlift all the injured Australians out of Bali, and needed his consent for his daughter's evacuation.

Rada had not wanted to add to his distress by telling him that Therese was fighting for her life in the ICU, or that the surgeons were not optimistic that she would survive the flight back to Darwin. She tried to focus on the positives and told him that

Chapter 6

Therese's urine output was good and that the surgeons had said she should be airlifted home.

But the distressed father was in shock and appeared to be struggling to grasp the gravity of the situation.

'Can you put Therese on the phone so that I can speak to her please?' he asked crisply, unaware of her dire situation.

Rada patiently explained that Therese could not talk to him right now. From his home in Queensland, a distraught Chris Fox gave his consent for her emergency evacuation.

Rada and Cath returned to the ICU where Therese looked more helpless and fragile than ever. Despite their own fears for her survival, they assured her she was going to be fine and promised that they would catch up with her in Australia as soon as they could.

'Make sure when she's evacuated that her luggage goes with her,' Cath instructed one of the nurses monitoring her.

The doctors remained cautious. She had deteriorated even in the last hour. Privately, nobody held any real hope of her making it back to Australia.

Cath and Rada left Therese in the ICU fighting for her life. If she survived the airlift back to Darwin it would be a miracle. But Cath, who had been raised in the Catholic faith, believed in miracles.

Outside the hospital, Rada hailed a cab and disappeared to visit the French patient. With Therese now barely conscious in the ICU and awaiting evacuation, Cath decided to return to the hotel to pack.

The dried blood from Saturday night was still on the footpath and the mere sight of it made her feel physically ill. The blood brought back ghastly memories of the shocking scenes she had witnessed at the medical centre, and she could no longer bear to look at it.

She approached the hotel's reception desk and asked if they would mind cleaning it up and sweeping away the broken glass that still lay scattered around the hotel.

It had been such a chaotic and traumatic night and between fielding calls, tending to the injured and supporting their guests who were looking for missing friends and relatives, she understood that this had been a task the hotel staff had not had time to attend to.

In the hotel lobby Cath ran into Frank Morgan, who had been using his own phone to contact and connect people. He confirmed that the Australian Federal Police had been in negotiations with the Indonesian authorities and were on their way to Bali to take over the investigation into the terrorist attacks.

On her way back to her room, Cath encountered a few of the guests who had helped in the triage area the previous night. They asked her how she was holding up. The question had been paralysing. Cath had no idea how she felt, and no-one had asked her. She had been running on adrenaline for hours and there had been no time to consider how she felt with so much suffering around her.

'I'm okay,' she lied, hurriedly changing the subject to Therese's missing friend.

After they had gone, Cath had slipped into her room and closed the door behind her. She sat quietly on the bed, reliving the events of the most harrowing night of her life and finally broke down – unleashing all the tears and emotion that she had been forced to hold back at the hospital, for Therese's sake.

Chapter 6

Now that she was alone, her tears were unstoppable. She wept for Therese, who may not survive the night — and for Bronwyn, her beautiful friend who had been missing since the terrorist attack. She cried for Marie-Antoinette, Carren Smith, Melinda Kemp and Tracey Ball and for Brendan Barry, and all the other injured victims and their families whose lives would never be the same again.

She pulled off her clothes and took another shower. She rubbed more shampoo into her long brown hair and scrubbed her body even harder. Sadly, the smell of burnt flesh and smoke was still there when she dried herself.

Cath was wearing a clean change of clothes when Rada returned to the hotel, looking more relieved now that she had seen Marie-Antoinette at the hospital whose name she had forgotten.

To Rada's surprise, she had found the French patient looking brighter after her surgery. She was swathed in bandages and awaiting evacuation too. Rada said a French travel agency had been in discussions with Marie-Antoinette's insurance company, who were preparing to transfer her to a bigger hospital in Singapore. From there, she would be flown home to her family in France.

'That's great news,' said Cath, relieved to hear it.

Now that Marie-Antoinette's pain was under control, she chatted to Rada about her life. The young woman was a jockey, who lived in a town south of Paris where she trained horses.

In Marie-Antoinette's limited English, and Rada's basic high school French, she told her new Australian friend that when she recovered, she would like her to come to visit her in France. She would take time off work to show her around, she explained, using lots of gestures.

The doctor came to see his foreign patient before she left, his eyes full of compassion as he studied her heavily bandaged body.

'I'm so sorry,' he apologised, sadly shaking his head.

'Sorry for what?' asked Marie-Antoinette, smiling at him. 'This was not your fault – I am still alive.'

Before Rada left, the women swapped names and phone numbers and promised to stay in touch.

Her new Australian mother-figure kissed the patient on the cheek as they parted ways.

'Take care of yourself,' said Rada, promising she would stay in touch. Marie-Antoinette watched her leave. She was certain that neither of them would ever forget the tragic circumstances that had brought them together.

Rada was making her way out of the hospital when she spotted Marie-Antoinette's doctor standing in the corridor. He had given her the biggest wave and the brightest smile.

Should I go over and speak with him? she wondered, hesitating. In the end, Rada had decided no words were necessary. It was clear from the doctor's warm smile that they understood one another already.

Back at the Masa Inn, Rada began to pack up too. The friends were ready to leave their hotel where they had not yet slept in their beds.

At 8pm on Sunday night, they caught a cab to Danielle's house in Seminyak, where she lived with her husband and two young sons. The house was a beautifully restored traditional Balinese property, hidden away behind secure wooden gates in its own lush, tropical oasis. After the horrors of the past 20 hours, this tranquil pocket of paradise was a million miles away from the chaos and carnage they had witnessed in Kuta.

Philippe met them outside in the street and led them into Danielle's kitchen to fetch some fresh water for the jugs in their rooms. They followed him back through the gardens to the guest bungalows where they were staying. Danielle, who owned fashion boutiques, had prepared a beautiful welcome meal for her exhausted guests.

Sitting around the table in these peaceful surroundings with their generous new friends was surreal after the ghastly sights they had seen.

After dinner, Cath and Rada retired to their separate bungalows ready for a good night's sleep. Cath dumped her bags on the floor, taking in her luxurious new surroundings. The moonlight was flooding in through the open shuttered windows and the stars gleamed down on her from the peaceful night skies.

Cath sank gratefully into the sprawling bed, which was opulently draped with mosquito nets. The sheets smelled fresh and comforting, and for a few moments, Cath lay under the canopy letting the calmness wash over her. She tried not to think about the outstretched hands of the poor souls piled in the van leaving the Gates of Hell, or Therese's gut-wrenching screams as she poured the cool saline over her burnt body.

Cath thought about the three young women lying side by side in the ICU beneath sheets that could not touch their skin. They were all somebody's daughters, and God willing they would survive their horrific injuries. With any luck, when Cath woke in the morning, Therese would be on her way back to Australia. There were no guarantees that she would cope with the journey, but she believed she had a better chance of survival if she could make it home.

She sunk her head into the softest feather pillows, where she could hear the gentle drone of approaching planes in the skies over Bali. The soft, rhythmic humming of the RAAF aircrafts grew louder as they began their descent into Denpasar to begin the evacuation.

It was the most beautiful sound Cath had ever heard.

Chapter 7

FIGHTING
FOR HER LIFE

At 4am on Monday morning, while Cath and Rada were sleeping, Therese was taken from the ICU to Denpasar Airport, where the evacuation of Australian casualties was already underway.

The first RAAF C 130 Hercules plane had touched down in Denpasar early on Sunday evening for what would be the largest Australian aero-medical evacuation since the Vietnam War.

For the past 26 hours, the Royal Darwin had been in emergency mode after a patient with shrapnel wounds arrived at the emergency department saying he had just arrived on a flight from Bali following an explosion in Kuta.

The injured patient told shocked medical staff that he had fled the scene of the devastation in Kuta's nightclub district and headed straight to Denpasar Airport where he had caught the first flight back to Australia.

The medical staff on duty had immediately raised the alarm with the hospital's senior executives, who alerted government authorities that an incident was unfolding in Bali.

At 2am on Sunday 13 October, while Therese was being transferred to Prima Medika, members of the Australian public had started contacting the AFP's National Assessment's Centre (NAC) reporting calls from concerned relatives and friends in Bali describing a major explosion at a nightclub or hotel in Kuta. The callers reported massive confusion and multiple fatalities and were immediately referred to DFAT's Consular Operations for further information.

In Bali, the Australian Consulate General had also been notified about two bomb blasts in Legian Jalan and the AFP had received calls from Federal agents on the ground in Kuta, describing the scenes of destruction and reporting that there were mass casualties from the explosions.

After visiting the scene of the blasts, Federal Agent Glen McEwen phoned the AFP headquarters back saying the carnage was extensive and many people were dead or injured. He also described the giant crater where the Sari Club had once stood and said the place was on fire.

As phone calls began to fly between Australian government departments and various police agencies, DFAT established an Emergency Call Unit to handle the growing number of calls from concerned friends and relatives in Australia.

By 6.40am the Prime Minister, John Howard had been contacted by a senior staff member appraising him about the bombings at Paddy's Irish Bar and the Sari Club.

AFP chiefs and the General Manager of National Operations were immediately called to an emergency summit at the AFP

Chapter 7

Headquarters and by 10am on Sunday morning, two separate RAAF Hercules planes were already on their way to Denpasar.

Each aircraft carried a team of seven doctors, nurses, surgeons and anaesthetists along with vital medical supplies.

When the planes reached Denpasar Airport some of the medics established a triage inside the departure lounge where they began identifying, triaging and treating some lesser injured casualties who were queuing for commercial flights back to Australia. Other medics set about establishing a make-shift triage hospital on the tarmac outside in preparation for an evacuation that would begin later on Sunday.

By the time Therese left ICU at 4am on Monday, the first Hercules had already returned to Darwin with 15 Australian casualties on board, and a second plane was preparing to leave with another 22 injured patients on board.

As Therese was being assessed in the make-shift hospital on the tarmac, an Orion aircraft was getting ready to take off with a cabin full of less injured patients.

In Australia, the Royal Darwin Hospital had sprung into disaster mode. It had emptied its emergency department and begun transferring patients to smaller private hospitals and clinics. A team of medical experts were arriving in Darwin to help staff deal with the flood of critically injured patients who had suffered the sorts of injuries that were normally seen in combat.

In Sydney, staff at the Concord Repatriation Hospital – the burns centre for NSW – had also activated its disaster plan. Additional staff were called in and air mattresses delivered to the hospital which was also on standby for an influx of critically ill patients who would be transferred by air from Darwin.

By the time the day was out, more than 66 badly injured patients had been airlifted to Darwin, where military doctors were assisting with the ongoing transfer of patients to other major hospitals all over Australia.

But Therese had not been one of the first patients to be evacuated out of Bali as Cath and Rada had anticipated. When they woke on Monday morning she remained in the makeshift hospital at Denpasar Airport where she was fighting for her life.

During the two hours she had been waiting, the morphine she had been given in the ICU several hours earlier had worn off. By daylight, she was screaming in agony again. The supplies were running out in the triage under the tarp, the morphine and anaesthetics had almost gone, and she could hear herself screaming out in pain.

'Don't leave me here to die,' she begged. 'I have to go home to my children.'

Two Balinese nurses sat beside their critical patient, who was in great distress from the pain. By mid-morning, Therese's cries were primal howls and the staff caring for her been reduced to tears by her suffering.

They begged the doctors to make room for her on the next flight home before it was too late.

'I'm so sorry,' whispered one of the doctors, examining Therese's bloated limbs again. 'She's too injured – we're not sure she can cope with the flight,' she heard him say.

Therese felt herself slowly disengaging – as if she was watching the dreadful scene from another place. For a few moments, she hovered above the tarp, looking down on the horrifically burnt patient shrieking on the trolley below. It was like a hideous movie that made you cringe as you watched through your fingers.

Then another emotion took over and she was back in the moment again.

'You don't know me,' an angry voice whispered in her head. 'I'm going to survive this. How dare you assume I'm going to die.'

The flash of anger sapped the little energy she had left; she closed her eyes again, willing someone to come and rescue her. She had to get out of this place. If she was as injured as everyone appeared to be saying, why hadn't she been taken home already?

Over the four hours since she had arrived in Denpasar Airport, her swollen body had continued to balloon. From the vague discussions going on around her head, she inferred that the medical experts believed the pressure in the Hercules would prove too much for her. Perhaps the swelling would affect her airways and she would have to be intubated.

It was now mid-morning in Bali. The sun was beating down on the tarp, and the mercury was climbing. Many of the casualties that had been brought in from the different hospitals and clinics around Kuta and Denpasar were already on the two hours and 45-minute flight to Darwin.

The pain was so all encompassing that even though Therese was floating in and out of consciousness, she remained vaguely aware and orientated.

In her rare moments of lucidity, she felt angry and despairing. She did not want to die alone on the tarmac in this strange foreign land that had been so cruel to her. She wanted to go home. If she was going to die, she wanted to leave this world surrounded by the people she loved – by her children.

But Alex and Katie needed her. How could she possibly leave them to grow up without her? The thought of leaving them without saying goodbye would break their hearts, and her own. The very idea of leaving them at all sparked a fierce flame deep inside her, and she began to cry out for help again.

It had worked for her in BIMC the previous night when she had taken Cath's advice and screamed so loudly that she had received the morphine she needed before it was gone. On Monday morning she screamed even louder. She screamed for her life and for her children. She needed someone to put her on that bloody plane before it was too late!

More time passed and when her eyes flickered open again, a familiar figure was sitting beside her, soothing the panic rising again in her stomach.

'It's okay, Taze ... it's me ... you're not on your own. I'm here with you,' whispered Bronwyn's voice. Therese closed her eyes and the familiar voice of her friend drifted slowly away.

A young Balinese male nurse came into the triage and spoke with the nurses who had been monitoring the patient. They had been weeping.

'She wants her children,' said one of the nurses, visibly distressed.

The discussion continued around the bed in Bahasa. For a moment, Therese felt invisible. Am I dead already? she wondered. Then she felt the rushing of wheels against the tarmac as the male nurse pushed the trolley as fast as it would go towards the last plane on the ground.

Chapter 7

'Please take her home ... please,' the male nurse begged the army medics. 'She has two children.'

And to Therese's great relief, she felt herself being lifted into the plane's cavernous cargo hold and registered the sound of heavy metal doors closing behind her.

She had spent hours on the tarmac waiting to die, and against the odds was still fighting to live. Her condition had deteriorated during the morning and although she was close to death, she was still acutely aware of what was happening around her.

Therese begged the female RAAF doctor examining her for some water.

'I'm so thirsty,' she pleaded, her throat burning.

The medic stared at her sympathetically.

'I'm so sorry,' she replied. 'But I can't give you anything because of the risk of aspiration.'

If by some miracle this patient survived the 1760-kilometre flight back to Darwin, she would need emergency surgery. Giving her water to drink was too risky, though the doctor's heart went out to her.

A male army colleague came over to examine Therese. Her entire body was red, raw and severely bloated. Her limbs alone were three times their normal size. The reports from the Balinese doctors at Prima Medikia were right. Her burns were extensive and appeared to be full-thickness burns. There was every chance that she might develop an infection that would kill her.

A short discussion followed between the medics about her chances of surviving the cabin pressure with such swollen limbs. Her only hope was medical intervention before the plane took off.

'I'm so sorry, Therese,' said the male doctor, looking her directly in the eyes. 'But I'm going to have to cut you, to release some of this pressure and restore the blood supply to your limbs. If I don't, the flight will kill you.'

Therese did not argue.

'Only with anaesthetic then,' she said optimistically.

But the number of seriously injured casualties who had already been evacuated during the past few hours while Therese lay on the tarmac had depleted the supply of anaesthetics. Even the heavy-duty opiates that would have afforded her some relief during the procedure had now gone.

She was given something to bite on, and the doctor carried out the agonising procedure without any pain relief or anaesthetic.

Therese felt the searing pain of his blade cutting into layers of burnt flesh and fatty tissue. Her screams echoed across the tarmac as the doctor repeated the procedure on her other arm and went on to make long horizontal slits down each of her swollen legs. It was the most indescribable and painful experience of Therese's life and she immediately lost consciousness.

On Monday 14 October 2002 – two days after the Bali Bombings – Therese Fox was finally evacuated from Denpasar Airport with fourteen other casualties. She was on the third RAAF plane to leave Bali and would not remember the journey home or ever know how close she came to death during that flight. She would spend the entire trip back to Australia unconscious but still fighting for her life.

When the Hercules finally touched down in Darwin at 12.35pm, a new team of paramedics was waiting on the ground to transport her to the Royal Darwin Hospital. As the doctors had predicted, the journey had proved too great, and she had briefly 'died' enroute. The doctors had had to resuscitate her before she could be taken from the plane to the waiting ambulance.

At the Royal Darwin Hospital, Therese was rushed into the ICU where she was placed in an induced coma. The doctors there would spend the next 12 hours trying to stabilise her so that she could be airlifted again to a bigger specialist burns unit in Sydney.

Therese's life was still hanging in the balance when the Careflight Service arrived the following afternoon to airlift her to Sydney's Concord Repatriation Hospital. The nursing staff watched her being stretchered out and taken to the waiting plane with another survivor of the bombings. Nobody expected her to make it.

Chapter 8

A DARK DAY

While Therese was screaming for her children in the makeshift hospital at Denpasar Airport, the masterminds behind the terrorist attacks were holed up at secret locations around Indonesia celebrating the shocking aftermath of the tragedy.

It would later emerge that Imam Samudra, who had led the preparatory meetings for the bombings, had stayed on in Bali for several days after the tragedy to survey the destruction and the reaction of those whose lives had been destroyed.

In the 30 hours that had followed the attacks, the death toll from the two simultaneous explosions had continued to climb, confirming what the international media had reported on Sunday – that many of the fatalities were Australian.

The message the Jihadists had intended to send to the world was clear. No-one was safe; not on their own soil, or on anyone else's!

On Monday morning, the Australian news was filled with stories of selfless acts of courage, miraculous escapes and tragic loss.

For those who had relatives or friends who were missing since the terrorist attacks, the fear that they may be among the dead was paralysing and many families had already begun to make plans to fly to Bali to wait for news. One of them was Bronwyn Cartwright's frantic family.

While Therese had been fighting for her life in the triage hospital at Denpasar, in Australia, the Government's National Security Committee had been summoned to an urgent meeting in Canberra. The emergency summit was called to examine the adequacy of Australia's domestic legislation on terrorism, which had only recently undergone a significant review following the terrorist attacks by Al-Qaeda on the US mainland on 11 September 2001.

Just as the Australian Prime Minister, John Howard, would tell parliament in an impassioned address later in the day, the 'barbaric' attack on innocent Australians on holiday in Bali had highlighted the nation's vulnerability for a potential terrorist attack on its own soil.

Saturday's bombings had taken place on Australia's doorstep, and anyone who thought another attack closer to home was not a possibility was deluding themselves. He said no-one had believed that the events of 11 September had been possible until they happened!

The meeting of National Security advisors followed telephone discussions on Sunday 13 October between the Australian Prime Minister and the Indonesian leader, President Megawati, who had expressed her nation's outrage over the bombings. They had agreed that the only likely explanation for the two separate blasts was a terrorist attack.

During the conversation, both leaders had agreed that the Indonesian and Australian authorities should form a collaboration to track down those responsible – and anyone harbouring them – and bring the perpetrators to justice.

A few months earlier, John Howard had travelled to Jakarta where he and his Indonesian counterpart had signed a 'memo of understanding' against terrorism. The agreement was sparked by growing concerns from the US and Australian Governments about the existence of extremist groups in Southeast Asia with links to al-Qaeda – specifically Indonesia.

The response of both governments to Saturday's bombings in Kuta was swift and decisive. Within hours of their telephone discussion, the Indonesian National Police (INP) and Australian Federal Police had established 'Operation Alliance', a joint investigation into the terrorist attacks and a partnership to coordinate the identification of the dead.

Late on Sunday, 14 AFP officers had arrived in Bali to join more than a dozen colleagues who were already on the ground – including those on leave from East Timor. Joining the taskforce were specialist identification officers, scientific crime scene investigators and post–bomb blast investigators.

In the days ahead, an average of 40 Australian federal agents and analysts would liaise with the INP on everything from disaster victim identification and forensic investigation, to criminal intelligence and bomb data analysis. Operation Alliance would become the most significant and resource-intensive operation the AFP had ever undertaken, and by its conclusion more than 500 officers would have played a part in the investigation.

Chapter 8

At Monday's security meeting, it was agreed that the Commissioner of the Australian Police, Mick Keelty – and the head of ASIO, Dennis Richardson, would join their officers and agents in Bali to oversee the collaboration between the two police authorities.

Meanwhile, the Australian Minister for Foreign Affairs, Alexander Downer, and the Minister for Justice and Customs, Christopher Ellison, had been preparing to travel to Jakarta to conduct a review of the terrorist legislation and initiate discussions to apprehend the culprits.

After the meeting of his security advisors, Mr Howard gave a heartfelt address to Parliament. He condemned the terrorist attack on innocent holidaymakers as a 'brutal and despicable act of indiscriminate violence' and said the outrage was a 'dark day' for the Australian people.

Early reports from Bali on Monday revealed that 181 people from different countries had lost their lives in the terrorist attacks and that at least 14 Australians had been identified among the fatalities.

But Mr Howard said it was estimated that as many as 70 Australians may have lost their lives in the bomb blasts while another 113 citizens were already known to have been seriously injured. He said the Australian authorities were still trying to establish how many casualties had been evacuated back to Australia, but it had been reported that another 220 citizens remained unaccounted for.

The Prime Minister said it was important to remember that not every missing person was necessarily dead. But because of the large number of Australians believed to be in the two nightclubs at the time of the blasts, the nation should prepare itself for the likelihood that the death toll would climb 'significantly' over the coming days once a formal identification process had been put into place.

'For the rest of Australian history, 12 October 2002 will be counted as a day on which evil struck, with indiscriminate and indescribable savagery,' Mr Howard said. Most of the casualties were young innocent Australians who had been having fun and relaxing. He said the tragedy was more poignant, coming at the end of Australia's winter football season when lots of AFL players and rugby league and rugby union teams were in Bali enjoying their annual breakups.

He said the word terrorism was too 'antiseptic' for what he believed was a 'barbaric, brutal mass murder without justification'. That was how it was perceived by the Australian people and the rest of the world.

Mr Howard said he had already received condolences from US President George Bush, and Tony Blair, the British Prime Minister, as well as Helen Clark, the Premiere of New Zealand, and many other world leaders. The Queen had also sent her sympathies to the families of the victims and the Australian people.

Mr Howard said the bombings were a terrible reminder that terrorism could strike anyone, anywhere and at any time. No-one was immune and nobody could hide from it. His government's thoughts were now with the families of those who had lost their lives or had suffered injuries, and those who were still missing.

His heart went out to the many families dealing with the agony of waiting by the phone, not knowing whether their loved ones were dead or alive. And his prayers were for those who had already been told the worst, and for the many casualties battling the horrendous burns suffered in the bombings.

The Australian Government also sent its condolences to the families overseas whose relatives were killed or injured in this evil act of terrorism – particularly the peaceful Balinese who lived in a beautiful part of Indonesia that so many Australians loved. They too had lost friends and relatives, and Bali's fragile economy and tourist industry would inevitably suffer because of this 'foul deed'.

'Those who did this are not friends of Indonesia – those who did this sought to inflict misery and deliver hatred, not only to the people of Australia and the people of other nations who have lost their sons and daughters, but also to the people and government of Indonesia,' said Mr Howard. He vowed to continue to support the war against terrorism, saying any other action would be pure folly.

But Australia should remember that this was not a war against Islam – and those true adherents of the Islamic faith would abhor the tragic events that had happened in Kuta on Saturday.

He also thanked the Department of Foreign Affairs and Trade and the Australian Defence Forces – particularly the members of the Royal Australian Air Force and medical personnel who had been involved in the evacuation of casualties and had worked in the most difficult circumstances in Bali.

Mr Howard warned that the true death toll of the bombings in Bali might not be known for several days and announced a National Day of Mourning for the victims the following Sunday. A national memorial service would take place at a future date.

Amidst this international denouncement of terrorism, Therese Fox's family were praying she would not be one of the growing number of fatalities from Saturday night's bombing attack.

At her home in Grovedale, Dawn Fox's strong Christian faith had become her lifeline. Just as the Prime Minister had predicted in his moving address to Parliament, she and her former husband were two of the many Australian parents grappling with the agony of waiting by the phone, not knowing whether her daughter had survived the night, or whether she would make it home.

Dawn had been replaying in her head the ominous conversations she'd had with Damien about his premonition of danger in Bali. At the time it had all sounded so random and silly, Now, she blamed herself for not taking his warnings seriously, and for not trying harder to talk Therese out of her holiday.

Fortunately, Therese's children had spent the weekend with their paternal grandmother, Pam Symons, in Little River, which is located 45 minutes up the Princes Freeway on the other side of Geelong. The stayover had been a blessing as it had spared the youngsters witnessing Dawn's anguished phone calls to the Foreign Affairs hotline and her conversations about their injured mother with their grandfather in Queensland.

The last thing Dawn wanted to do was frighten her grandchildren before she knew exactly what their mother's situation was. On Sunday, she was informed that the Australian authorities were planning to airlift the casualties from Bali back to Darwin. Someone would contact her when the evacuation had begun, and flights would be arranged to reunite her with Therese, who would be transferred to a hospital closer to home.

Chapter 8

On Sunday morning, while Dawn was waiting by the phone for updates about Therese, her grandchildren were watching cartoons at their grandmother Pam's house. Their father, David Dorling, who had the care of his children on alternate weekends, had spent the weekend in Adelaide on his local football team's end-of-season trip.

In an ironic twist of fate, the team had also been planning to go to Bali for their breakup but had changed their minds at the last minute. Officials had decided Bali was too expensive and that some of the players may be deterred by the expense and pull out. Instead, they had opted to hold their celebrations in South Australia, believing more of their team would go.

Not wanting to disappoint Alex and Katie, who enjoyed their time with his mother, David had arranged for his children to spend the weekend with their nana in Little River.

David was still in Adelaide on Sunday morning when his mother received a call from the children's other grandmother, telling her that Therese had been seriously injured in the terrorist attack in Bali that was all over the morning news.

Pam had listened with a sinking heart as Dawn shared the information she had already shared with Bronwyn's mum.

The two shocked grandmothers decided it would be better to spare Alex and Katie the shocking details about the terrorist bomb. They agreed Pam would keep the explanation simple but truthful, and would tell them that mum had been involved in an accident and was in hospital in Bali.

The two children were watching cartoons when their grandmother returned to the living room, picking her words carefully so she did not frighten them.

'I'm afraid Mum has had an accident in Bali and has had to go to the hospital,' explained Pam, keeping her voice matter-of-fact and even.

Alex had given no response at all and continued to watch his cartoons as though he had not heard her. But Katie, observing the worried expression on her nan's ashen face, had immediately sensed that something was seriously amiss. She had wondered if her mum had hurt herself swimming, or cut her leg, or broken an arm. She had known that to happen to kids at her school.

But the brief explanation coming out of her nan's mouth did not match the fear on her face and Katie had climbed onto her lap and began to cry.

Pam's sudden silence and her sudden distracted behaviour had frightened Therese's little girl. She looked at her older brother with worried eyes, wondering if this 'accident' was something they ought to be concerned about. But Alex had remained transfixed on his cartoons.

He finally broke his silence with a random question for his nan.

'Can I go out to play with Austin' he asked.

Alex was a highly sensitive and caring child, and his father would later realise that his son had known something was terribly wrong and had been putting on a brave face because he was so scared. Later, his dad and his nan concluded that he had unconsciously detached himself from the situation, to protect himself from whatever it was the grown-ups had felt unable to say.

Shortly after the phone call from Dawn, David rang his mum from Adelaide to check on his children and she told him about Therese and her missing friend.

Chapter 8

David had already seen the news about the terrorist attacks in Bali on the hotel TV that morning. But he was shocked to discover that Therese and Bronwyn had been involved. He had known that his former partner was on holiday in Bali with her friend, but he had no idea where they were staying. He did not make the connection until his mother told him about Dawn's phone call.

David immediately offered to catch an earlier flight home, but his mother said his premature return might alarm the children. There was nothing he could do. He should stick to his original plan and return home on Monday morning with the rest of his footy team. They would tell the children together when they had more information on their mother's condition.

'It sounds bad,' said Pam, sounding choked.

David returned to his football breakup, still reeling from the shattering news. Although their five-year relationship had not worked out, they shared their mutual love of their children and had remained on good terms. He could not believe this had happened.

'Bloody oath – we could have been there too,' remarked one of his mates, reflecting on their lucky escape.

Later that day the team had gone to a hotel overlooking the water in Glenelg, and another update on the bombings was aired on the TV in the bar. The pub was packed, but the noise and the banter died immediately as the crowd listened in silence to the shocking eyewitness accounts from Kuta.

Survivor Peter Hughes' badly burnt and swollen face gave Australians at home a glimpse of the suffering as he humbly told news crews that he was 'good' while awaiting treatment for burns to 50 per cent of his body.

Hughes, 42 – who was from Perth – had gone to Paddy's bar because the queue outside the Sari Club on Saturday night had been too long. He had been heading to the bar to get the first round of drinks when he saw an Indonesian-looking man with a backpack at his feet.

The blast had propelled a girl into him, knocking him to the ground and he had pulled her outside with him onto the footpath when the second bomb went off across the road and threw him back inside the crumbling pub. He was glad to be alive.

David, watching the footage of the devastation, felt as detached as his son had felt when his nan had delivered the news. The whole thing was completely unreal.

In seconds, the crowded pub had come to a complete standstill as people took in the giant crater where a club full of people – just like this one – had once stood.

The blasts that had claimed hundreds of casualties had included dozens of footy players just like themselves. The mood was sombre and pensive. David had never experienced the kind of silence that he glimpsed in the pub in Adelaide that Sunday afternoon – and he never would again. And it was even more surreal just knowing that the mother of his children had been involved in the nightmare.

What David did not know as he made his way back to Adelaide Airport the following morning was that his children's mother had been lying in a makeshift hospital at Denpasar Airport, where no-one expected her to survive.

When he arrived at Melbourne Airport an hour later, he found his mother and stepfather waiting with his children. The adults were careful not to talk about the terrorist attacks, or mention that their mother's life now hung in the balance.

From his mum's house, David rang his former mother-in-law, who told him that the evacuation of the casualties had already begun. They were on standby to fly to Darwin where the authorities were planning to reunite them with their injured daughter. Because it was likely that Therese and some of the other casualties would be transferred to hospitals closer to home, it might be better for the children if they remained in his care for the time being.

After the call, David sat his children down and gently explained that Mum had been burnt in the accident in Bali and might be in hospital for a while.

'Just until she's better,' he assured them. He told them not to worry and said he would continue to take them to primary school in Grovedale until things settled down. Katie cried again. Alex said nothing.

Later that day, he drove them back to their home in Grovedale and helped them pack some of their clothes and suggested that they should bring some of their games and favourite toys to play with. It was important to keep their lives as normal as possible in these uncertain times.

For now, they would be living at his place in Werribee and spending more time at Nana's in Little River while their other grandma took care of Mum.

'We will go to see her very soon,' he assured them. Privately, he had no idea when that might be – or if Therese was going to make it.

In Grovedale Dawn had spent an anxious Monday afternoon waiting by the phone for updates on the evacuation.

She was grateful that Therese had remained on such good terms with her children's father and knew he would step in and help. David was a great dad and Dawn had every confidence that he would handle the news that Mummy had been badly hurt with the utmost tact and sensitivity. In truth, the family had been given very little information apart from the fact that Therese was badly burnt and was in a critical condition. Her father had given his consent for her to be evacuated on one of the RAAF planes, but on Monday, nobody appeared to know where she was.

On Monday night, Dawn's prayers were finally answered when she received a call informing her that Therese had finally arrived at the Royal Darwin Hospital where she had been placed in an induced coma. Her condition was still critical, but it was hoped that she would be airlifted to Sydney the following morning as soon as her condition had stabilised.

Dawn was told that her daughter would be taken to the burns unit at the Concord Repatriation Hospital and that flights and accommodation were in the process of being booked and would be paid for by the authorities. Someone would call her to let her know when Therese was on her way.

The family were relieved but frightened. The situation sounded desperate, and they had no idea what to expect.

On Tuesday morning, the call they had been expecting finally arrived. Therese's transfer was imminent, and Dawn and Damien had been booked on flights from Melbourne to Sydney where they would be reunited with her at the Concord Repatriation Hospital. They had been warned that she was still in a coma and her condition remained critical. Her dad would be flying down from Brisbane and would join them at the hospital.

Chapter 8

Upon their arrival in Sydney, Dawn and Damien caught a cab straight to the hospital where Therese had just been admitted to the ICU in the burns unit. The staff at Concord had been shocked by the extent of her injuries and amazed that she had made it to Darwin at all, let alone survived the flight to Sydney.

The family were immediately taken into a private room where one of the specialists treating Therese came to speak with them.

'Please don't have any hope that she can possibly survive this,' he said, looking Dawn directly in the eye.

He explained that Therese needed urgent surgery to remove more debris from her badly burnt body, using more sophisticated equipment than had been available at the hospital in Denpasar.

Unfortunately, their plans to perform the emergency procedure were abandoned because her temperature had plummeted.

'It's now dangerously low,' explained the doctor, who explained that it was unlikely that she would survive the anaesthetic.

'It is a grave concern, because without the surgery she runs a real risk of developing an infection which could be life threatening in itself,' he said.

Dawn, too shocked and too numb to think straight, asked if she could see her daughter.

One of the nurses led them into the ICU where Therese lay in a coma. She was bandaged from head to toe, apart from a 2-inch gap around her eyes, which were so swollen they had closed. Dawn surveyed the lifeless 'mummified' patient attached to the respirator. She was fitted to a tangle of tubes which were hooked to a multitude of different machines which flashed and beeped at intervals. The entire scene was confronting and terrifying.

Dawn approached the bed, panicking at the realisation that she did not recognise the woman in the bed as her own daughter.

'We're here for you, Therese ... you're home now,' she whispered, too traumatised to cry.

The family had been told Therese was in a coma and could not hear them, but Dawn had not been convinced. Her belief that her daughter could hear them had been confirmed, because within minutes of the conversation, Therese's temperature had miraculously started to rise.

'She *knows* we are here,' wept Dawn, convinced that underneath the bandages her daughter was fighting to stay alive.

The specialist and the nurses looked surprised but remained cautious and non-committal. They would see how she went during the night and would review the life-saving surgery in the morning.

Therese's family had not slept since the news on Sunday. They decided to take the doctor's advice and catch up on some of the sleep they had lost and pray that things improved overnight.

They were provided with accommodation near the hospital. But Dawn was so shaken she had spent a restless night suffering the same frightening nightmare. In her dream, she had watched the doctors and nurses peeling away the layers of bandages – only to discover that the injured woman beneath them had not been her daughter at all.

It had all been a ghastly mistake and under the dressings, another mother's daughter had been fighting for her life, while her beautiful Therese lay buried beneath the wreckage of Paddy's bar in Bali.

Chapter 8

The harrowing nightmare had left Dawn sweating under the covers and would haunt her in the days ahead, though she was too afraid to share her darkest fears with anyone.

When they returned to Concord on Wednesday morning, Therese's condition had still been critical, but by a miracle her temperature had continued to rise during the night. The surgical team, after reviewing the patient, had been reconsidering the surgical procedure.

After warning the anguished family that Therese might not survive the procedure, the doctors wheeled her off to theatre. Dawn had watched them disappear down the corridor, terrified that she may never see her daughter again.

Damien thought they should get some fresh air away from the ICU and had called a cab to take them down to Sydney Harbour. They sat together in the sunshine trying to make sense of it all.

Despite the doctor's warnings, Damien felt inexplicably optimistic. After spending months secretly worrying that this holiday spelled danger for his sister, the same sixth sense that told him she was alive now told him she was going to pull through.

'She's going to be okay, Mum. I feel it,' he said, putting a reassuring arm around his mother.

Therese's friend Michelle Larkins had said the same thing in her comforting phone calls to Dawn.

'She'll come through this, you'll see,' she kept saying.

'Her kids are the world to her – she loves them far too much to give up the fight. She's tough – and she has the determination to do anything. She will survive – for them!'

Dawn, desperately trying to push her doubts to the back of her mind, prayed Michelle would be right.

Back at the hospital, Therese had returned to the ICU. She had survived the procedure, but she was not out of danger by a long way. The doctors warned that the next few days would be critical.

More debris had been scraped from Therese's skin and her burns redressed. She was now on a cocktail of super-strong intravenous antibiotics to prevent an infection from setting in, but the doctors remained cautious about her chances of survival.

'The antibiotics will flush out any bugs she may have picked up in Bali,' they told the family, picking their words carefully.

The procedure had allowed them to examine the full extent of Therese's injuries and they were able to confirm what the specialists in Bali had determined. She had sustained a fractured skull and had suffered burns to 85 per cent of her body. Around 65 per cent of them were serious third degree full-thickness burns.

The heat from the explosion had been so intense it had calcified her elbow joints, and melted the skin from her face, hands and feet. The specialist said Therese was the most severely burnt patient he had ever treated, and that he held little hope of her being able to survive such extensive injuries.

'Her body is very weak,' he said frankly. It was a miracle she had survived at all.

Dawn and Chris were told that the next 48 hours were crucial and that they would have to wait and see whether her situation deteriorated over the following days. As he left the private room, the doctor warned them again not to get their hopes up.

But leaving the hospital that night, her brother reassured his mother that some miracles took longer than others. The miracle Therese needed was going to be a work in progress.

Chapter 9

DEFYING

THE ODDS

When the Australian Consulate contacted Cath and Rada on Monday night to let them know that Therese had survived the flight back to Darwin, they were relieved and elated.

'She made it!' shouted Cath, hanging up the phone to tell Rada the news they had been waiting all day for.

They had woken that morning to the comforting sound of the RAAF planes disappearing back into the skies on their return to Australia, hoping that Therese had survived the night and had been evacuated with all the other injured casualties.

After their impassioned pleas to John Wilkinson from the Australian Consulate, and the urgings of Therese's doctor and their new friend, Philippe, they imagined that she would have been one of the first patients onto the Hercules and that the military doctors would have understood it was her only hope of survival.

So, it had been a shock on Monday afternoon when Therese's father rang the Prima Medika Private Hospital to ask where she was, and they discovered she had not been among the casualties who had been arriving at the Royal Darwin Hospital since early morning.

The good Samaritans had been at the hospital performing a welfare check when Chris Fox's call had come through to the reception.

One of the Balinese nurses had immediately handed the anxious Australian father over to Rada.

'Therese wasn't on the planes,' he told her, sounding completely beside himself.

Rada was shocked but explained that all the seriously injured Australians had already been evacuated from Bali. The hospital had already told them that Therese had left the ICU at 4am and had been taken by ambulance to Denpasar Airport. The evacuation had already been underway then.

'B…b…but that was hours ago,' said Chris, panicking again.

He had told Rada that they had been assured by someone at Foreign Affairs that they would receive a call as soon as Therese arrived at the hospital in Darwin. But they had heard nothing all day, and when he'd telephoned again, nobody could tell him where she was.

'Where can she possibly be?' he asked, frantic.

He said he had been informed that there were paramedics on the tarmac at Darwin Airport waiting to take the casualties to the Royal Darwin Hospital. If Therese had been among them, she would have told them her name and who to call.

Rada's heart broke for Therese's dad. Chris was assuming his daughter would be conscious, when it was possible she had not survived the flight, or even made it onto one of the planes. It was clear he had not understood the gravity of his daughter's critical situation.

Cath and Rada had no idea where Therese was. After her surgery on Sunday, Therese's condition had deteriorated so rapidly that Dr Kubera had warned the Consulate official that unless she was evacuated quickly, she would die.

She had still been alive when she left for the airport at 4am, but where was she now? Had she made it onto the army planes – and if she had, had the flight ultimately proved too much as the doctors had cautioned? If she had not made it, they felt certain the family would have been told. So, where was she?

Sitting beside the phone in Australia on Monday afternoon, Therese's shattered parents had begun to imagine the worst. And as the day wore on in Bali, Cath and Rada had begun to imagine it too.

It was an enormous relief when the Australian Consulate rang on Monday night to inform them that Therese had finally arrived at the hospital in Darwin, where she was now in a coma in the intensive care unit.

'She's unconscious – but alive!' said Cath, convinced that Therese's chances of recovery were greatly improved now that she had made it safely home.

She had felt even more hopeful on Tuesday afternoon when Chris Fox rang back to tell them Therese had been transferred to the Concord Repatriation Hospital in Sydney and that arrangements had been made for them to be reunited with her.

Chris told her the doctors were speculating that there may have been Napalm in the bomb at Paddy's Bar, which might explain the extensive nature of Therese's severe chemical burns, though it was subsequently ruled out.

* * *

While Therese was defying the odds in Concord, Cath and Rada were supporting other devastated Australian families through the painful process of identifying the fatalities from Saturday's terrorist attacks.

For so many families, the anguish of waiting by the phone, not knowing if their loved ones had survived – or were among the bodies now lying in the morgue at Sanglah – had become the living agony that John Howard had predicted it would be.

For some, the pain had been too much, and they had booked seats on the first flights they could get. By Tuesday they had begun to arrive in Bali in their droves, where they faced the nightmare of trying to find the people they loved, and negotiating the painful identification process to determine if they were among the dead.

After witnessing Therese's heartache over Bronwyn, and the distress and frustration of the young women from Queensland who had been trawling the hospitals in the middle of the night looking for their missing friends, Cath and Rada wanted to support other people through the nightmare.

As the Prime Minister had cautioned, not everyone who had been listed missing had necessarily lost their lives in the terrorist attack. Cath had already seen the relief that her phone call had given distraught father Ron Kemp when she told him that his daughter Melinda had been found alive and was being treated at the Prima Medika Private Hospital.

Chapter 9

Rada would later experience the same satisfaction when a young Norwegian tourist who had been registered missing was finally found at a hospital in Denpasar. He had not been injured but had spent days sitting beside the hospital beds of two of his friends who had.

Since Therese's evacuation, the TV had continued to replay the ghastly events on Saturday night, until the Australian teachers could no longer bear to watch.

They had decided to focus on what they *could* do, rather than dwelling on the horrors that could not be undone.

They had begun first thing on Monday morning by contacting the Australian Consulate and registering Bronwyn missing. They had also given the authorities the names of Carren Smith's friends – Jodi Wallace and Charmaine Whitton – and the names of the Queensland girls whose friends had prayed with Cath in the reception at Prima Medika in the early hours of Sunday morning.

Afterwards, they had done a ring-around of the different hospitals to see if Bronwyn, or any of the others, had been admitted there. Unfortunately, the volume of overseas phone calls in and out of Bali had caused problems with the telecommunication lines and their calls kept cutting out.

Philippe had driven them into Denpasar where they had visited each hospital in person to see if the names of the missing friends had been added to the register of casualties posted on hospital walls.

The teachers were hoping they might still find Bronwyn at one of the hospitals. It was possible she had suffered a head injury during the explosion at Paddy's Irish Bar and was in a coma in one of the intensive care units, like Therese.

Perhaps some kindly stranger had found her, and taken her to hospital, only to be turned away as they almost had, and was caring for her at home.

There was, of course, another more worrying possibility, but they had not wanted to think about it.

Over the past couple of days, the streets had become even more chaotic than they had been over the weekend. The Indonesian police were out in force and with the arrival of the Australian Federal Police on Sunday, the authorities were clearly on high alert.

The destruction caused by Saturday's terrorist attacks had created widespread panic and uncertainty across Bali. When rumours began to circulate about the possibility of further bomb attacks on the island, more anxious foreign tourists packed their bags and left. Even the locals who had come to visit places like Kuta had been fleeing the major tourist spots fearing they may be a target.

While the remaining foreign visitors were scrambling to book flights out of Denpasar, the grieving families of the victims of the terrorist attacks began arriving in Bali. On Monday, so many Australians arrived at the airport that there had not been enough hire cars for them. A local travel agent came to the rescue and offered to provide buses to transport them into Kuta. As the week wore on and the bomb threats escalated, the numbers of arrivals dwindled, and the buses sat empty at the airport.

At the site of the bombings – and at many of the hospitals and shops along the streets – the Balinese paid their respects to the dead and apologised to the families as they passed by.

Chapter 9

They had placed wreaths of flowers and sweet-smelling posies, and lit candles and incense before pausing to say prayers for the victims.

The relaxed and happy holiday atmosphere that had greeted Rada when she arrived in Kuta on Saturday morning had been overtaken by a deep sorrow that was felt by everyone.

The RAAF evacuation of Australian casualties late on Sunday and into Monday had significantly eased the burden on the local hospitals whose exhausted medical staff remained traumatised by the suffering of their injured patients. When Cath and Rada returned to the Prima Medika Private Hospital on Monday morning, the ICU that had been so chaotic and overwhelmed over the weekend was now calm and deserted.

The only remaining patients were the two badly burnt Japanese girls, who were still fighting for their lives. Rada observed them with sorrowful eyes, wondering who they were and whether their poor mothers had been told that their daughters had been caught up in this barbaric act of violence. She wished she could help. But they did not even know the girls' names.

Cath stood quietly beside their beds and silently recited the Lord's Prayer for them. It was all so heartbreaking and senseless. Sadly, they would not survive.

Since the evacuation, Melinda Kemp and her sister, Tracey Ball, were now in the Royal Darwin Hospital, and so was Brendan Barry – the badly burnt Australian whose suffering Cath and Rada had witnessed at BIMC. Barry, who had been at the Sari Club with a group of friends, would later discover that his good friend and fellow Queenslander Jodie Cearns had been critically injured in the explosion.

The teachers were told that Sari Club survivor Carren Smith had discharged herself before the RAAF planes had arrived to begin the evacuation as she had told them she would.

In a strange twist of irony, the young woman who had gone to Bali intending to take her own life had been in flight and fight mode, and had been focussed on her survival.

After witnessing the valiant efforts of the staff battling to treat the flood of critically injured patients – many of them with complex and potentially fatal injuries – she had become more convinced that her best chance of surviving was a return flight to Sydney.

It was clear that vital medications, like painkillers and anaesthetics, had started to dwindle along with the hospital's supplies of syringes, dressings and medical aids, due to the sheer volume of critical admissions.

The Balinese doctors had been pressuring her into having the life-saving surgery, but Carren decided to organise her own flight home, believing it would be faster than waiting for the RAAF planes that she had been told were on their way to Bali to begin the evacuation.

In the triage area at BIMC where she had waited for hours to be seen it was already clear that there were many other casualties in a far worse condition than she was.

Carren was concerned that she might be one of the last patients to be airlifted in an evacuation that could take several hours.

If the Balinese doctors were right, the clock was already ticking, and her situation was already time critical. The sooner she got herself home, the better.

Chapter 9

On Sunday, while Cath and Rada were collecting her bags from the hotel, Carren phoned her brother in Australia, telling him vaguely that there had been a slight 'incident' in Bali, and that while she was okay, she really needed him to organise her a flight home.

'As soon as possible,' she said, trying not to sound as desperate as she was.

While her brother looked into flights, Carren's sister rang the hospital to tell her that Qantas were arranging a special emergency flight from Denpasar to Sydney for all the casualties of the bombings.

The plane would have Australian doctors and paramedics on board who would have the expertise and medical equipment that the small private hospital in Bali unfortunately lacked.

The flight was leaving Bali at 10.30pm on Sunday night and Carren's sister urged her to get herself to Denpasar Airport to ensure she got a seat.

When the doctors at Prima Medika discovered their patient was planning to discharge herself, they were horrified. Her head wound, which had been temporarily fixed at BIMC, was held together by 38 stitches. But she required more complex emergency surgery to insert a plate in her depressed skull and they urged her to reconsider.

'Without this surgery, you have a maximum of six hours to live,' said one of the doctors bluntly.

But Carren had not been convinced that she would survive the delicate surgery even if she stayed. Conditions were difficult, and the lack of specialist expertise and shortage of medical supplies might increase the risk of introducing an infection that might prove fatal. As the Balinese doctors had already told her, even her burns required more specialist treatment than the hospital in Denpasar could provide.

Refusing to listen to the doctors' urgings to reconsider her decision to discharge herself, Carren had urged the nurses to fix up the bandages on her stapled head. She did not want her wound to look too confronting, or she might alarm the medical staff, who may refuse to allow her to board the Qantas flight back to Sydney and make her stay for the evacuation.

Before she discharged herself, the doctors at Prima Medika were so concerned that they wanted Carren to sign a disclaimer, accepting responsibility if anything went wrong on the flight home. They had warned her that she was leaving against their advice and her decision might prove fatal.

Clutching her bags, and the passport that Cath and Rada had recovered from under the sink in the hotel bathroom, she was taken by ambulance to Denpasar Airport, praying that the flight to Australia would depart on time.

The plane left was leaving at 10.30pm and with a six-hour flight ahead of her, the last thing she needed were unforeseen delays. When the plane finally landed in Sydney, she would be first passenger off and would take herself to the nearest hospital.

At the airport everything had gone smoothly, and Carren had boarded the flight, making light of the bandages covering the life-threatening head wound that had attracted so much attention on Saturday night. The true extent of her predicament remained secret until the plane was safely out of Indonesian airspace.

Everyone on the flight had been talking about the terrorist attacks in Kuta and Carren had spent the entire six-hour journey back to Sydney holding a drip for a teenage girl who was severely dehydrated.

But twenty minutes before the plane began its descent into Sydney, one of the paramedics who had come to check on the patient, noticed the colour draining from Carren's face and raised the alarm.

Taking the drip from her hand, he lay her flat on the cabin floor and asked her again about her head injury. Carren admitted that she had fled the explosion at the Sari Club and had been told she had a depressed skull fracture which required emergency surgery.

The horrified medic panicked, suspecting the cabin pressure might be the reason for her sudden loss of colour. He immediately alerted the cabin crew about the patient's serious head injury and by the time the plane landed an ambulance was waiting to take her to Sydney's Royal North Shore Hospital.

Carren had still not heard from her two missing friends but was hoping they had found their way back to the hotel, or had been taken to another hospital. She intended to contact them once she was safely in hospital in Sydney to let them know she was okay.

On Tuesday, at around the time that Therese was being airlifted to the Concord Repatriation, Carren was in theatre undergoing life-saving surgery. Part of her skull had to be removed and a plate fitted in her head.

Like Therese and many of the other survivors of the Bali bombings, she would require ongoing treatment for her burns. But she felt thankful to be alive.

OUT OF THE ASHES

* * *

By Monday morning, a crisis centre had been set up at the Sanglah General Hospital, which Cath and Rada discovered was exactly that – a centre in crisis! The centre had immediately become a focal point for distraught relatives arriving in Bali to look for their missing children and grapple with the identification process. The Australian teachers observed them wandering around the centre looking confused and distressed – not knowing what to do.

The hospital had posted a register of names listing all the people who were still missing. Cath and Rada added Bronwyn's name to the register and checked to see if any of the other young women's names were on the list. They already were.

Tragically, Rodney Cocks had also checked the hospital lists that day, his heart sinking when he noticed Therese and Bronwyn's names were among the fatalities.

A notice had also been pinned to various hospital walls and shop windows asking for donations of blood, particularly types A and O. So many of the casualties had lost so much blood because of the injuries they had suffered, and many others had undergone complex surgeries requiring multiple transfusions. Blood supplies were running low across Bali; with local patients still requiring ongoing surgery, everyone was being urged to roll up their sleeves and help to save lives.

The Sanglah hospital had also organised a telephone service offering free international calls, as well as providing complimentary hot coffee and food for the families and friends who were still waiting to hear if their loved ones had been identified among the dead.

Chapter 9

Like the shocked and weary doctors and nurses that Cath and Rada had seen at the hospitals over the weekend, the staff at the Crisis Centre looked exhausted as they grappled with the overload of inquiries. It was a similar scene at the Australian Consulate, where the staff appeared to be drowning in people and paperwork.

'There are just so many inquiries,' explained the woman on the Consulate's information desk, where Cath and Rada had gone to register Bronwyn's name and provide documentation for identification purposes.

The enormity of the tragedy appeared to be taking its toll on the woman, who told them she had collected so much information from so many people that she was struggling to remember it all.

Rada remembered how she had felt at the Dharma Usadah Hospital on Sunday morning; she had become so overwhelmed that she had completely forgotten the name of the place. Now this poor woman was losing bits of paper and had forgotten who she had spoken to. The devastation was too much to bear.

'Can we help you in any way?' asked Cath, wondering if they might be useful as volunteers. Perhaps they could be support workers to those who had been told their children were among the dead, or counsellors for the Australian families grappling with the detailed forms they were required to fill out for the formal forensic identification process?

Sadly, Rada was very well qualified for the role after experiencing the heartache of losing her only son. She would be able to relate to these parents because she understood their helplessness and grief – and she had felt their pain. They had immediately returned to the Crisis Centre and volunteered their help.

One of the first parents they had supported was an Australian mother who told them that her daughter had been missing since the bombing at the Sari Club on Saturday. Her daughter's name was Jodi Wallace.

Cath and Rada had recognised the name immediately. Jodi was one of Carren Smith's missing friends who they had been trying to locate. Her father and brother had arranged flights and were coming to Bali to join her mother in the search to find her.

'We just want to bring her home,' said Jodi's distressed mother, bursting into tears.

The teachers had taken a detailed description of Jodi Wallace. Her mother said Jodi had birthmarks on her right lower arm, pierced ears and a belly button ring. She also wore a toe ring, a silver chain, a silver ring and bracelets. They collected all the information and noted Jodi's mum's contact details.

On Tuesday they had met Charmaine's grieving parents too. Cath had found Len and Pauline Whitton standing in the middle of the Crisis Centre at Sanglah, looking lost.

'Can I help you with anything?' Cath had asked, introducing herself.

Pauline Whitton was distraught. They had just been told their daughter had been identified among the bodies in the morgue.

'They can't find Charmaine's passport,' said her mum, bursting into tears. 'It was not among her possessions at the hotel. Nobody knows where it is.'

Cath knew immediately where the passport would be found. She explained how Carren had told them about hiding their passports under the bathroom sinks.

Chapter 9

'That's where we found Carren's passport,' Cath explained.

Charmaine's mother smiled through her tears. 'That's always where Charmaine used to hide things when she was away,' she said sadly.

Cath was confident this is where they would find Charmaine's missing passport. Little things like this were important to parents who were grieving. They needed their children's precious belongings to take home and treasure.

It was one of the reasons why Bronwyn's mother, Jenny Hobbs, had called the Bounty Hotel, asking about her daughter's belongings. She had never been to Bali and had no idea if the belongings of the missing victims might be looted by unscrupulous people. It had been very reassuring to hear that Bronwyn's bags had been locked in the hotel's secure baggage room.

Jenny had told the Bounty's manager, Kossi Halemai, that her family would be travelling to Bali to collect them. Later, when Cath had called the hotel with a query, the manager had given her Bronwyn's mum's contact details.

Cath had immediately called Jenny Hobbs to ask if she could email a recent photo of Bronwyn, along with her dental and medical records, and any scans and X-rays she might have on file. This would help enormously in the identification process. Bronwyn's mother had sounded distraught on the phone.

During their conversation, Jenny had provided Cath with a detailed description of her daughter. Bronwyn was slim, five feet eight inches tall, with long blonde hair, a belly button piercing with a small cross, and a tattoo of a blue butterfly on her shoulder. She had also had a plate in her ankle following a horse-riding accident when she was younger. Her date of birth was 24 May 1974.

Jenny had also told Cath that her brother-in-law Michael, her sister Libby, and her brother Ross were in the process of booking flights to Bali to look for Bronwyn.

Within hours, the family had emailed everything Cath needed to help with the identification process, including up-to-date photographs of Bronwyn. Their French hosts had driven them back to the Sanglah Hospital to determine whether Jenny's daughter was among the unidentified victims of this tragedy.

Cath and Rada were directed to a private room where the authorities had compiled dozens of photographs of the fatalities. They had the painful task of scrutinising the photographs of all the bodies recovered from the two blasts to determine whether the ones they had been sent by Bronwyn's family matched any of the young women in the morgue.

Cath had become worried about Rada and wondered how her friend would cope with such an upsetting task when she was still mourning the death of her son. But Rada, who had been demanding answers about her son's death, had known how important it was to deliver answers to other grieving parents like Jenny.

Together, the friends had carefully examined every snapshot, catching their breath as they flipped through image after image of beautiful young people cut down in the prime of their lives. Some of the faces in the snapshots bore a strong resemblance to one another. Cath and Rada's hearts felt even heavier when they realised that some families had suffered multiple losses. So many lives would never be the same again, they said, their hearts breaking for their families.

The teachers lingered over two photographs of a young woman who bore a striking resemblance to the snapshots Jenny's family had sent of Bronwyn. Was this Therese's friend? they wondered. One of them looked so much like her that they were 90 per cent confident it was her.

Unfortunately, the photographs had already been marked with another young woman's name which created doubt in their minds. They decided to ask Bronwyn's mum for some clearer shots and try again tomorrow.

Among the compilation of photographs was a snapshot of a handsome young man who bore a close resemblance to Rada's son, Matthew. He appeared to be around the same age and looked so much like him that it had taken her breath away. My poor, poor son, thought Rada, stifling a sob. The photo was a reminder of her own devastating loss and all the dreams that Matthew – and all these other young people – would never fulfill.

Someone – probably the parents of the youngster in the photo – had written along the top '100% match'. Reading the words, Rada was completely overwhelmed. The pain those poor parents must have felt when their worst fears were confirmed and they realised their son was gone.

Rada felt so distressed she had left the room in tears. She sat quietly outside on a bench, in an area of the hospital where seats had been placed for families dealing with this harrowing identification process. On the table was a hot thermos of coffee and some nibbles. Rada doubted anyone would even feel like eating as they waited for answers.

Cath had followed her friend outside to the bench; Philippe and Danielle had made their way upstairs and were comforting her.

'This is my beautiful son,' said Rada, producing a photo of Matthew, and bursting into tears again.

Cath felt her friend's anguish. They sat in silence for a few moments reflecting on all the wasted young lives and all the dreams that had been taken from them in this hideous terrorist attack.

An Italian friend had joined Phillipe and Danielle at the hospital. She was a warm and kindly woman who shared her time between Bali and her home in Italy. She had been helping them as they drove from place to place, trying to source essential items – like medicines and bottled water – for local people who had injured relatives in the hospital.

This barbaric attack had not just hurt foreign visitors. It had caused pain to the peaceful Balinese people too. Many local families had now gathered at the hospital to support relatives and friends who had been injured by flying shrapnel and debris, or who had suffered terrible burns.

Danielle told her new Australian friends that it was customary in Bali, when a relative was in hospital, for the entire family to stay and support them.

'This means no-one can work and things become very hard for them to survive,' she explained.

Despite their own hardship, even the poorest Balinese family had been donating something small to help the victims of the bombings.

A local charity, called HATI, had been collecting donations to help improve conditions for local families who needed support while their relatives remained in the hospital where they had been undergoing surgery or required complex critical care.

Later, Rada would donate 1000 rupiah to Hati – the equivalent of $20 (Aus).

Danielle told her that this was more than a month's wages for some Balinese people.

'Your generosity means one family member can carry on working,' she said.

At a time when many Balinese faced a lengthy stay in hospital, every rupiah counted.

Rada would later relate Danielle's story to the principal of her former primary school in Tewantin. He was so moved by the plight of the Balinese that he shared this with his school community. His students ultimately raised more than $1000 for HATI.

They were preparing to leave the hospital when news came through about another bomb threat in Ubud. It would turn out to be a hoax, but it added to the growing unease.

That night, Cath lay in bed reflecting on their challenging day and meditating on a scripture from the Bible. It was from The Philippians 4.13 which read: 'I can do all things through Christ who shelters me.'

The scripture had once hung on the wall at Cath's grandmother's home in Brisbane and her nan had always found the words comforting.

In times as painful as these, Cath thought they could all do with some help. She hoped the scripture that had served as a spiritual reminder for her grandmother would give her the strength to keep going.

* * *

After the AFP arrived in Bali on Monday to join forces with their Indonesian counterparts, strict new procedures had been put into place to ensure that the identification process, which had been so chaotic, was now properly coordinated.

New confidentiality rules meant families were no longer permitted in the photo identification room to view the photographs of the dead. Neither were they allowed into the morgue to make physical identifications. By Tuesday, notices had been put on the door of the morgue instructing families to go to reception.

The arriving Australian families had so many questions that the Australian Consulate had begun to hold daily meetings at the Hard Rock Café, where relatives and friends of the victims could be updated on the status of the identification process.

During these briefings, Australian experts in forensic investigation carefully explained the process that now had to be followed. Crucial criteria had to be met for them to accurately confirm the identities of the victims – specifically DNA, fingerprints and dental – as well as medical records including scans and X-rays.

At the meetings, the officials warned the families that this would be a slow process. In some cases, it might take up to three months to identify some of the victims. But by cross-checking DNA against fingerprints and dental and medical records, there would be no room for error.

For the grieving families who had spent days tormenting themselves about whether their children had survived and had been admitted to one of the local hospitals – or were in the morgue – the prospect of a long wait prolonged their agony.

Chapter 9

They were already shocked and traumatised, and the prospect of delays in identification created discord in the meetings. The fear and tension at the daily briefings was tangible and the growing frustration inevitably erupted into anger as parents began to feel the strain.

Cath and Rada's hearts went out to the shattered families. So many people were doing their best in the most horrific circumstances. Everyone was trying so hard to be brave and hold things together in the aftermath of this horrific tragedy.

After one particularly heated briefing, Cath had gone outside to get some air and was shocked to find herself caught in a blaze of cameras and flashlights.

Not sure how to deal with this attention from international media, she had bolted into the toilets to compose herself. When she emerged, a reporter from Sky News had approached her, wanting to know what had happened in the meeting, and how the families were dealing with this aftermath of this atrocity. Cath tactfully replied, saying everyone looked lost and was doing their best to comfort each other. It was a very painful time for everyone, she said.

Later she and Rada had caught a cab back to Danielle's place where they had made notes of the day's events in their journals. So much had happened over the past few days, and they wanted to keep a contemporaneous record of events to ensure they did not forget anything important.

'Started writing notes and compiling this story,' wrote Rada on Tuesday night.

'So much to tell I can't write. So many memories come back. I want my daughter to read this story.'

Chapter 10

MORE BOMB THREATS

Everywhere had looked so serene when Rada woke the following morning that she had decided to take a walk along Seminyak Beach, where a week earlier, Therese and Bronwyn had watched the sunset over the Indian Ocean.

Afterwards, she had slipped into the pool in the gardens of Danielle's tropical oasis, closed her eyes and let her body float weightlessly around in the water.

It was a picture postcard morning. The palm trees were swaying, the sky was blue, and the birds were singing in this pretty Balinese resort, which really was paradise on earth.

The peaceful scene was a tragic juxtaposition to the horrific scenes they had glimpsed on Sunday morning in Kuta when the barrier blocking the road to the Sari Club had resembled the Gates to Hell, and the Devil's work was evident everywhere in the devastated landscape behind.

Chapter 10

After breakfast, Cath and Rada had moved into the small spare cottage in the grounds of Danielle's sprawling home to make room for Bronwyn's relatives, whose plane was due later on Wednesday morning.

It was agreed that Michael, Libby and Ross would move into the bungalows that had been Cath and Rada's sanctuaries for three days, and they would share the smaller property. Given the tragic circumstances surrounding the trip, nobody wanted this grieving family staying in a hotel in Kuta. Having everyone together at Danielle's place would allow them to support the family through this nightmare.

Before they headed to the airport that morning, Cath and Rada had called in at the Hard Rock Café for the daily briefing, where emotions were running high and the patience of distraught families was wearing thin. The crowd that had gathered for the morning update complained angrily about the painstaking identification process that was fraught with delays.

It was taking too long, complained the traumatised parents. Why couldn't they be shown the photographs that had been in the hospital's photo ID room? Why couldn't they identify the anonymous casualties lying in the morgue?

The frustrated parents looked for someone to blame. They berated the AFP and the Australian Consulate, saying the identification process had become disorganised and confusing, and that there had not been enough support for the victims' families.

Representatives from the various authorities had tried to calm the proceedings down. They agreed that things had been confusing and chaotic in the immediate aftermath. But now that the Australian and Indonesian police were working together and had a process was in place, there were strict protocols to follow to avoid mistakes being made.

Cath and Rada had realised that if the AFP had been involved on Sunday morning, they would never have been able to access Therese's hotel room to collect her bags. And they would not have been permitted to remove her passport from the hotel's safety deposit box, or Carren Smith's bag and the passport from under her bathroom sink. Carren would not have been able to leave the country and would have had to have her life-saving surgery in Bali. She may not have survived. Therese would most certainly have died.

Sadly, Rada had witnessed first-hand the distress that not having a proper process could cause to survivors. The day before she had been helping at the morgue and been given the painful task of breaking bad news to families whose relatives had been formally identified.

She had just informed one young Australian woman that her friend was dead. A few minutes later, an AFP police officer who had been assigned to the investigation had called her over to explain that just because her friend's name had been on the list of confirmed fatalities did not necessarily mean that the information was correct.

The young woman's friend had been identified by a hotel key found in his pocket. An official had telephoned the hotel the key belonged to and was given the name of the guest who had been staying in that room. Based purely on that information, his name had been added to the death register.

But without DNA, fingerprints and dental records, this identification had been unreliable, the officer said. The keys could have belonged to anyone. To make a positive identification based on the key to a hotel room without other supporting information was the reason this stringent process had been put in place.

Rada had had the dreadful job of telling the distressed woman that her friend may not necessarily be dead after all. She had looked as confused about the information as Rada had felt.

By following a strict forensic process which required DNA, dental and medical records, and fingerprints, these sorts of mistakes would no longer happen.

Unfortunately, this meant inevitable delays, which for the exhausted and traumatised families waiting for answers was unacceptable. At the meeting that morning, the voices had grown louder and angrier and a stranger in the crowd had risen to his feet and tried to calm things down.

Paul Featherstone was an Australian expert in disaster and rescue management and a close friend of Charmaine Whitton's parents, Len and Pauline. Featherstone had been involved in the 1997 rescue of Australian ski instructor Stuart Driver, who had been buried under tons of rubble after a landslide destroyed two ski lodges in the NSW alpine resort of Thredbo.

Diver, aged 27, had spent almost three days trapped up to his neck in mud and freezing water. He had been the only survivor of the landslide which had killed his wife, Sally, and 17 other people.

Featherstone had also been an expert in the investigation into the arson attack at the Childer's Palace Back Packer Hostel in south-east Queensland in June 2002, which had killed 15 young people – as well as the 1977 Granville train disaster, where 83 people had died.

He understood the process and the complexities of forensic investigation better than anyone. But he wanted to be sure that these heartbroken families understood it too.

Featherstone diffused the escalating situation by suggesting that they itemise 10 points for discussion and resume the meeting again at 3pm with the answers. Cath and Rada were relieved. This would allow them enough time to meet Bronwyn's family at Denpasar Airport and bring them back in time for the meeting.

Danielle and Phillipe accompanied their Australian guests to Denpasar to meet the family. It was another perfect day in in Bali, though they doubted the picture postcard scenery and idyllic weather would mean anything to the shattered relatives who were arriving under such terrible circumstances.

Bronwyn's mother had decided not to come with them. She had not been able to sleep since the news on Sunday and had wanted to stay with her four other children who were waiting for news.

Jenny was so distressed that she had developed a heavy crushing feeling in her chest, and Jess had decided to stay in Geelong with her mum and wait for updates. Too upset to sleep, they had dragged a mattress into the lounge and had laid side by side, hugging and comforting each other.

In the small hours while the rest of the world was sleeping, they had reflected together on the gregarious nurse with a heart of gold. Bronwyn would do anything for anyone, and she did it all at the same pace – a million miles an hour! She had always been able to see the upside in the worst situation and had always been laughing about something. Jenny recalled that in 2000, she and her girls had been on a six-month working holiday to the UK.

During their holiday they had enjoyed a boat trip down the Thames, where another tourist's pink chiffon scarf had repeatedly blown across Bronwyn's face, blocking her view of the river.

Every time it had happened, she had eyeballed her mother through the pink chiffon scarf and had laughed out loud. Now, every time Jenny closed her eyes, all she saw was Bronwyn's face, laughing at her through a haze of pink chiffon.

Jenny had been torn about the pilgrimage to Bali. Her four younger children were shocked and grieving and needed her at home. But Bronwyn was missing, and her mother felt compelled to go to Bali. Ross had urged her to stay at home with her other children. They would be her eyes and ears in Bali and would keep her updated as developments unfolded.

Cath and Rada recognised Bronwyn's family the moment they came through the sliding doors into the arrivals area of Denpasar Airport. Their faces looked familiar from the family snapshots they had emailed or faxed them over the past few days. None of them felt like strangers meeting for the first time.

The teachers had also been in regular contact with Jenny over the past few days. She had told them she was still considering joining her family on a later flight with her older brother, Peter. Jenny was one of nine children, and her large close-knit family always took care of one another.

Cath and Rada had greeted Bronwyn's family in silence. After all the telephone conversations no words were needed.

Bronwyn's Aunt Libby's face looked pale and worn, and her uncles had the same look of disbelief that they had observed on the faces of the other shocked families they had met during the week.

Cath and Rada helped them into the car with their bags. Their pain was raw. Sadly, the friends had now become accustomed to connecting with strangers in an intimate way through sadness and grief.

The group returned to the Hard Rock Café with Bronwyn's family; it was a more settled meeting.

The Head of the Australian Forensic Team, Dr Chris Griffiths, addressed the afternoon session. Griffiths had explained again that there was an international protocol to follow in the identification process. It was a painstaking process that took time, and confidentiality rules had to be adhered to. If mistakes were made, two families suffered, so it was important they got it right first time.

Griffiths continued to field questions, looking visibly moved by the anguish of the devastated families. He had his own personal connection with the tragedy. His friends' son was also among the missing.

Cath understood the logic behind the identification process, but remained convinced that if Bronwyn's family could see the photographs in the identification room, or give them her dental records directly, it would fast-track the process and confirm immediately whether she was among the fatalities.

When she explained that the 'not knowing' was causing everyone such distress, Griffiths handed them his mobile number and told them they could call him.

Other points of discussion at the meeting had included problems in completing identification forms and the slow progress of the police investigation. One of the AFP officers reminded everyone that the Australian authorities were working with the Indonesian police and could not be seen to be taking over the investigation in their country. If the terrorist attack had happened in Australia, they would not permit a foreign police force to come in and run their investigation. They had to be thankful for the collaboration and were doing what they could.

Parents wanted to know if there would be a memorial placed at the site, and they wanted to know if they could see it. They were told that a memorial was already being discussed, and that arrangements were underway to transport people to the bomb site in Legian Jalan at 11am the following morning.

'When should families head home?' asked one of the relatives.

Featherstone said there was nothing to be gained by staying. It would not hasten the process that had to be followed. Emotions immediately erupted again. Who was he to tell them what to do? They would listen to the experts!

Rada and Cath looked at one another in despair. Featherstone clearly was an expert, they thought. The meeting was adjourned for a tea break.

Over coffee, Danielle admitted she was impressed by the forthright approach of the straight-shooting Australians, who had not been afraid to demand answers. She doubted the more conservative and compliant French would have challenged authority figures in this way. It was impressive, she said.

Everyone disbanded after someone burst in to warn everyone that the Hard Rock was rumoured to be the next terrorist target.

Afterwards the family had made their way to the Bounty Hotel to collect Bronwyn's suitcase and her passport from the safety deposit. They were given the luggage but were informed that the new confidentiality rules meant the hotel required a letter from the Australian Consulate before they could release the passport.

The delightful manager, Kossi Halemai, warmly welcomed the Australian family. He told them he remembered Bronwyn and Therese very well and had seen them around the hotel during the week, chatting to the Aussie football players – always smiling and laughing.

They had come into his office the previous Saturday morning in high spirits to tell him they were going bungy jumping.

'I told them not to go – it was too dangerous,' he said, his voice trailing away.

Afterwards the family had done the rounds of hospitals to see if Bronwyn had been admitted anywhere, or if her name was on any of the casualty lists on the hospital walls. Sadly, her name was nowhere to be found – except on the missing register at Sanglah. Until now, the family had hoped to find her at one of the hospitals – either as a patient or volunteering her services as a nurse. They wouldn't have been surprised to find her tending to the injured – too busy to call home.

But it had become clear that most of the seriously injured Australian survivors had already been evacuated home. And she had not been among the remaining hospital patients who were mostly foreigners. There were still so many unidentified casualties in the morgue that they had reached the upsetting conclusion that this was probably where Bronwyn would be found.

In the late afternoon, they called around at the Australian Consulate to get the letter for the release of Bronwyn's passport and were handed her wallet. It had been found in the debris at Paddy's bar by a local man who had immediately handed it in.

Chapter 10

Miraculously, the wallet was unscathed with the crisp dollar notes inside, untouched. The destruction had been so random, the family sorrowfully agreed.

While the family was touring around the hospitals, Cath and Rada called in at BMIC and photographed the nurses who had kept Therese alive until her transfer to the larger private hospital in Denpasar. The medical staff still looked traumatised from the sights they had seen at the weekend but had agreed to pose for the camera. Cath and Rada hoped to show Therese the faces of the people who had helped her when they visited her in hospital in Sydney.

Later they tracked down the young Balinese man who had found the wallet. He had discovered it among the ruins at Paddy's during the recovery effort. A man had been lying beside it, but there had been no sign of Bronwyn. When the family offered him something for his kindness, he had refused to accept anything and apologised for what had happened to their niece.

Bronwyn's family were so humbled that they had donated the money to HATI instead, to help the Balinese people.

Ross later rang Bronwyn's mother and told her about the wallet. He did not want to tell her that the chances of finding her daughter alive was looking unlikely now that all the survivors had been accounted for.

Jenny told him she had booked flights to Bali tomorrow with Peter. They would be in Kuta in time for Thursday's memorial service, which the Prime Minister would be attending.

But the family in Bali were cautious. CNN had just revealed that Australia was bracing itself for another terrorist attack –

the news sparking heightened security fears for the safety of Australians in Bali.

Amidst the concerns about another terrorist attack, the Arab satellite channel Al-Jazeera aired an audiocassette carrying a recorded voice message – purportedly from Osama Bin Laden – claiming that the Bali Bombings were in retaliation for the United States' war on terror and Australia's role in the liberation of East Timor.

The message carried a dark warning:

> *'You will be killed just as you kill, and will be bombed just as you bomb – expect more that will further distress you.'*

Although the feared terrorist organisation had not specifically claimed responsibility for the bomb blasts in Bali, former FBI agent Ali Soufan would later confirm in his book, *The Black Banners*, that al-Qaeda had financed the bomb plot. Other reports were more specific and stated that al-Qaeda had sent Jemaah Islamiyah's figurehead – Hambali – $30,000 to fund the terrorist attacks on the Sari Club and Paddy's Irish Bar.

Chapter 11

CANDLES AND PRAYERS

Thursday morning had begun with a series of distressing telephone calls between Bronwyn's family in Bali and her mother, Jenny, who was waiting at Sydney Airport for her connecting flight to Denpasar.

The stressful days without news and the long nights without sleep had left her too exhausted to think. Making the decision to travel to Bali had been torture. She desperately wanted to attend the memorial service, but her own four children and her brother Peter's children were all in shock and needed them.

The bomb threats had made her afraid for herself, and for her family in Bali. That morning, the authorities in the Philippines had thwarted a terrorist bomb plot in Manila and all Southeast Asia – and Indonesia in particular – was now on the highest alert.

Jenny had heard that there would be increased security surrounding the memorial service at the Australian Consulate for the Australian, New Zealand and Canadian casualties of the terrorist attacks. Jenny was in a quandary. Her flight was due to leave Sydney very shortly and she had no idea what to do. In the end, the anguish had become too much to bear and she had collapsed on the floor in tears.

In another call, Libby's husband, Michael, told Jenny that he had just spoken to a federal police security officer who had personally guaranteed her safety at the memorial service. But she had made her mind up – she would not be coming, and she begged her family not to go to the memorial service. She had already lost her beloved daughter and did not want to lose anyone else she loved.

The family was reconsidering attending the memorial when they arrived at the Hard Rock Café on Thursday, where the Australian Prime Minister was preparing to address the meeting before the service later that day.

The botched bomb plot in the Philippines had prompted a more noticeable security presence at the Hard Rock Café. Because of the concerns for the Australian families, armed AFP officers would be accompanying the convoy on their visit to the site of Saturday's terrorist attacks.

The Prime Minister listened to the morning update, which had confirmed that the death toll was continuing to rise. With so many bodies still awaiting formal identification, it was likely there would be more Australians among the dead.

The victims' families told him the waiting was torture.

'I just want to take my daughter's body home,' wept Charmaine Whitton's bereft mother, Pauline. John Howard was visibly moved by the distress of the relatives in the room and had a message for everyone.

'We will do everything to get those bastards!' he promised.

Later, Mr Howard spoke to Jodi Wallace's anguished father, Barry, who had flown out from Byron Bay to look for his missing daughter.

'When you get home, don't forget you have 19.5 million mates waiting for you.' The Prime Minister had taken this attack on Australians very personally. It had happened on his watch and was a cowardly malevolent attack on every Australian including himself!

By Saturday Mr Howard's compassionate remark was headlines everywhere, The Daily Telegraph running the story on its front page under the banner *Nineteen Million Mates*. The story went on to say that travel warnings had been ignored and that the joint police taskforce was hunting 57 suspects believed to be involved in the bombings.

Sadly, Jodi Wallace's parents would later discover that their beloved daughter had been identified among the fatalities from the Sari Club. Tragically, she had spent what should have been her thirtieth birthday in the morgue at Denpasar.

At 11am, the convoy of minibuses took everyone to the site of Saturday's terrorist attacks. An AFP officer sat on each of the buses, which were permitted beyond the barrier to view the scene of the destruction where so many had lost their lives or had suffered terrible injuries.

Surveying the 1-metre-deep crater where the Sari Club had once stood – and the wreckage of Paddy's bar where Therese had left Bronwyn dancing – the full magnitude of the horror was overwhelming. For her shattered aunt and uncles, the visit had quashed any lingering hope that she might have survived.

'How am I going to tell my family?' Ross asked Rada, looking devastated.

After viewing the scene of the carnage, they had found a quiet spot on the other side of Paddy's bar away from the photographers who had followed the convoy of heartbreak. There they said a prayer and held their own private memorial service for the effervescent fun-loving nurse with everything to live for.

They placed posies of fresh flowers and lit candles and lanterns and placed in the rubble where Bronwyn had died doing what she loved best – dancing.

Among the flowers, they placed photographs of her with two poignant letters from her heartbroken mother and sister. Jenny said goodbye to the daughter who had packed so much into her short life – and Jess told her how much she loved her and needed her to come home.

Despite their letters, they had been struggling to accept the dreadful reality that Bronwyn had perished in the blast at Paddy's. Since the news, they had felt her presence around them – as though she had been lingering to ensure they were okay. It was time to rest now, wrote Jess, giving her big sister permission to leave them.

Earlier that morning, Rada had picked a posy of pink frangipanis, which she placed in the rubble. She had also lit incense and had said a prayer for her son's spirit too.

'This is for you, Matthew,' she whispered. Just like Jenny and Jess, she had sensed her own son's presence very strongly during these sad days.

At the service, Rada had been joined by a young man called Michael Baldacchino, who was mourning his mother, Sylvia, who had died in the explosion at the Sari Club. Rada had noticed him sitting alone at one of the meetings at the Hard Rock Café and had befriended him.

Michael had told Rada that his 56-year-old mum had been a frequent visitor to Bali and loved the place. Before her holiday, they had discussed travel insurance and he had jokingly asked her what she wanted him to do if anything should happen to her.

'Scatter my ashes on Kuta Beach,' she had told him with a big smile. Rada lit candles for his mum and they sadly reflected on the tragedy that had left so many families in mourning.

'I don't hate the people responsible for my mother's death – I have forgiven them,' said Michael. He saw no point in hating and blaming. It wouldn't bring his mum back.

At the site of the Sari Club, friends and relatives placed wreaths beside those of the Balinese people, who said prayers for everyone who had lost their lives in the attack. They told the grieving families they were sincerely sorry.

As they left the site, Rada paused to photograph a pile of shoes that was heaped on the footpath outside the Sari Club. The blackened items had belonged to the victims who had lost their lives on Saturday night. They were a haunting reminder of everything these families had lost.

Danielle went shopping for more flowers for everyone to take to the official memorial service at the Australian Consulate on Friday, to honour the Australian, New Zealand and Canadian victims who had lost their lives on 12 October.

At the ceremony, the Australian Prime Minister offered heartfelt words of comfort to the relatives of the dead, and to the families of those who were still in hospital battling burns and other serious injuries.

'As we grapple inadequately and in despair, to try and comprehend what has happened, let us gather ourselves together, let us wrap our arms not only around our fellow Australians, but our arms around the people of Indonesia and Bali.

'Australia has been affected very deeply, but the Australian spirit has not been broken. The spirit remains strong and free and open and tolerant.'

After the service, everyone lit more candles which they placed in front of a cross that remains inside the Consulate building. Rada, who had sat next to Pauline Whitton during the service, lit candles for Bronwyn and Charmaine and all the other beautiful young people who had died before their time.

At the reception that followed, Cath and Rada shook hands with the Prime Minister and spoke with other dignitaries. Cath recognised a doctor among the crowd. She had seen Dr Arthur Sorrell at BIMC on Saturday night assisting the overworked staff. She had since learned that he was one of many foreign doctors who had helped with the casualties. After she left with Therese, Dr Sorrell, had gone on to help at the Sanglah where most of the seriously injured survivors had been taken.

During the reception the Prime Minister came over to offer his condolences to Bronwyn's Aunt Libby. She noticed he had tears in his eyes and seemed genuinely distressed. This had happened on his watch, and he shared the grief of all the

Australian families. She gratefully shook his hand, touched by his genuine compassion.

After the reception, they wandered across to sign the guest register recording the names of those who had attended the memorial.

Jenny's brother, Ross, had unwittingly signed his name below the Prime Minister's, which was supposed to stand alone on an empty double page.

'You are not supposed to sign there – that's for the Prime Minister,' sniffed a member of the Consulate staff.

Rada stared at the official in utter disbelief. After the pain of the last few days, the mistake sounded as trivial and unimportant as it was. Rada took the pen and promptly signed her own name next to Ross' – and Cath and the rest of the family followed. They all agreed that Bronwyn would have appreciated the humour behind their rebellion.

The following day, the family returned to Melbourne with an extra passenger. Jenny was so grateful to the women who had supported her family and had tried so valiantly to find her daughter that she wanted to meet them for herself.

'Why don't you both come back to Melbourne with us? My sister would love to meet you,' suggested Libby.

But Rada had already booked a flight Sydney to spend some time with her sister, Kira, and visit Therese at Concord Hospital. She had decided that some time in Sydney would give her an opportunity to process what had happened and talk through the grief that the tragic events had unearthed about Matthew's death. So much had happened, but Rada had not had the space or time to think about her own feelings while others needed her support.

Some time with her sister would leave her in better emotional shape before she returned to her 24-year-old daughter, Dannika, who was waiting for her in Queensland.

But Cath had decided a trip to Melbourne to meet Jenny might bring the grieving mother some comfort. As the authorities in Brunei were also on high alert as a result of the ongoing bomb threats in Southeast Asia, she had decided to postpone her return to school. She had told the principal she needed time to recover from the harrowing events of the past week.

The tragedy had overtaken their plans to travel to Ubud, and Cath had decided the time would be better spent visiting Bronwyn's mum in Geelong and Therese at Concord.

Afterwards, she planned to take some extended leave from the international school in Brunei, to be with her parents in Brisbane, who were worried about the impact of the bombings on her own emotional health.

They had been following the news from Australia, and were very concerned about Cath's decision to stay on in Bali where there was a real risk of another terrorist attack.

Before Cath and Rada left Bali, they had bought a big bouquet of tropical flowers for the generous French neighbours who had so willingly opened their homes, and their hearts, to complete strangers.

Amidst all the hatred and wickedness that had spawned the terrible events that had brought them all together, what the Australian friends would remember most was the goodness and kindness of people.

On Saturday 19 October – exactly one week after the Bali bombings – Bronwyn's family packed their bags and returned to Australia without her.

Chapter 11

Her grieving Aunt Libby had watched her niece's suitcase disappearing into the hold of the plane – with all the gifts she would never get to give, and all the new clothes she would never have the chance to wear – and wept all the way home.

Chapter 12

THE MIRACLE
WOMAN OF
BALI

During the harrowing days that Bronwyn's family had been trawling the hospitals in Denpasar looking for her, Therese's parents had remained by her bedside at Concord praying for a miracle.

Despite the doctor's pessimism that it was not possible to survive such devastating injuries, Dawn Fox had continued to cling to the hope that her daughter would still pull through.

Therese might look fragile, but underneath those bandages lay a strength and stubbornness that too many people had underestimated. As a teenager, Therese had been incredibly wilful and determined, and Dawn had lost count of the number of times she had been punished for her defiance at home, or for playing up at school. But despite all the lectures, punishments and groundings, nothing had ever curbed Therese's quiet defiance.

Damien had been an easy, compliant child; however, his twin sister had always been more of a challenge to deal with.

If Therese was told she could not do something, it had always made her even more determined to do it. Drawing on her own experience with her daughter and her unshakeable Catholic faith, Dawn hoped that all the qualities she had found such a headache during Therese's adolescence would give her the strength to defy the odds and prove everyone wrong.

Despite the doctors' reluctance to perform the urgent surgery she had needed on her arrival at Concord, Dawn remained convinced that the sound of their voices had already ignited the fight in her. In her mind, this had been the reason that Therese's temperature had inexplicably risen on Tuesday night. Now she was hoping that same fighting spirit would help her in her battle for survival.

Every day since her admission to Concord, Dawn had reminded her daughter how much her children needed her – and how much she needed her back. As a mother, she knew how important Therese's children were to her. If anything could inspire her to keep fighting, it was her unstinting love for Alex and Katie.

If Dawn had learned anything in her life, it was the healing power of a mother's love for her children. As a young woman, Dawn had never been able to have children of her own. During the early 1970s, she had undergone several rounds of the new IVF treatment that Australian fertility specialists had been pioneering. When that had failed to work, Dawn and Chris – a good-living church-going couple – had been fortunate enough to be approved by the adoption services.

On 5 February 1973, she had received a double blessing when the beautiful six-week-old twins were placed in her care. They were born at Melbourne's Royal Women's Hospital on 6 December and surrendered for adoption by their biological mother, who already had multiple children and could not care for any more.

Their birth names had been Paul and Joanne but their proud new parents had renamed them Damien and Therese.

Dawn had been ecstatic with her twins, who brought new purpose to a life that had been marked by periods of anxiety and depression. Her marriage to Therese's adoptive father Chris had been comfortable, but not the fulfilling relationship she had hoped for.

Her husband had been a successful accountant who had been an active member of their local Catholic church. But over time, he had become dissatisfied with his marriage and the distance between the couple had grown with the constraints and responsibilities that came with being a father.

For the maternal and nurturing Dawn, fulfilling her dreams of becoming a mother had brought new healing into her life and her babies quickly became the centre of her world and her reason for living.

Although the marriage had not survived, Dawn's love for her children had been infinite, as was the love she later felt for her grandchildren.

Dawn was convinced that Therese's love for Alex and Katie would help to heal the scars of the Bali bombings and bring her back to them.

Chapter 12

Therese's friend Michelle Larkins had said much the same thing in her anguished phone call to Dawn after hearing the news that her friends had been caught up in the terrorist attack she had so narrowly escaped.

When Therese's mother had told her that there was little hope of her surviving such dreadful burns, she had reassured Dawn that her friend loved her children too much to leave them alone in this world.

'Alex and Katie will be the reason she gets through this – you'll see,' she told her.

Dawn desperately hoped that Michelle would be right, and reminded Therese about her children every day since she had arrived in Sydney.

'Keep fighting, Therese,' she whispered, hoping that she could hear her voice through the layers of bandages and the perforated eardrums. 'Alex and Katie need their mum – and I need you too.'

***

Sadly, Therese had not been the only badly injured survivor of the Bali bombings who had been transferred from Darwin to the specialist burns unit at Concord.

Of the 86 most seriously injured survivors of the blasts who were evacuated from Bali, 77 critically wounded casualties were airlifted to major hospitals in other Australian states. By the time the Prime Minister addressed the memorial service on Friday 18 October, at least two of those casualties had died and others were still fighting for their lives.

Multiple casualties had been transferred to Concord's burns unit where the staff had been instructed to make 12 beds available for some of the most badly injured patients. The unit's Director,

Peter Haertsch, told media that his staff had been grappling with 'war-like' injuries that they had never seen before.

'It's something you wouldn't see in civilian life and something I haven't seen in 22 years of burns surgery,' Haertsch had told reporters from CNN on Thursday 17 October.

Over the past three days, his staff had been treating a combination of serious injuries, which included horrendous burns complicated by deep glass and shrapnel wounds. Doctors had also been dealing with other complications such as renal failure and thermo-regulatory shutdown, primarily because many of the casualties had not been able to access specialist medical treatment in the crucial first hour following the terrorist attacks.

Haertsch said that even those patients who had received treatment for penetrating burns had failed to have their injuries expertly closed in a sterile manner, which meant their wounds were contaminated with debris, wood, dust and dirt.

This increased the risk of potential infections and possible sepsis which could prove to be life threatening. He said the biggest risk to patients was not having access to proper treatment during the 'golden hour' after the injuries had occurred. Trauma shock was also a significant issue for many of the patients.

The medical expert said the unprecedented number of serious casualties admitted to Concord with complex burns had exhausted Australia's supply of bioengineered skin, which specialists rely on when treating badly burnt patients. But the hospital anticipated that all major burns surgeries would be completed by the end of the week, though for some of the most serious patients, the treatment would continue for weeks – even months.

Chapter 12

Meanwhile, the ABC reported that two of the most horrifically injured victims had been admitted to Concord – including a Melbourne woman who had suffered burns to 85 per cent of her body.

They were referring to Therese.

The other injured patient was Australian businessman Ben Tullipan, 38, whose life was also hanging in the balance in the burns unit at Concord. Not only had this patient suffered full-thickness burns to 63 per cent of his body but he had also lost his legs and most of his stomach muscles.

He had also arrived in the ICU in an induced coma after being airlifted out of Bali. He had been taken from the wreckage of the Sari Club in the back of a ute to the Sanglah Hospital where he had been placed in a corner of the emergency room with a sheet over his face. The nurses had thought he was already dead. But another Australian saw the sheet move and raised the alarm.

The businessman was the first of the critically wounded casualties to be evacuated from Bali by the RAAF in the biggest aero-medical response since the Vietnam War.

Ben had been in Bali on a buying trip and had slipped into the Sari Club to buy a bottle of water when the car bomb went off outside. He was standing just 5 metres away from the Mitsubishi van when the deadly 1-tonne bomb ripped through the premises and had borne the full brunt of the powerful explosion.

Concord had also agreed to treat some of the more critically wounded foreign casualties who had been airlifted to Australia for urgent medical treatment. One of the patients was a young German woman in her late twenties called Ingrid who had sustained severe burns to her back and arms during the blast at the Sari Club which had killed three of her friends.

As surgeons worked around the clock to meet their surgical objective of completing all their major operations by Friday, Therese was wheeled back into the operating theatre for her second procedure in a week.

Her first operation, the day after her transfer from Darwin, had not included clearing the debris from the skin on her back. At the time, her critical condition had left doctors fearing that she might not be strong enough to survive the general anaesthetic and that treating her entire body would require her being under for longer.

The burns on her back covered a large area and would require more time and attention. The doctors had decided to treat the burns on the rest of her body, and perform another operation in a few days on those on her back.

With the risk of infection now posing a very real threat to her life, her name was added to the list of complex surgeries on Friday 18 October.

During the procedure, the surgeons had also taken a small sample of skin from her buttocks, which would be taken to the labs to grow new skin cells that would be grafted onto the burnt areas of her body.

They told Dawn that the growth cycle for the new skin cells generally took around 10 days and that she would be undergoing repeated surgeries under general anaesthetic for skin grafts, which they warned would be a painful but necessary process.

Unfortunately, with third-degree burns covering 65 per cent of her body, finding samples of skin had been problematic as there was very little viable skin left for them to remove. Chris Fox had telephoned Rada to update her on his daughter's progress.

* * *

The following morning, while Therese remained in her coma in the ICU, Bronwyn's family were on their way back to Melbourne with their new friend Cath Byrne.

Returning home without her beloved niece was the hardest thing Libby had ever had to do. The idea of not bringing Bronwyn home to her mother, or providing Jenny with any answers, only added to her sense that they had failed her.

Cath met Bronwyn's mum at Michael and Libby's home in Geelong the following day. It was an emotional meeting for everyone, and Jenny's face looked strained and stressed after her week without sleep and her conflict over abandoning her trip to Bali for the memorial service.

Despite her anxiety and fear, there had been a quiet, stoic resignation in Jenny's demeanour that broke Cath's heart.

Although they had never met before, the two women felt they had known each other forever – probably because of the countless phone conversations and emails that they had shared over the past week.

Jenny warmly embraced the compassionate teacher who had been on the other end of the phone line in Bali at all times of day and night. She was as warm in person as Jenny had sensed on the phone. Bronwyn would have loved her, she thought.

They showed Cath photographs and shared their most cherished memories of a fun-loving young woman with a zest for life that had been exhilarating, and sometimes exhausting.

It was clear to Cath that Jenny was still in a state of shock and disbelief about what had happened, and without official confirmation that Bronwyn had been identified, she had become trapped in a painful limbo.

Every day was tinged with the 'not knowing' that John Howard had alluded to in his speech to Parliament after the terrorist attack. While the family reflected and remembered, the wait for news continued to prolong their agony.

The family listened in tears as Cath described Therese's terrible injuries, and recalled how she had begged them through the pain to look for her missing friend.

Cath also told them about the wonderful holiday the girls had had in Kuta, just as Therese had told her and Rada at their triage at the Masa Inn.

Cath had thought it was important for the family to know this and hoped they might take some small comfort from the knowledge that Bronwyn had lost her life living it to the full.

The family laughed through their tears as they shared their precious memories of Bronwyn with one of the women who had tried so hard to find her. They had spent hours looking through photographs that captured the milestones in the life of a feisty young nurse who had been such a bright light in all their lives.

Jess recalled how her discerning older sister had given the seal of approval to her new boyfriend, Adam Barnard, and told her he was a keeper. Her mother remembered how, even as a toddler, Bronwyn had always been so hyperactive and busy. With hindsight, it was as though she sensed – even then – that there was no time to waste and needed to fit in as much as she could while she had the time.

Although Cath had never had the chance to know this dynamic young woman in her lifetime, the intimate and powerful bond she had forged with this warm family through her death would be one she would treasure for the rest of her life.

With a heavy heart, Libby sadly returned Bronwyn's suitcase to her mother. The family gathered around in silence while Jenny opened it. Among the items was a Calvin Klein designer handbag that Bronwyn had handpicked for her little sister. At the time, Jess had assumed it would have been one of the designer 'knock-offs' that Bali is renowned for. It would be months before Jess would discover that the gift was the real deal and that Bronwyn had spent a fortune on the handbag, knowing it would be something her sister would treasure. Tragically, this parting gift from Bronwyn would now be even more precious for so many other reasons apart from her generosity and thoughtfulness.

In among the clothing and gifts, Jenny found the wallet that the Consulate had handed to her family in Bali. It was as perfect as the crisp dollar notes inside it. Jenny began to weep. How could it have survived the inferno when it now seemed almost certain that her beautiful daughter had not.

She had also found the poignant note that Cath had hastily scribbled, telling Bronwyn they had packed her things, and that Therese was in the hospital with burns.

'We were hoping that she may have been taken to one of the other hospitals and might come back to the hotel and wonder where her things had gone,' explained Cath. 'We had hoped, when I wrote that note, that she was still alive.'

Bronwyn's mother nodded. They all had.

Cath watched as Jenny Hobbs examined the contents of the suitcase that she and Rada had hurriedly packed at the Bounty Hotel the day after the bombings. Among the bathers and shorts and holiday clothes were children's clothes and gifts that had obviously been intended for Therese's children.

'That's our fault,' explained Cath, describing how Therese had asked them to call around at her hotel to collect her suitcase before her evacuation, and they had not known whose suitcase belonged to who. They had just packed up everything and had obviously bundled these items into the wrong suitcase.

Jenny sadly put the items on one side. Her heart was breaking for the young mum who was fighting for her life in Sydney. She hoped that Therese would pull through, so she could give her children these gifts herself.

* * *

Cath had still been in Melbourne on Sunday when Rada's plane touched down in Sydney. After the others had left, Danielle had treated her to a relaxing massage to make up for the one she had missed in Ubud. Afterwards she had scoured the market stalls looking for an album for all the precious photographs she had taken in the days after the terrorist attacks.

They were not the happy snapshots she had imagined herself taking on her first trip to Bali. But despite the pain and suffering they were a record of the tragic events. They had also captured the generosity of strangers who had become friends, and the compassion of the Balinese people who had mourned with them.

The photographs told a story of sadness and inspiration that Rada had been struggling to find the words to tell. Her snapshots included pictures of the locals praying for the casualties who had survived, and the beautiful wreaths and dedications from the Balinese people to those who had lost their lives in the terrorist attacks.

They poignantly captured the notices in Kuta's empty shops appealing for donations of blood from people with types 'O' and 'A'. They also reflected the depth of a loss she could not put into words – from the pile of charcoaled shoes outside the Sari Club to the candles and flowers at the memorial service where the Prime Minister had been reduced to tears.

Rada had also recorded the images of the exhausted staff at BMIC who had helped to keep Therese alive, and the doctors at the hospitals where she had been taken. Rada's photo montage was not just a historic record of the tragic events of 12 October 2002 but a record of Therese's journey too.

She hoped that one day soon, she would be able to show her the photographs, so Therese would know everything that had been happening while she had been fighting for her life.

Rada had chosen the album that was to hold these treasured memories very carefully. She had settled for a simple hessian and cardboard design with a dove on the front edged in fine rope. This simple symbol of peace felt fitting given the scenes of devastation and sorrow on the images inside. The album had been bound by string and had a pencil-shaped piece of wood attached to its spine. These simple items had created an unexpected dilemma when she arrived at Sydney Airport.

'You can't take that through without having it fumigated,' sniffed one of the custom's officers, studying the inoffensive piece of wood which he claimed contravened the regulations of incoming goods made of natural materials.

Rada was told that unless she paid to have the item treated, she would have to surrender the album. After the horrors she had witnessed in Bali, Rada could hardly believe her ears.

'The album only cost me three bucks!' she said, sounding incredulous. 'To pay over $100 to have it treated is more than it's worth.'

A more senior customs officer had come over to find out what the problem was.

When Rada had explained what the album was for, he had resolved the issue by removing the offending stick and tossing it in the bin. He said this way she could keep her memento without having to pay for it to be treated.

The official was very apologetic. Their job required them to enforce the rules even in terrible circumstances such as these. He said it had been upsetting having to confiscate items made of seashells and straw, knowing that some of the returning Australian travellers had come home mourning people who had been killed or badly injured in the terrorist attacks.

On Sunday night, Rada showed the album with its poignant memories to her sister, Kira, hoping her photographs would give her a small insight into the nightmare they had been a part of in Bali.

'And to think that I thought Afghanistan was too dangerous,' she observed wryly.

* * *

In her induced coma on the other side of Sydney, Therese continued to float between life and death in the ICU. In her dreamlike state of sedation, she could hear the distant sound of familiar voices. They seemed too far away for her to hear their words, but she had found the voices vaguely comforting.

Her body felt limp and lifeless as if it did not belong to her. It was as if she was swimming underwater – so weighed down that she could not swim to the surface to reach the voices that spoke to her through the darkness.

Over the past 24 hours the doctors had begun to reduce the medication that had been keeping their patient in her induced coma, and the distant voices had gradually crept closer, their words sounding less muffled.

On Sunday, as the drugs slowly wore off, two unfamiliar women's voices filtered into her consciousness. They sounded closer than the other voices had, and Therese could hear their conversation as they spoke to one another.

'I would rather be dead than suffer like that,' remarked one of the voices, unaware that the seemingly lifeless patient in the bed could hear their conversation.

Who were they talking about? wondered Therese, confused and disorientated. Where was she? Who were they?

Her eyes began to flicker, and she could hear the faint sound of running feet and beeping alarms. Suddenly, she heard her father's deep, distinctive voice speaking her name. His tone was softer and gentler than it normally was, but she recognised his voice immediately.

'It's okay, Therese,' he whispered. 'You are safe now – we are here.'

Her mother's face came into view as she leaned over the bed to study Therese's face, her eyes brimming with tears of pure relief.

After all the sleepless nights she had spent worrying that another mother's daughter lay beneath those bandages, she had known those soft brown eyes anywhere.

'Therese, it's Mum, you're in the hospital,' said Dawn, choked.

Damien leaned over the bed and smiled at her too. The same gut instinct that had told him Therese was in danger now told him she was going to make it.

Therese's eyes darted wildly around and she began to panic. She scanned the unfamiliar hospital surroundings, her eyes flitting from face to face. What were these tubes and machines for? she tried to ask, unable to speak because of the tube in her throat that was helping her to breathe. Gripped by panic, she wildly plucked at the tubes and wires, frantically trying to free herself.

She was immediately sedated again, and slowly drifted off into a lighter, calmer sleep. One of the ICU doctors told the distressed parents that being confused and disorientated was a normal reaction for a patient who had been in an induced coma.

For the next few hours, Therese floated in and out of sleep, suffering the horrific post-coma hallucinations that were another side effect of the drugs that had been keeping her calm and pain free. For the first time in eight days her mother slept that night.

Dawn was back in the ICU very early on Monday 21 October, awaiting Cath and Rada's arrival. Over the past week, Cath and Rada had been in regular contact with Dawn and Chris, who told them that the doctors were preparing to reduce the drugs to bring Therese out of her coma.

Rada had been Therese's first visitor that morning and thought she appeared to be very groggy and disorientated. She assumed this was due to the high dose of morphine she had been given to control her pain.

Chapter 12

'Hi Therese, do you remember me?' asked Rada, though it was clear from the recognition that had swept across her face when she entered the IC, that Therese had immediately known she was one of the teachers from Queensland who had helped her in Bali.

Rada's visit to the hospital was brief because she thought Therese seemed very weak and out of it. But it had been good to finally meet Dawn. Rada told her how brave her daughter was, and how determined she had been to make it home to her children. She said Therese had astonished everyone in Bali with her strength and courage.

'It really is a miracle that she has made it this far,' she told Dawn. Rada left the hospital saying she would be back again tomorrow.

Not long afterwards, Cath arrived from Melbourne. Cath had been hoping that Therese would remember her. She had decided to wear the same bright yellow polo-shirt that she had been wearing over her nightie on the night they met. If Therese was still in a confused state, she would hopefully recognise the distinctive top and remember her as one of the teachers from Queensland who had helped her during those agonising hours in Bali.

Cath was desperate to see Therese, who she had last seen in the ICU at Denpasar, awaiting evacuation. She had also been eager to meet Dawn, who she had only spoken to on the telephone.

Her first meeting with Therese's mum at the Concord Hospital was as emotional as her introduction to Bronwyn's mother had been two days earlier in Melbourne.

Hugging Cath tightly, Therese's mum had expressed her gratitude for the compassion and kindness that she and Rada had shown to her critically injured daughter during those crucial hours in Bali. Their kind faces may well have been the last ones Therese ever saw, and Dawn would never be able to thank them enough for being there when she could not.

Cath wished Rada could have been here to hear Dawn's words for herself. After losing her own son in such dreadful circumstances, Rada would appreciate better than anyone how comforting this must have been to Therese's mum.

'The doctors have told us not to have any hope at all that she can survive this,' said Dawn, her voice dropping.

Cath recalled being told the same thing at the Prima Medika Private Hospital in Bali when the doctors had asked her to consent to the emergency procedure that had caused her such a personal dilemma.

'They didn't think she would survive then either,' she said, squeezing Dawn's arm. 'And they didn't think she would make it back to Australia – but here she is!'

Dawn wiped away her tears and led Cath into the ICU where Therese lay sleeping on the bed, still intubated.

Cath stepped closer to the bed and observed the patient, who was heavily bandaged and wearing a full-body compression suit. Therese was still attached to an assortment of IV drips and tubes. Some were attached to beeping machines whose alarms sounded at intervals and brought the nurses running. It was such a relief seeing Therese back on Australian soil after the precariousness of her situation in Bali and the evacuation that nobody thought she would make.

Cath recalled how she had called in at BMIC to grab a photo of the nurses who had kept Therese alive before her transfer to Prima

Medika. They had remembered the two Australian tourists who had held morphine drips and fluid bags over the injured patient as she lay screaming on the floor of their overwhelmed clinic.

Kathryn, the English administrator at the ex-pat private hospital, was surprised when Rada told her that Therese had survived the evacuation and was back in Australia. They had been told that she had not made it and had listed her name in their files as 'deceased', which was what Rodney Cocks had also been led to believe. Cath was happy to tell her it was a mistake.

In Concord, Cath wanted to know about Therese's children and wondered if Alex and Katie understood the circumstances surrounding their mother's injuries. As a primary school teacher, she knew first-hand the impact that serious injury, or illness and death had on the lives of young children.

'Are they having professional support?' she asked. Dawn said her grandchildren had been offered counselling to help them understand what had happened, and to prepare them for a reunion with their badly injured mother. But it was still early days, and Therese's condition was still so uncertain.

'At the moment, Alex and Katie are staying with their father,' explained Dawn. But they would be coming to see their mother if things improved. Dawn, realising what she had said, immediately corrected herself.

'I mean *when* things improved,' she added.

Cath told her that she had every confidence that Therese would improve now that she was back in Australia and having the specialist care she needed.

'Your daughter was so brave in Bali,' she said, recalling Therese's confronting injuries and the stench of burnt flesh that had hung like a noxious cloud over the ICU. She told the weeping mother how her daughter had walked almost 2 kilometres after the bomb blast back to their hotel. Her injuries had been so shocking that even the Balinese doctors had been amazed by her courage.

Therese was certainly a fighter, they agreed.

The sound of voices brought Therese out of her sleep, and her eyes flitted around the room and over Cath's distinctive yellow polo-shirt until her gaze lingered on her familiar face.

'Hi, Therese, do you remember me?' asked Cath hesitantly.

Therese's eyes smiled weakly at her through the pain, and though she had not been able to answer because of the tube helping her breathe, Cath saw the flicker of recognition in her eyes.

Cath moved closer to the bed.

'We did it! We got you home after all,' she said, feeling elated.

Later, she watched the nurses carefully removing the bandages covering Therese's face. Her mother struggled to retain her composure as the doctor inspected the red, raw skin beneath the dressings, though Cath could already see the improvement.

When Cath left Therese in the ICU before the evacuation, she was naked and horribly bloated, and her body resembled rare-cooked meat. Her face had been swollen and burnt, and her lips had been so swollen she had been struggling to speak. It had only been nine days and the swelling had already begun to reduce all over her body. Although the skin on her face remained angry and raw, it was already showing signs of healing.

'It truly is a miracle that she's here at all,' said Cath, putting a comforting arm around Therese's weeping mother.

Cath left the hospital that afternoon, reflecting on the painful circumstances that had brought her and Rada into the lives of survivors like Therese and Marie- Antoinette and Bronwyn's family. The terrorists had intended to inflict so much suffering, and they had certainly achieved that.

But powerful new bonds were forged in the ashes of Bali that overshadowed the suffering and the evil. As the Prime Minister had said in his moving address at the memorial service, they had not broken the Australian spirit – and they had not destroyed this remarkable survivor.

Rada and Cath had been at the hospital the following day when Therese's suitcase finally caught up with her. It had disappeared in transit, and when they had followed it up, had discovered it had been put in the wrong ambulance and had gone to Denpasar Airport with Melinda Kemp, who was about to be transferred from Darwin to a hospital in Perth with her sister. After that, it had gone to a few other places until it had finally found its way to Sydney.

They hoped that having her belongings back might be another small step forward in Therese's journey back to recovery. They also thought that having her own things around her might bring her some comfort.

Sadly, the sight of all the new holiday clothes and bargain shopping had had the same painful effect on Therese's mother that Cath had witnessed Jenny Hobbs grappling with in Geelong.

'And these gifts were in Bronwyn's luggage by mistake,' explained Cath, showing the clothes and games Therese had bought for her children in Bali.

But Therese could not bear to look at them. She had closed her eyes and drifted off to sleep.

'The children will love these presents,' said Dawn, wiping a tear from her eyes and putting them on one side. She didn't know when Therese would be able to give them to Alex and Katie, but hoped she'd hang in there so that she could do it herself.

Dawn found some undeveloped film from Therese's camera in the suitcase, which Chris Fox later took to a photo lab to be processed. The film contained snapshots of the girls' dream holiday in paradise, before it descended into their worst nightmare.

Among the happy holiday snapshots was a photo of Bronwyn and Therese on their snorkelling trip, which was taken by another tourist just a few days before the terrorist attack.

The photo showed the friends sitting side-by-side on a boat in the Indian Ocean. They were smiling for the camera and obviously having the time of their lives. It brought a tear to Chris Fox's eye seeing the girls looking so happy. They had had no idea when they posed for that photo, that before the week was out, one of them would be lying in bandages fighting for her life, and the other would be missing, presumed dead.

One of the young female doctors had been outside the ICU when Chris had showed the photographs to Dawn. The medic had burst into tears at the sight of the two pretty nurses smiling for the camera. The poor patient fighting to stay alive in the ICU looked nothing like the girl in the photo.

'How could anyone do this to their fellow human beings?' the doctor had asked, wiping the tears from her eyes. Chris and Dawn shook their heads. They could not fathom it either.

It would be months before Dawn would mention the holiday photos to Therese, who flatly refused to look at them. The snapshots were a painful reminder of a life she had lost and friend she had loved, and she found it all too upsetting.

Before Cath left for Brisbane, she called at the hospital to say goodbye. Therese was heavily drugged, and her eyes were cloudy, but she was no longer intubated and smiled at her when she walked in.

'I will be back to see you very soon,' promised Cath.

Therese smiled and closed her eyes again.

Therese was awake when Rada next called at the hospital with her sister, Kira to see how things were progressing. She was propped up against the pillows and while she still seemed groggy, she was pleased to see them.

But her courage had astounded everyone who had encountered her. As the chief nurse consultant in Concord's ICU would later recall in a sensitively written piece for December's Nursing Review, that although there were many examples of bravery among their Bali patients, Therese's determination and courage was super-human.

And this astonishing will to survive had earned her a new nickname among the staff at Concord. They called her – the most badly burnt patient they had ever seen – 'The Miracle Woman of Bali'.

Chapter 13

COMING
HOME

Eighteen days after the terrorist attacks in Bali, Bronwyn Cartwright's formal identification had led to her name being added to the growing number of fatalities from the bombings in Bali – the shattering confirmation bringing an end to the agonising wait that had been eating her family alive.

For the past two and a half weeks, Jenny Hobbs had spent every day dreading a knock on the door that would bring the news she could not bear to hear.

Her family's time in Bali had told her that the coroner's findings had generally followed the day after his autopsies, which meant most families were informed the next morning whether their loved ones had been identified as one of the unfortunate casualties whose bodies had been recovered from the new 'ground zero' in Kuta.

This had left Jenny feeling highly anxious and unsettled until the late afternoon, when, for a few hours at least, no bad news was good news. Unfortunately, by the following morning, the waiting began all over again.

The first inkling that Bronwyn had been found had initially come with a phone call from the Australian coroner, who had contacted Jenny wanting information about a tattoo on her daughter's shoulder.

'Can you tell me more about your daughter's butterfly tattoo?' he asked.

Jenny gave him a detailed description of the brilliant blue butterfly that Bronwyn had decided to have emblazoned across her shoulder and the coroner jotted it down.

'You have been very helpful,' he said.

In the detailed description of Bronwyn that Jenny had already given to Cath and Rada in Bali, she had described her daughter as tall and slim with beautiful long blonde hair.

When the family had flown out to look for Bronwyn, Jenny had given them more information that could help with the identification process, such as the plate in her ankle and the belly button ring with a small silver crucifix. Bronwyn also owned a gold wristwatch that she liked to wear, and a gold locket that she had bought on their working holiday in London two years earlier.

Their shared hunger for adventure had taken Jenny and her two daughters to the UK for a year, where Jenny and Bronwyn had found work in different hospitals in the south of England, and Jess had landed a job in admin.

On a train ride home from work one day, Bronwyn had proudly showed her mum the unusual square gold locket she had bought herself. Jenny had thought it was the ugliest piece of jewellery she had ever seen, though she had been too tactful to say so.

Jenny could not be sure that her daughter had taken these items on her holiday, let alone know if she was wearing them on that fateful night in Paddy's bar. For this reason she had not mentioned it as another possible means of identification.

The coroner had Bronwyn's dental and medical records, and the X-rays of the ankle injury at his disposal. Yet the only thing he had seemed specifically interested in had been the blue butterfly tattoo and it was that distinguishing feature which finally helped him to formally identify Bronwyn.

When the coroner confirmed that Bronwyn had been among the fatalities, her mother had been distraught. For almost three weeks, she had been torturing herself with horrific images of her beautiful daughter lying horribly burnt in the morgue, her long blonde hair scorched from her head, and her pretty face disfigured beyond recognition.

But during her discussion with the coroner, it had occurred to Jenny that for the butterfly tattoo to be a significant identifying factor, Bronwyn could not have been severely burnt at all, or the artwork would not have survived.

When she asked him how Bronwyn had died, he confirmed that her body had been untouched by the blaze. His autopsy had found that her only physical injury had been a broken leg. There had been no traces of dust in her lungs, which meant she had not had even had time to draw breath when the bomb went off. Her death had been instantaneous, and she had not suffered.

Chapter 13

The coroner's explanation brought great relief to the grieving mother, who found it comforting to know that Bronwyn had not suffered a slow and agonising death, as she had been dreading she may have. Like her wallet, Bronwyn had been unscathed apart from her injured leg.

But could anyone really die of a broken leg? Jenny, a critical care nurse, did not think so and immediately rang one of the doctors she worked with to query this. He explained that in a major explosion, the impact itself acts as an accelerant, causing a high-pressure shock wave that passes through every cell in the body in zero seconds. The instantaneous process causes such a shock to the body that death is instantaneous.

That night, Jenny's close-knit family had gathered to hold their own vigil for Bronwyn, the effervescent young nurse who had shone as brightly as any star. Their world already felt like a dimmer place without her.

Over the coming days, Jenny had been at Libby's place when a photo in the newspaper leapt out at her.

'Oh God, that's Bronwyn,' she gasped, grabbing the newspaper. But when she looked more closely, she realised that it had not been Bronwyn in the photo, it had been another young woman who looked uncannily like her with the same long blonde hair and striking features.

Accompanying the photo had been a story about a grieving husband whose young wife had lost her life in the terrorist attack in Bali. In his shock and grief, the man had mistakenly identified another young woman for his wife, because she was slim and blonde and bore the same blue butterfly tattoo across her shoulder.

He had realised his mistake when he discovered the woman he had wrongly identified as his wife had a belly button piercing. His wife had not had any piercings on her naval and this simple error – made in trauma – had resulted in his wife's name being added to the list of fatal casualties from the Bali bombings, when the woman he had identified had not been his wife at all.

'Bron had a belly button ring, long blonde hair *and* a blue butterfly tattoo,' said Jenny, stunned.

Had an unfortunate case of mistaken identity been the reason that the authorities had taken so long to identify Bronwyn? Had the photo that Cath and Rada identified in the photo ID room at the Sanglah Hospital two days after the bombings been her daughter after all? They had been 90 per cent certain that the woman in the photo was a match for Bronwyn, but had discounted it because another young woman's name had been written on the photo.

After faxing through a clearer photo of Bronwyn, Philippe had also been convinced that he had seen her face before. He had immediately driven to the Sanglah Hospital to check it against the photos in the photo ID room. But the image had been removed because the woman in the photo had already been identified.

Was this also the reason why the forensic expert, Dr Griffiths, had not been able to find a match when Bronwyn's aunt and uncles had handed him more photographs of their niece when they met him at the morgue?

To Jenny, this could be the only reason why the coroner had specifically asked her to describe the blue butterfly tattoo on Bronwyn's shoulder.

Chapter 13

It was so ironic, thought Jenny, who had frowned on the tattoo that Bronwyn had decided to have emblazoned over her shoulder a few days before her mother's 40th birthday.

Jenny came from a conservative Australian family and did not approve of tattoos. With her birthday celebrations just days away, Jenny was sure her then 19-year-old daughter's flashy new fashion statement was certain to attract plenty of unwanted attention from her discerning relations.

'You're going to have to cover it up for my party,' she had told Bronwyn, who had laughed, unfazed by her mum's obvious disapproval.

On the night of Jenny's party, Bronwyn had defiantly slung a cardigan over her shoulder – the wrong shoulder – and had shown it off for all the world to see.

'It's not a permanent one – it will wash off,' fibbed Jenny, not wanting to tell her family the truth. But Bronwyn had spent the party dancing and laughing and hadn't given a toss what anyone thought.

Who would have thought that the tattoo Jenny had complained about would be the one distinguishing feature that had enabled the authorities to identify Bronwyn, and bring her home?

When Bronwyn's coffin finally arrived in Melbourne two days later, the entire family had been waiting at the airport to pay their respects.

Before they left Geelong, Jenny's older brother Peter had arrived at his sister's house with a giant bunch of pink lilies that one of his young apprentices had sent for her, to mark the sad occasion. Jenny had picked three of the prettiest flowers from the bunch and had wrapped them in a ribbon and taken them to the airport for Bronwyn.

Qantas had allocated the grieving family a private area to meet the coffin, which they had organised would be collected by Tuckers Funeral Services in Grovedale. At the airport, they had discovered three coffins had arrived from Bali as other casualties of the bombings were returned to families who had been as shaken and distraught as their family was.

Jenny had immediately untied the bow around the bunch of pink flowers and had placed a single lily on each of the coffins before they were driven away.

'Bronny would never have wanted to have them all while the others got nothing,' she said, choking back tears.

'She would have wanted me to share them.'

Later, the AFP had come to see her to return some of the personal effects that Bronwyn had been wearing on the last night of her holiday. Jenny was heartbroken to see Bronwyn's wristwatch, and the ugly locket that was now bent and blackened with smoke.

* * *

Sadly, the Hobbs and Cartwright families had not been the only families in Geelong who had lost people they loved in the terrorist attacks on the two nightspots in Kuta.

The close-knit community of Geelong – which sits on the other side of the city's Westgate Bridge, an hour's drive from Melbourne – was in mourning for three other young locals who were also believed to have perished in the terrorist attacks.

Geelong brothers Aaron, 33, and Justin Lee, 31, along with Justin's wife Stacey, 30, were also among those who had died when the bomb ripped through the Sari Club on 12 October.

The brothers had been in Kuta for a little over a week when Stacey arrived to join them on the day before the bombings. She had just discovered she was pregnant.

In a place like Geelong, which is more like a big country town than a city, everyone knows everyone else and the whole community was grieving. Therese's former partner David Dorling knew one of the Lee brothers from around the football traps. And Michelle Larkins' sister Linda had known Stacey Lee and her sister Kelly Thornburgh. The beating heart of this small town was now bleeding for them and for their families.

By a coincidence, Therese and Bronwyn had run into the Lee brothers on the flight from Melbourne to Denpasar that they had nearly missed. They had chatted to the boys and one of their friends on the plane journey over and had discovered they were all staying at the Bounty Inn in Kuta.

Like the girls, the brothers had all grown up in Geelong and had been well-known faces in their local area. Aaron, a plumber, had been well known in community sports and his younger brother, Justin, worked as a truck driver for his uncle Shane Grainger, who ran a local steel fabrication company. His wife, Stacey, worked in administration at the Geelong campus of Deakin University. They had all gone to school in Geelong.

The couple, who had known each other since their mid-teens, had been married since 1999 and were described by friends as the 'most in-love couple you could ever meet'. The community had wrapped its arms around the stricken families.

Justin and Aaron's brother, Randall Lee, travelled with his Uncle Shane to Bali to search for the boys and his pregnant sister-in-law. They had been among the frustrated relatives who had struggled to cope with the prolonged process of identifying the victims. Their grieving father, Graeme Lee, had told the Melbourne media that that his close-knit family had lost four of their own – including his unborn grandchild. The couple had been intending to share their good news on their return from Bali.

On 27 October, a memorial service was held for the trio at the KD Stewart Centre of Deakin University, where more 600 mourners turned out to pay their last respects.

A friend of the couple had told the service about Justin and Stacey's joy as they looked forward to a new chapter in their lives, as parents.

'Justin loved his family, his in-laws, his workmates, and most of all, Stacey,' he said.

Another friend, Craig Hassan, described Aaron Lee as the most upbeat person he had ever known – a man who looked at the positive side of live.

'For him, life was to be enjoyed,' said Hassan.

Although the service was a celebration, the terrorist attack that had claimed their lives remained at the forefront of everyone's minds. The Rev Denis Tomlins spoke for everyone when he said their deaths had been an 'unbelievable and unacceptable loss'.

The Chaplain of Deakin University, the Rev Bart Croon, condemned the 'evil people' who had taken their lives and praised the friends and family who had travelled to Bali to search for them. He said the entire nation had been so deeply touched by the atrocity that it was difficult to come to terms with.

At the time of their memorial, the family had still been waiting for answers, but during their visit to Bali, they had resigned themselves to the inevitable news that they had perished during the attack on the Sari Club.

* * *

While the Lee family and Bronwyn's relatives were struggling to come to terms with the death of the vibrant young people they had loved, Therese's mother was in a quandary about how she would break the shattering news about Bronwyn to her critically injured daughter.

Therese's doctors, aware of the distressing new development, had strongly advised Dawn not to tell her for the time being. She was too seriously ill to cope with such devastating news.

'Your daughter's body is very weak,' they advised. 'It might be better to wait until she is stronger before telling her this sort of news.'

Studying Therese, who had since been placed on a higher dose of morphine for her pain, Dawn had to agree. Her daughter was not out of danger yet and the painful procedure of scraping embedded debris from her wounds was still being repeated every few days to avoid infection.

Therese was already on a cocktail of high dose antibiotics, but the doctors knew from the other victims they were treating that many had developed superbugs which were proving resistant to even the strongest antibiotics. Because Therese was still so weak, they believed an infection might be enough to kill her. Most patients with serious chemical burns from hyperbaric explosions like this, died of infections rather than their primary injuries. And as most had suffered complex injuries caused by penetrating shrapnel, the risks of infection were greater.

Therese had been in a great deal of pain since the surgery on her back and had already begun the painful process of skin grafts. She had also been having daily physiotherapy to overcome mobility issues caused by her burnt skin contracting and tightening. The doctors had said it was important to keep the skin stretching or she would not be able to move at all. They had not told her that physiotherapy would be even more agonising than the skin grafts and the dermabrasion procedures.

To make matters worse, bone had started to grow over her calcified elbow joints, which made it agonising to move her arms and hands. The specialists had explained to Dawn that the body's response to such severe injuries had been to go into 'overdrive' and the bone had grown over the injury to protect the area.

This required intensive physiotherapy which meant cracking and breaking the new bone in her arms every time they worked on her. The pain was so horrendous that Therese wanted to die.

'You have to keep fighting,' her mother kept reminding her sobbing daughter. But nobody appreciated how tired she was, or how hard it had become to keep up the fight.

Therese's full-thickness burns had penetrated through layers of skin and fat almost to the bone. This had caused injury to her muscles and tendons as well as significant nerve damage.

The specialists had warned Dawn that the nerve damage might take years to heal, and it was possible that some of the damage might be irreparable. Even if the nerves began to regenerate, the pain she would suffer during the healing process would be excruciating.

She would need lots of physiotherapy and long-term pain management, as well as psychological support to deal with the trauma and the impact of her debilitating injuries on her life.

The delicate skin grafting process was also fraught with problems. Therese had so little viable skin left on her body that the doctors would have to rely on synthetic skin samples to repair her wounds. But the sheer volume of seriously burnt casualties from Bali undergoing skin grafts in hospitals around Australia meant that the demand had already depleted the supplies of synthetic skin, and Concord had been forced to order more.

Even when artificial skin is used to close the burns, it is not a permanent solution. Synthetic cells promote the growth of a new layer of skin and when grafts fail to take, the wound breaks down, leaving the patient open to infection.

With her daughter still fighting for her own survival, knowing how to break the news of Bronwyn's death left Dawn in an impossible dilemma. She understood how important it was to keep Therese calm and positive to give her the strength and the will to keep fighting. But hiding her own distress about Bronwyn's death when her heart was breaking for her family was absolute torture.

After Therese emerged from her coma, her mother had promised she would never leave her alone again. Whatever the journey held, they would travel it together. But the news about Bronwyn would have to wait until she was strong enough to deal with it.

* * *

Rada was at her sister's place in Sydney when she heard that Bronwyn had been found. She had immediately telephoned Jenny Hobbs to offer her condolences.

As a grieving mother herself, Rada understood the shock and disbelief that parents had to deal with when grappling with the sudden death of a child. There had been no goodbyes for Rada and her son, and she knew only too well the heartache this caused to those left behind.

'At least she did not suffer,' said Jenny, telling Rada what the coroner had told her about Bronwyn dying instantly. Rada understood how comforting this must have been to her. She too had endured the anguish of wondering whether her child had died alone or had suffered in his final moments.

Ever since the terrorist attack, Jenny had been tormenting herself for not taking the time to drive Bronwyn to the airport to say goodbye. She had spoken with her a few days before the trip to Bali and had been happy to hear her sounding so excited about the holiday. How could she have known then that this would be their last conversation?

While Jenny Hobbs was planning a funeral for Bronwyn, Therese's condition in Concord still hung in the balance. The repeated trips to theatre to clear away debris from some of the deeper layers of skin, and the regular skin grafts, had sapped what little strength she had. Sometimes she barely had the energy to open her eyes.

Therese still required additional morphine just to have her dressings changed, and remained heavily sedated. Most of the time, she felt as though she were not present.

Therese had been in this sedated state when the nurse had arrived in the ICU to take more blood. She had vaguely asked them what they were testing her for.

'We're taking some blood to test for HIV,' explained the nurse as she accessed the central line for her pathology sample.

Therese had looked confused.

'Why?' she asked, not sure why she was in even in the hospital. 'Have I been raped?'

The nurse shook her head. Sometimes the drugs prompted this crazy scrambled talk. She thought no more of it, and labelled her sample and disappeared.

But somewhere amidst the cloud of opiates, Therese had recalled a dark secret that she had been harbouring for years. As random as her question had sounded, she *had* been raped, though she had never told a soul.

Therese had been 13 when it happened. She had attended a New Year's Eve party in Geelong with her father and brother and during the night had wandered out of the house to a local park. There, an older youth appeared from the shadows. While her family partied, he had forced her onto the ground and raped her. It had happened so fast that Therese had been too paralysed with fright to resist or scream.

Afterwards the young man had casually wandered off across the park, leaving her in shock on the wet grass. Therese had felt so distressed and ashamed that she was not sure if anyone would believe her and had decided not to tell anyone what had happened. Instead, she had returned to the party and asked to go home. In all these years, she had never shared her secret and when she had, her disclosure had been blamed on the drugs and she would not recall ever sharing it.

Later, the nurses told Dawn about Therese's peculiar question, but her mother had not given it a second thought either. It would be years before Therese would share the story of her rape again, and the next time it would be with a professional counsellor.

On another occasion, not long after her admission to Concord, Therese had woken to find a male nurse leaning over her bed. His olive skin suggested he might be foreign, but he was Australian. When she opened her eyes and saw his face it triggered a terrifying flashback of the man who had slipped past her in Paddy's Bar in the seconds before the explosion.

'Get away from me ... get away!' she had shrieked, flailing around on the bed in terror. The nurse had been badly shaken by the outburst and a colleague had immediately hurried him away from her bed.

'Don't worry,' said the nurse. 'The patient's very traumatised – that's all.'

Afterwards, Therese felt terrible about her reaction. But the sight of a foreign face had dragged her back to that hideous night and had been a terrifying reminder of her worst nightmare.

In the early days after Therese's admission to Concord, two AFP officers had been posted outside the doors of the ICU to monitor the injured casualties of the terrorist attacks. When these patients emerged from their comas and were well enough, they would be questioned about the terrorists to determine if they had any information that might help bring the perpetrators to justice.

With Therese now out of her coma, officers from the joint taskforce had come to the hospital to interview Therese, who had no idea that her injuries had been caused by a bomb, or that she had been hurt in a deliberate act of terrorism.

On the advice of the hospital-appointed psychologist who had been counselling Therese and her parents, Dawn and Chris had been instructed to give their critically injured daughter only tiny pieces of select information. The psychologist had been concerned that giving Therese the whole ghastly truth would have been too traumatic for her to handle.

If her parents told her too much too soon, it might have an adverse impact on her emotional wellbeing and on her physical recovery.

With this advice in mind, her mother had simply told Therese that there had been an explosion in Bali and that she had been hurt.

When the police arrived at the hospital, they had been sympathetic and had kept their questions very general. They had asked Therese what she remembered about the explosion at Paddy's Irish Bar.

'There was something ...' she said, describing the man she had seen walking towards the dance floor where Bronwyn had been dancing. She thought she might have been by the bar at the time but had no idea what had happened to her.

What *did* she remember about the man? they asked.

Therese thought he had been Indonesian but could not tell the police whether he was young or old or remember anything about his physical appearance.

She also described the incident in the car park a few days before the explosion, when she and Bronwyn had been lost. She told police about the group of men who had been gathered around a car but could not remember the make of the car or anything else about them. She wasn't sure if they had even said anything. But she had remembered feeling uneasy.

How many men were there? asked one of the AFP officers. Therese was not sure. Perhaps five or maybe six. She thought they might have been speaking in their own language, so she could not tell them what the men had been saying, or even if they had been doing anything wrong.

Sadly, due to her injuries, Therese's recollection had not been very helpful to the investigators.

By the time the officers interviewed Therese, they had already interviewed thousands of Australians returning from Bali about their experiences before, during and after the terrorist attacks in Kuta. In the first 10 days after the bombings, they had interviewed more than 7000 tourists in a bid to catch the people behind the attack. A total of 7340 questionnaires were handed out to passengers on 19 different flights arriving at various Australian airports from Bali. The exercise produced 450 relevant leads which they AFP followed up.

One of those returning passengers was Rada van der Werff, who had been contacted at her sister's home in Sydney to determine if she remembered anything that might help their investigation.

Rada said she doubted it. She had only arrived in Bali on the morning of the bomb blasts, but as she was in Sydney, she had agreed to make a formal statement in case she had any information that might help apprehend the people responsible. She had seen first-hand what the bombs had done to Therese, Marie-Antoinette, Carren Smith and the broken family members like Len and Pauline Whitton and Jenny Hobbs. She wanted the perpetrators to be caught and brought to justice for the destruction they had caused to so many innocent people.

In her statement dated 28 October 2002, Rada told the police how she had arrived in Bali on the morning of the terrorist

Therese pictured with her children Alex and Katie
at their home in Queensland in 1999.

Therese and her friend Bronwyn on a snorkeling trip off the coast of Bali in 2002 - just days before the bombings.

Therese and Bronwyn enjoying a quiet dinner for two
at the Bounty Hotel in Kuta on 8 October 2002.

A view of the destruction in Legian Road, Kuta after the terrorist attacks at Paddy's Irish Bar and the Sari Club in 2002.

Rada's photograph showing the shoes that have been left behind by patrons fleeing the Sari Club on 12 October.

The local Balinese people paying their respects to the victims of the terrorist attacks in Legian Jalan.

Bronwyn's family at the Bounty Hotel in Kuta in 2002 -from left to right: Bronwyn's Uncle Ross, Cath Byrne, Uncle Michael, Rada van der Werff and seated, Kozzi Halemai the hotel manager, and Bronwyn's Aunt Libby.

Tributes to Bronwyn sit amid the ashes of the Sari Club
where her family lit candles beside a photo of their
missing niece during their own private memorial.

Prime Minister, John Howard addresses the Memorial Service at
the Australian Consulate in Denpasar to honour the Australian,
New Zealand and Canadian victims of the Bali bombings.

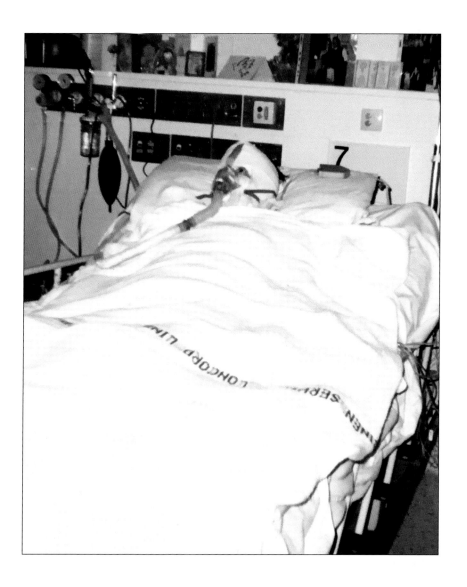

Therese pictured fighting for her life in the ICU at Sydney's
Concord Hospital after her evacuation from Bali.

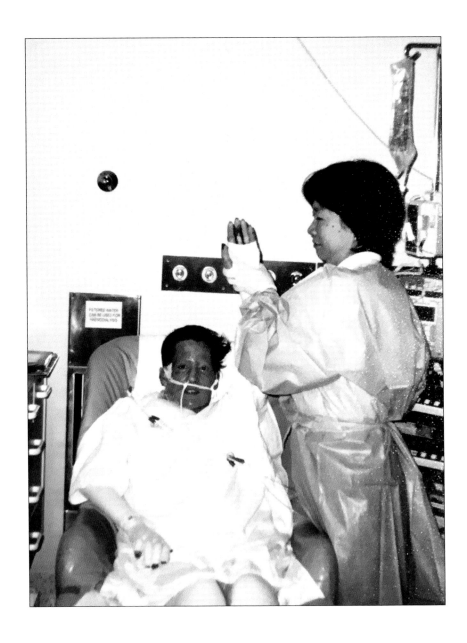

A nurse at Concord's burns unit attends to Therese after
she emerges from her coma in October 2002.

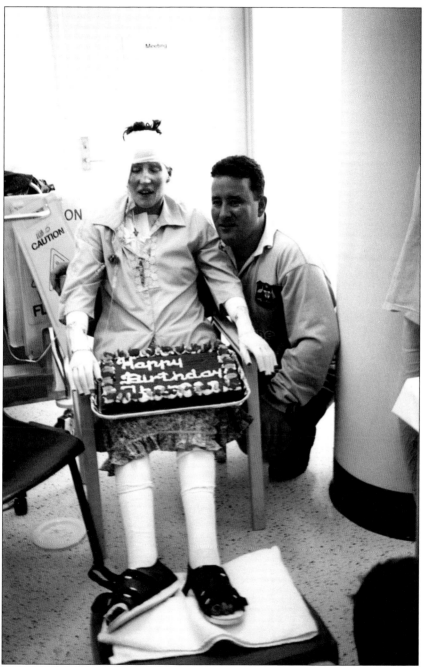

Therese with her twin brother, Damien, celebrating
their 30th birthday on 6 December 2002 - a milestone
nobody imagined she would ever live to see.

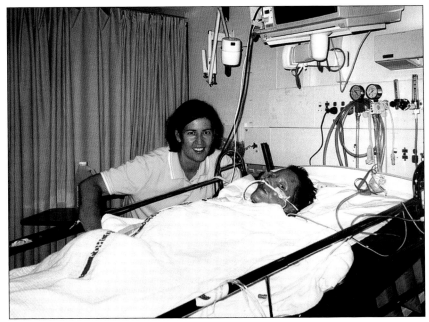

Cath in her yellow polo shirt beside Therese's bed in
ICU at Concord on their first reunion after Bali.

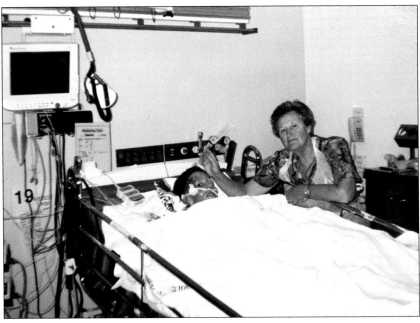

Dawn with Therese after she came out of her coma in October 2002.

Therese with her son, Alex in ICU at Concord
days before she turned 30.

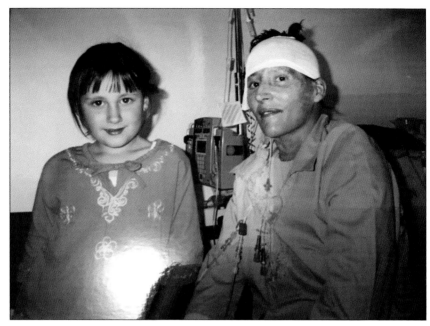

Katie poses with her injured mum in Sydney on her 30th birthday.

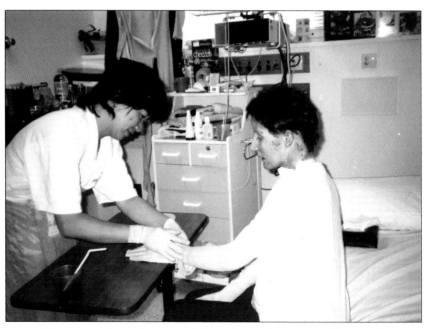

Therese undergoing agonising physiotherapy in Concord.

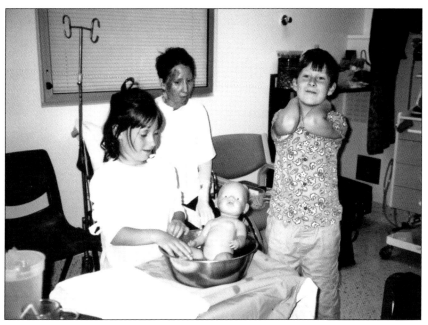

A heavily drugged Therese with her children at
the burns unit in Concord in late 2002.

Therese pictured saying goodbye to her
physiotherapists at Concord in January 2003.

Rada van der Werff and Therese in Concord ahead
of her transfer to Melbourne. Rada flew to Sydney
especially to witness the momentous occasion.

The Miracle woman of Bali on the day she left Concord.

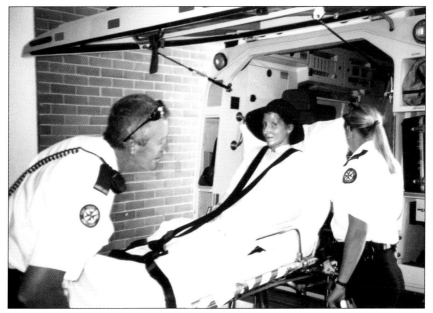

Paramedics lift Therese into the ambulance outside
Concord Hospital for her trip to Kingsford Smith Airport
to be airlifted to Melbourne in January 2003.

Therese with her beloved children on Mother's Day 2003
celebrating another milestone on her long road back to recovery.

Cath poses with Therese's mum Dawn at the Therese
Fox Benefit Appeal in Geelong that was organised by
her local community on 7 December 2002.

Therese looking bloated on her steroid medication,
poses with her dad, Chris at her welcome home
party in Grovedale in October 2003.

Therese and Dawn in her new courtyard at her home in Grovedale
after the Backyard Blitz big reveal in September 2003.

Proud grandma, Therese holds her newborn baby grandson, Flynn in April 2015 and celebrates a new chapter in her life.

Dr Dina Hadiningsih and surgeon Dr Kubera who
saved Therese's life at the Prima Medika Private
Hospital in Denpasar after the Bali bombings.

The medical staff at Bali International Medical
Centre who treated Therese on 12 October 2002
and were amazed to hear she had survived.

Taken in 1999, the three musketeers with their nursing
colleagues from Geelong's Gordon Tafe, Therese is pictured
back row third from the right, Her friend Michelle Larkins is
in the front row in a red cape with Bronwyn to her right.

attack. Her room hadn't been ready, so she had lazed around the pool before doing a spot of shopping and exploring her surroundings. She described how they had gone to bed that night at around 11pm and that her friend had been fiddling with the air conditioner when they heard a muffled explosion a few blocks down the road.

'Cathy actually thought that she had done something with the air conditioner and that had made the noise and the power go out,' she explained.

'We then saw mushroom-like smoke bellowing from the direction of the Sari Club. Frankly, I just did not hear the second bomb go off.'

Rada went on to describe the tourist bleeding on the hotel steps with shrapnel wounds to his arm.

'A short time later, people started returning to the hotel. Some were just shaken, and some were burnt in various degrees. Interestingly, the first person I saw returning was another AFP officer and I think his name was Tim Fisher. His hands appeared to be badly burnt.'

The schoolteacher described how she and Cath had met Therese and the French girl, Marie-Antoinette, who was also burnt. And they described their night at the hospitals and the terrible scenes they had witnessed there, and again the following morning at the site of the bomb blasts.

'Cathy saw trucks coming out of the scene with charred bodies inside,' she said, feeling sick as she thought about it.

She had told the officers that Therese had sustained severe burns all over her body and that the Balinese doctors had said they had known people who had died of far lesser injuries.

Rada had gone on to describe how she and Cath had attended the daily meetings at the Hard Rock Café where they had met lots of families and Australian Federal Police officers.

'As this was my first trip, I cannot say if the mood of the people was any different than usual,' she said.

'The Balinese were extremely compassionate and helpful in every step. They constantly kept saying how sorry they were for the Australian and the taxi drivers were fantastic. I cannot say that any Balinese that I saw took advantage of the situation and were more than helpful.'

Rada concluded her interview by handing federal agent Tarun Shivanna the 36 photographs she had taken in Bali after the bombings. She asked him to return them to her as soon as possible.

Throughout October, many stories emerged about ordinary people performing extraordinary acts of bravery – either by helping to rescue the injured from the two infernos or staying on to assist others as Cath and Rada had.

There were many acts of heroism on that Saturday night, including accounts of seriously injured people risking their own lives to help others who had been hurt, and tourists with medical skills working side by side with the Indonesian doctors and nurses to tend to people at the site of the atrocity and at the nearby hospitals.

By the end of October, it was confirmed that 201 innocent people had lost their lives in the Bali bombings, and hundreds more had been seriously injured. The fatalities had come from 21 different nations and had included 88 Australians. Sadly, Brendan Barry's friend, Jodie Cearns from the Gold Coast, who had fought for her life for ten days in Melbourne's Alfred Hospital, had finally succumb to her injuries. And a few weeks later, another young victim's name would be added to the death toll. Her name was Simone Hanley from Western Australia, whose older sister Renae had been one of the first to die when the bomb ripped through the Sari Club. Simone had spent 58 days battling for her life in the burns unit at the Perth Hospital. She had been the 88th Australian victim to lose her life from the bombings in Bali – taking the total death toll to 202.

Chapter 14

A COMMUNITY
IN MOURNING

After her brief trip to Melbourne, and her visit with Therese at Concord Hospital, Cath returned to Brisbane to spend some time with her own family, who were worrying about the impact of the bombings on her emotional health.

Cath had always been a strong and resilient personality, but she had seen so much tragedy in Bali that her parents were relieved to hear that she was having a break from teaching to spend time with them before her return to Brunei.

Her time with her parents had been emotional and therapeutic. Cath's mum and dad had been panic-stricken about her decision to remain in Bali with all the new bomb threats they had read about in the newspapers. They were relieved to have their daughter home for a while, so they could give her some loving of their own.

After all the loss and the heartache that she and Rada had witnessed after the terrorist attacks, her time with her family had been very precious.

Cath had still been in Brisbane when she heard that Bronwyn had been found. She had felt heartbroken for Jenny and the family, but relieved that the agonising limbo of '*not knowing*' had finally ended.

'It has been comforting to know that Bron didn't suffer,' said Jenny, explaining the coroner's findings that her daughter's death had been instant.

The bereaved mother had gone on to tell her about the misunderstanding about the blue butterfly tattoos, which she believed had been the reason for the delay in identifying Bronwyn's body.

Although they had been resigned to the news, when it came, the finality of her death had still been a dreadful shock. But it had been a comfort to the family to know she had not died alone or in agony and had taken her last breath doing something that made her happy.

Jenny had another reason for calling Cath.

'I've got something I need to ask you,' she faltered. 'My family would love you to say a few words at Bronwyn's memorial service.'

Jenny thought it fitting that Cath should speak after the role she and her friend had played in Bali supporting the family's quest for answers.

'Would you do that for us?' Jenny asked.

Cath said it would be a privilege. She had not known Bronwyn in her lifetime, but through hours of intimate discussions with the people who had loved her, she felt as though she had come to know this dynamic young woman personally.

She would not be able to speak about Bronwyn's life, but she could talk about the family's determination to find her and bring her home to her mother.

Bronwyn's funeral was arranged for 7 November in Geelong. Cath immediately booked a flight to Melbourne but decided she would go via Sydney and visit Therese on the way.

On 2 November, Cath returned to Sydney and made her way straight to Concord, where she found Therese in a bad way, physically and emotionally.

On her first visit, Cath had felt the elation and relief of knowing Therese had overcome incredible odds and had made it safely home.

But on her second visit she had glimpsed the suffering that Therese would have to endure, and had been struck with the stark reality that the road to recovery was going to be a long and painful ordeal.

'How are things going?' asked Cath, sitting beside Dawn, who was intently massaging Sorbolene into her daughter's burnt face. Over the past few days this had become Dawn's daily routine and was an act of love that had made her feel a little less helpless.

Cath had noticed that although Therese's skin was still red raw, and beginning to scab, it appeared to have improved slightly – probably due to Dawn's healing hands and the creamy moisturising cream that she had been rubbing over her face and into her neck.

Therese had already undergone a couple of skin grafts which had not taken, and according to her mother was due back in surgery any day for more.

'This is so hard for her,' Dawn explained, in tears. 'But having the dressings changed is the absolute worst.'

Chapter 14

Cath had been in the ICU when the nurses arrived to change Therese's dressings, which they had to do every other day, to check that they were healing and to keep them clean. It had been important that the wounds did not become infected. But it was such a painful procedure that Therese had required extra morphine before they could begin.

Cath had tactfully made her way towards the door to give them some privacy while they performed their task, but Therese had begged her to stay.

'Please don't go,' she said, her brown eyes cloudy with morphine. Cath had returned to her seat, trying to keep the patient distracted with small talk while the nurses gently peeled away the bandages. Her body looked angry and lacked any surface skin, and her back was shocking after the agonising surgery to erase more debris from her burns.

Therese had howled in pain throughout the process, and her suffering was unbearable, even for Cath, who thought she had seen her at her worst. Afterwards, she had felt so shaken by the upsetting scene that she made an excuse to go outside and had wept. Dawn followed her outside.

'It's a nightmare that never ends,' Dawn said to Cath. 'I'm sorry,' she sniffed, wiping her nose on her tissue. 'It's so very hard for her.'

It was hard for her mum too, Cath noted sadly.

'Well, we can't fix Therese's pain, but we can be here for her,' she said, leading Dawn back into the ICU.

The women sat in silence as the nurses finished the last of the dressings. After they left, Cath produced some of the photographs she had taken of the doctors and nurses in Bali.

'These are the people who saved your life,' she told Therese, recalling how shocked and exhausted the poor medical staff in Bali had been when faced with the sort of injuries that belonged in a war zone.

Therese studied the strangers in the photo. So much of that terrible night remained a blur, and she wondered if they would have been better letting her die, though she did not say this out loud. She did not want to cause her mother any more pain.

Over the past few days her pain had been off the scale, and she had wanted to close her eyes and never wake up. But whenever those dark thoughts crept into her head, she thought about Alex and Katie. The idea of them growing up without her was unthinkable and it gave her the strength to keep fighting.

When the doctors came to examine her the following morning, Cath made an excuse to go for a walk to allow her some privacy.

As she wandered around the corridors, she had encountered Ingrid, the German girl who had been airlifted out of Bali by the RAAF during the evacuation. Ingrid had suffered severe burns to her arms and back in the terrorist attack and had also been transferred from Darwin to Concord, where she was now being treated. Cath had found Ingrid walking with her mother, who had travelled from Berlin to support her injured daughter.

'I'm staying in accommodation near the hospital – it is good to be here,' said Ingrid's mother in her crisp German accent. Cath had chatted with the two women about the impact of the terrorist attack on innocent people's lives. She had also told them about Therese.

'Their bombs hurt so many people,' said Ingrid sadly. 'And for what?'

Chapter 14

Before Cath left, they had swapped phone numbers and emails and had promised to stay in touch.

When she returned to the ICU, she found Dawn massaging her daughter's face. Therese had been exceptionally quiet that morning, though she had not yet told them why.

In a moment of lucidity, Therese had begun to remember the conversation she had heard while she was coming out of her coma, when she overheard someone saying she would rather die than suffer like her.

At the time, the conversation had felt so unreal and dreamlike that she had not known who the voices belonged to, or who they had been referring to. Now the conversation had returned to her, and it had occurred to her that whoever it was they had been talking about her. When she finally told her mother, Dawn had been devastated that anyone could be so insensitive, though she imagined they hadn't realised Therese had been able to hear them.

'Well, I'm not bloody well dead!' Therese had spat, a new fire rising in her belly. 'I'm here and my kids need me to get better.'

Later the nurses had come in to change her dressings and, despite the morphine she had been given, her cries had echoed all over the ICU.

'Is there anything I can do to help?' Cath had asked as Dawn continued with her moisturiser.

'I don't think so,' she answered, focused on the labour of love.

Cath looked at Therese's raw feet and recalled the horror that she and Rada had felt when they had witnessed the soles falling off in their makeshift emergency triage in Kuta.

She thought about all the new shoes that the friends had bought during their shopping sprees in Kuta and wondered if

Therese would ever be able to wear them. It was so cruel it was heart-breaking.

Cath pulled up a chair and sat at the bottom of Therese's hospital bed where she gently began to massage the Sorbolene into the new skin on the soles of her feet. The entire time, Therese lay back on the pillows and sobbed.

When Cath came to the hospital on 4 November to say goodbye, she thought Therese looked drained and disconnected. Cath told her she was on her way to Melbourne to see Bronwyn's family, though she had not mentioned the funeral. But Therese's own battle for survival had become so all-consuming that she no longer had the energy to ask about Bronwyn. Perhaps on some deep subconscious level, she suspected her friend had gone. Her mother did not mentioned Bronwyn much these days, and Therese had stopped asking. Life had become too hard.

The nurses had provided her with a morphine pump so that she could control her own pain relief as she needed it. But her hands were so heavily bandaged that she could not press the button to activate it and required her mother's help even for that simple task.

Observing Therese's low mood, Cath explained that she would not be visiting her for a while. After her trip to Melbourne, she had to return to her teaching job in Brunei, but she promised she would keep in touch.

'I'll write to you, or fax you on the ward,' Cath promised as she left.

Therese had nodded lethargically. She was so doped out she had run out of words. Her mum had walked Cath down to the hospital reception to say goodbye.

Dawn knew the reason for Cath's trip to Melbourne but had asked her not to mention it to Therese, on the psychologist's advice.

'Give my condolences to Bronwyn's mother,' whispered Dawn, wiping a tear from her eye. Cath assured her she would.

'When are you going to tell Therese about Bronwyn?' asked Cath, looking concerned.

Therese's mother took a deep breath.

'Not just yet,' she answered cautiously. 'It's not the right time.'

She had watched Cath disappearing out of the hospital back into the normal world. In her old life, Dawn would have been in her kitchen right now, perhaps making lunch, or coming back from the shops.

But this was their new 'normal' now, she concluded stoically. She returned to the ICU with her brightest fake smile, hoping Therese would not glimpse the pain behind the mask.

Dawn had no idea how she was going to break this terrible news about Bronwyn. She only hoped that when she finally did, her daughter would understand that she had only kept her painful secret because she had been trying to protect her.

Still, her heart was breaking for Bronwyn's family, and it was becoming harder every day to keep up the pretense. She wondered if there would ever be a right time to tell Therese that her friend was dead, particularly when she had been fortunate enough to survive. She had been grateful that Therese's counsellor gave them sound advice about how to deal with these difficult situations, making suggestions about what they could say to protect Therese from further trauma. And she was always around to counsel them after these painful discussions with their daughter, to offer them the help they needed to keep going.

OUT OF THE ASHES

* * *

On 7 November, almost a month to the day that they had left for their holiday in Bali, more than 500 people gathered at Tuckers Funeral chapel in Bell Post Hill near Geelong to celebrate the life of Bronwyn Louise Cartwright.

The funeral had originally been planned to take place at Tuckers' smaller chapel in Grovedale, but because of the numbers of mourners expected to attend, the family had decided to hold the service at their larger venue. Among the congregation had been Bronwyn's best friend, Oriana, who had sat with Jess and represented Therese.

In the days before Bronwyn had been formally identified, her friends and colleagues at Melbourne's Epworth Hospital held their own memorial service for their missing friend. Bronwyn's devastated sister, Jess, was among the mourners who offered prayers for the popular nurse who had lost her life in Bali.

Some of the grieving colleagues travelled down for the funeral, which Damien Fox had attended on his sister's behalf. The family had chosen the songs 'Imagine' by John Lennon, and 'Forever Young' by Bob Dylan. Jenny thought the soulful words to the songs captured the spirit of the gregarious dreamer whose time on this earth had been too fleeting.

Since the news of Bronwyn's death had filtered around their community, a string of tributes had appeared in the local newspapers. The family had also set up a memorial Facebook page, where friends and relatives had placed tributes and lit virtual candles for her.

One memorial that touched Jenny's broken heart was a tribute from the mother of one of the patients Bronwyn had recently nursed at the trauma unit at the Epworth Hospital. The young man had been injured in a road accident and had sustained serious injuries that had requiring intensive rehabilitation. He had asked her one day in a low moment: 'Who is ever going to want me like this'?

His pain had touched Bronwyn's heart and a few days later, after she finished her shift, she had wheeled him out of the hospital to a local pub for a drink. She had watched him having the time of his life, chatting to girls in the bar and feeling normal again.

In Bronwyn's mind, socialising and having fun was better than any medicine the doctors could prescribe him. Later she had wheeled him back to the hospital with a huge smile on his face that rivalled the grin on her own.

'I never want to hear you say that stuff again,' she said, wagging her finger. And she doubted he ever would.

Michelle Larkins, the nursing friend whose new job had saved her from the fateful trip, sat with her husband, quietly remembering Bronwyn's no-nonsense approach to life. One of her fondest memories of her feisty friend had been of a night where they had been out dancing in Geelong.

During the night, a man in the bar had inappropriately groped Bronwyn, who had swiftly responded by grabbing the offender by his testicles and dragging him by them onto the dance floor, squeezing them so hard she had brought tears to his eyes.

'Next time you think of grabbing a woman like that, just remember, buddy, some girl like me is going to drag you by the balls in front of a crowded room and make you dance,' she hissed in his ear.

The incident had been so typically Bronwyn – the ballsy fearless gal who could hold her own in any situation and still manage to come out of it smiling.

Michelle had also been asked to write a small tribute to Bronwyn for one of the family to read. In it, she described her friend's incredible passion for life, her compassion and her desire to help people. For Bronwyn, life was as simple as the things she wanted from it. If her family and friends were happy, that had made her happy too.

Michelle, Therese and Bronwyn had met at Gordon TAFE during their training and had become inseparable. They had called themselves the three musketeers and Michelle could not imagine her life without them.

For the service, the family had chosen a special poem that Jenny believed spoke volumes about her daughter's life. It began with the words:

When I am gone, release me, let me go

I have so many things to see and do,

You mustn't tie yourself to me with tears.

Be happy that we had so many years …

So many years. Jenny had only had 28 years with her whirlwind of a daughter, and it hadn't been long enough.

In the weeks that Bronwyn had been missing, she had sensed her presence so strongly that she had been certain she had hung around to keep an eye on everyone – not wanting to leave this world until she knew the people she loved were going to be okay.

Chapter 14

Jess had said in the letter she had given her aunt to take to Bali that it was okay for her to go. Now that Bronwyn had been returned to them, her little sister gave her everyone's blessings and hoped she would finally rest in peace.

Cath read the eulogy she had penned to the girl she had never had the chance to know in her lifetime, and the family she had met through her death.

I have had the privilege of knowing the Hobbs and Cartwright families for only 26 days – and what an honour that has been.

Their love, strength, compassion, humour and gentleness shines from them all.

During this short time, they have helped me gain an understanding of the type of life Bronwyn lived and an understanding of the love that shone from her. I think them for this.

Some people come into our lives and go quickly......they touch our souls. We gain strength from the footprints they have left on our hearts, and we will never ever be the same.

Twenty-seven days ago, the name Bronwyn Cartwright first touched my soul. Her name was spoken by her friend, Therese, as she lay in my arms. Her plea was clear and simple – 'please help find my friend Bronwyn. Please find her.

We tried – we tried so hard.

We can now give thanks to God that the searching is over.

Instead of having flowers, the family asked for donations to HATI, the Balinese charity that Rada had supported after the bombings, to help the local people recover from the tragedy.

From the stories in the newspapers, and the things the family had seen on their recent trip, it had been clear that the terrorist attacks had impacted so many livelihoods and had decimated Bali's tourist industry, which had since ground to a halt.

On her recent stay in Melbourne, Cath had told Jenny Hobbs about the story that Danielle had shared with herself and Rada, outside the photo identification room at the Sanglah Hospital – about the hardship faced by the Balinese people.

Jenny had been as moved by the story as Cath and Rada had been. She believed that asking for donations to a worthy cause that would help others would be something Bronwyn would have approved of.

Her family had told her how sad and compassionate the Balinese had been in the days after the bombings. Her sister Libby had described the wreaths of posies and flowers placed outside the hospitals, the shops, and even the most modest homes in Kuta. Libby had also told her how the people had shared their sorrow as they paid their respects to those who had lost their lives, or who had been hurt by the bombs.

Libby had lost count of the apologies and condolences they had received during their time in Kuta as everyone – from the delightful manager of the Bounty Hotel to the sympathetic taxi drivers – apologised for the suffering that had not been their fault. The mourners at the funeral dug deeply and every cent went to HATI.

Bronwyn's family and friends were not the only ones reaching out to the Balinese people. The indigenous people of Geelong – the Wathaurong community – hosted a memorial concert for Bronwyn and Aaron, Justin and Stacey Lee, and all the other innocent victims who had been killed or injured in the terrorist attacks. The event had been entitled 'Bridges' and had been the Wathaurong's gift as they offered their comfort and support to the people of Bali.

Rada had not been able to make it down to Victoria for Bronwyn's funeral. She had returned to Brisbane to spend time with her daughter, Dannika, who had been relieved to have her mother safely home.

She had been receiving regular updates from Dawn about Therese's progress, and the journeys of some of the other casualties whose paths had crossed theirs in Bali.

'I've kept a journal,' Rada told her daughter. 'When you are ready to read it, it will explain everything.'

So much had happened in a few days, and it had been life changing for everyone.

* * *

While Jenny was mourning for her daughter in Melbourne and Rada was catching up with her own, Dawn had decided to tell Therese about her friend's death.

Over the past week, she had been slowly filtering more details about the explosion that had caused Therese's terrible burns. And in November, she approached the subject by explaining that the injuries had not been the result of an accidental explosion – but a suicide bomber.

Therese had looked panic-stricken as she tried to process this shocking revelation.

'A terrorist attack?' she asked, looking devastated. 'Why?'

Her mother shook her head.

'I wish I knew,' she said sadly.

Therese became so distressed that her mum left out the part about Bronwyn's death. She had not wanted to overwhelm her.

But later in the day, a giant bouquet of flowers arrived at the hospital from Jenny and the family in Melbourne and Dawn realised this was her opportunity to explain.

'I have something I have to tell you,' said Dawn, taking a deep breath.

Therese looked listlessly up from the pillows.

'What is it?' she asked.

Dawn swallowed hard.

'Unfortunately, Bronwyn didn't make it.'

Therese looked crushed and began to cry.

It was unbearable to imagine that her friend had been killed in a terrorist attack – and that she was still here.

Therese's chest felt heavy with grief. She had lost people before, including her adoptive grandparents. But the raw, aching grief and sense of despair she experienced when she heard about Bronwyn's death was a pain beyond all others and she was utterly broken.

Therese closed her eyes, her salty tears stinging her burnt face. She did not want to speak any more and she could not bear to hear how her friend had died, though she had imagined it probably was from burns like the ones she was battling.

Despite her suffering, she had never thought about ending her life before. But after hearing about Bronwyn, she would have been content if death crept up on her while she slept.

The struggle to live was too hard, and there was no end to the suffering. But the pain from these hideous burns – as

Chapter 14

excruciating and unbearable it was – was more bearable than the all-consuming sorrow she felt over Bronwyn's death.

The aching, raw guilt that Therese now felt was worse than anything she had suffered so far, and she had no idea how she was going to live with that.

Chapter 15

WANTING
TO DIE

In late October, Concord finally opened its hi-tech new
burns unit and some of the hospital's most seriously injured
casualties became the first patients to benefit from the state-
of-the-art facilities.

The new unit was modern, airy and well equipped, and
Therese had been allocated a room with separate partitions
which offered her a little more privacy than she'd had in the old
intensive care unit.

Rada found Therese there on her next visit to Sydney and had
been stunned to find her sitting alone on her bed in her room,
almost naked and morphine-affected.

'Where are the nurses?' asked Rada, looking around for the
staff. Therese looked at her blankly, not answering.

'Where's your mum?' inquired Rada, scanning the ICU for
Dawn.

Therese vaguely shook her head.

'I've had a shower,' she slurred through the cloud of opiates she had been prescribed to combat the crippling ordeal of having the cool running water trickling over her burns.

Therese had sobbed the entire time the nurses had showered her and had screamed even louder when they had patted her scorched body dry. The pain had been so indescribable that she had thought she would pass out.

If the pain from her third-degree burns had not been agonising enough, having a shower and her dressings changed had been even more of an ordeal.

Rada studied her dazed friend.

'Where are the nurses?' she asked again. And again, Therese shook her head, clearly out of it.

'They are fixing up my dressings,' she said.

Therese looked so vulnerable and helpless it was distressing seeing her like this – as dependent as a baby.

This undignified situation had been unacceptable to Rada, and only added to Therese's suffering. She strode off to find one of the staff.

Later, Rada had watched the nurses tending to Therese's dressings and wondered how soul-destroying it must be for this formerly independent young mum to find herself in such a depressing situation. A couple of months ago, Therese had been a nurse herself, responsible for the care of infirm and needy elderly patients who had been incapable of looking after themselves. Now, she was as helpless as they had been, relying on everyone else for everything. Rada imagined it must be a nightmare.

After the nurses had gone, Therese lay quietly on the bed.

'Have you heard about Bronwyn?' she asked.

'I have,' answered Rada.

As they sat in silence considering this development, a fiery new spark swept across Therese's foggy eyes. Until now she had felt nothing but overwhelming sorrow about Bronwyn's death, and guilt that she had survived.

But now she felt a feral rage towards the terrorists for murdering her friend and 201 other innocent people – and ruining her own life too.

'I'm gonna get those fuckers for this!' she spat.

Rada understood. It was appropriate for her to feel angry about this shattering news. She remembered how furious she had felt after her son's death. It was why she had been fighting the mining company for answers.

'Do you want to talk about it?' she asked. Therese shook her head.

'I can't,' she said, trying not to cry again.

She said she had been told that Bronwyn's only apparent injury had been a broken leg.

'How can that be?' she wondered, studying her bandages and the morphine pump she had been struggling to use.

How could she survive with these horrific injuries, and Bronwyn – without a mark on her – hadn't made it? It made no sense to Therese. But nothing made any sense anymore.

She laid her bandaged hands on the pressure suit and examined her feet, which were still swathed in dressings and looked enormous.

'Who is going to love me with these scars?' she asked.

Chapter 15

Rada pulled her chair closer.

'Time is such a healer,' she said, trying to comfort her.

When Rada called in on her the following day, Therese had been sitting alone on the bed, looking lost and hopeless.

'I wish I was dead!' she said evenly. 'It's too hard to keep fighting.'

Rada caught her breath.

'You don't wish that, Therese – you really don't,' she replied, her thoughts immediately turning to the son she was still grieving for.

In Bali, Rada had witnessed the anguish of too many grieving parents whose children had been taken before their time. She had comforted Pauline Whitton after she had broken down during one of the consulate meetings, distraught that no-one could tell her when she could take her daughter's body home.

Rada had supported Jodi Wallace's mother too, after her daughter had been identified in the morgue. She had not been able to attend Bronwyn's funeral, but she knew that her family were broken-hearted.

Rada sat beside Therese and shared her own story, describing the heartache she had felt over her son's tragic death and the enormous void it had left in her own life.

'You don't want to die, Therese,' she soothed. 'You've made it this far. Things will get better for you – I'm sure they will.'

Therese closed her eyes again. Would they? she wondered bleakly.

* * *

After Bronwyn's funeral, Cath had returned to her school in Brunei where she had continued to monitor Therese's progress in phone calls and emails.

Sometimes when she rang the ICU, her mother put Therese on the phone, though she had often sounded out of it. Mostly she faxed letters to Dawn at the hospital to give to Therese, telling her about her life as a primary school teacher and trying to inject some light into her difficult days and remind her that people had been thinking about her.

In one of their phone conversations, Dawn told Cath that Therese and Damien were turning 30 on 6 December. It was a milestone that nobody had expected Therese to survive to see, and she had been thinking about having a low-key party on the ward to mark the occasion. Cath wanted to return to Australia for this special event and agreed it was a birthday well worth a celebration.

On 20 November, Cath wrote:

Dear Therese,

Wish I could be there with you but will have to wait another few weeks.

Although I am not there in person, know that I am with you in heart and spirit. I hope to speak with you on the phone soon.

Your mum and dad have told me how you continue to improve each day. Of course – I wouldn't expect any other sort of news – after all you are an amazing lady and you have already shown so many of us your will, determination, and strength.

I am so proud of you and can't wait to see you again.

Cath went on to say that her four and five-year-old students had been keeping her on her feet and that there was never a dull moment in her classroom. She was looking forward to returning to Sydney to celebrate her 30th birthday in December.

Am trying to get on a flight back to Sydney for this special day. Until then – keeping eating those chocolates!!! Miss you heaps! With care and love always. Cath

A week later, Cath wrote again.

Well, not long now until I finish work and get back on the plane and be with you. I fly out of Brunei on the 4 December … I will stay overnight in Brisbane and get a flight to Sydney on the 5th. I am so looking forward to seeing you again. It was wonderful talking with you the other day. You sounded great!

Cath had gone on to say that work had been hectic and that she had been working Saturdays. She had reminded Therese about her own independent life as a full-time working mother, saying she had no idea how nurses managed shift work. As far as Cath was concerned, Therese might be a patient, but she still was still that same woman under those bandages, and there was light at the end of the tunnel.

In her letter, Cath had asked about Alex and Katie, and said she was sure they would be excited about coming to see her for her birthday.

Better go as there is a netball game about to star … I haven't played netball for years so should be a good laugh. Take care my friend and see you soon … Love Cath.

There had been a couple of other reasons for Cath's trip back to Australia. She had been planning to fly to Melbourne with Rada to attend a fundraiser being organised by Therese's close-knit community for the battling young mothere and her children.

The Therese Fox Benefit Appeal had been an initiative inspired by some of the mothers at her children's primary school, who had made a beautiful patchwork quilt, which they had stitched messages into, wishing her a speedy recovery.

The fundraiser was to take the form of a dinner dance and concert and had been shaping up to be a sell-out affair. So far, more than 200 supporters had already booked tables for themselves and their friends – including Bronwyn's sister, Jess, who had booked a table for herself and her partner, Adam – and for all her cousins and their partners.

The benefit concert was to be hosted by former AFL footy star and former Geelong great, Billy Brownless, who was now a TV celebrity on Channel Nine's *The Footy Show*, which had a cult viewing of footy fans all over Australia.

Cath knew from her regular phone calls to Jenny Hobbs that her family had been supporting the event and that lots of local businesses and private individuals had donated prizes for the auctions and raffles that would be run throughout the evening. But she was not sure if Therese had known about it, so she had not mentioned this in her letters.

Cath had also failed to mention that she had also been struggling since her return to Brunei, with the longer-term psychological impact of the bombings now obvious to everyone. Before Bali, Cath had been studying for her Master's degree, but since the tragedy she had not been coping with the work and had been forced to reduce some of her subjects.

Her friends and colleagues at school had noticed a distinct change in Cath since her return from Bali. She was quieter, almost distant at times, and had been doing things that she would not have done before – such as checking the exits and entrances everywhere she went, and making sure she found a seat close to the door in case anything happened.

The school where she worked in Brunei was close to an army barracks, and the sudden sound of guns or loud explosions from military training exercises startled her and left her feeling anxious. These days, Cath was in a perpetual state of hypervigilance, and looking for signs of danger in every situation.

Suspecting she might be suffering from a form of post-traumatic stress, Cath had seen a local doctor. But there had been no psychiatric nurse or appropriately qualified professional at the clinic in Brunei to help her.

Cath had been told that the Australian Government was offering financial support and psychiatric help for survivors and their families, as well as those who had lost people. She wondered if that applied to secondary survivors like her and Rada.

She had decided to apply for the counselling and had provided letters in support of her application from Therese's parents and from Bronwyn's mother.

Cath's teaching contract in Brunei was coming to an end, and when she was informed that Queensland Health had been willing to fund some counselling sessions for her, the principal at her school had agreed to release her from the arrangement so she could see a counsellor in Brisbane.

She would leave the school in May but had arranged to take unpaid leave during December to begin counselling.

This meant she would be home for Therese's 30th birthday and the fundraiser.

* * *

Therese, however, was unaware of these plans as she braced herself for more skin grafts and battled her way through the inevitable infections that the specialists told her now impeded the recovery of many of their burns patients.

The extent and severity of the burns Therese had suffered during the explosion had affected every part of her body except her scalp. And although her beautiful long brown hair had been scorched off her head, there had been no damage to the hair follicles and in time, her hair would grow back.

But with so little viable skin for the specialists to use in the grafting process, they had become reliant on the artificial skin grown in the labs.

The synthetic skin contained peeling factors produced from cells known as fibroblasts, taken from the foreskins of newborn babies. These special cells produced healing and growth properties and had been snap frozen in liquid nitrogen and stored until were needed for grafting.

The artificial skin arrived at the hospitals in strips, and the surgeons had been using them to close the wounded areas on their burns patients.

In the early days after the Bali bombings, there were so many seriously burnt casualties undergoing skin grafts in Australian hospitals that the demand for artificial skin had depleted the supplies.

Chapter 15

There had been instances where the grafts had failed to take and had broken down, leaving exposed open wounds that became infected.

This had been the case with a few of Therese's skin grafts, particularly on the badly burnt area covering her chest where the transplanted artificial skin had not taken. This left an exposed wound requiring antibiotic treatment to prevent a life-threatening infection from creeping in.

After weeks in the ICU, Therese's condition remained precarious and she was still on high doses of morphine, which had to be increased during her excruciating showers and dressing changes. She required even more before the gruelling physiotherapy sessions which had become so painful that she absolutely dreaded them. Every day brought another mountain to climb and most of the time, Therese felt too drained to function.

The recent surgery to remove the bone and the shrapnel in her elbow had not been successful and the wounds had not healed.

The constant physio she required for her arms was the most agonising ordeal of all because it broke the new bone that had formed over her injured elbows, making them painful to move. But without physio, her joints would stiffen and seize up and she would lose the ability to use her arms and would be in constant pain.

Therese felt hopeless and helpless. At almost 30 years old, she could no longer feed herself, brush her hair, clean her teeth, hold a pen or a newspaper, or even write her name on the constant flow of paperwork that her father brought to the hospital for her to sign. She had become so incapacitated that she even needed her mother's help to go to the toilet.

Because of Therese's unstable condition, it had been suggested that she grant her parents the power of attorney so that they could manage all her business affairs and act on her behalf until she could manage these things for herself.

Little by little, Therese had felt her identity slowing being stripped away from her. She had become so depressed that the doctors had upped the dose of antidepressants to counteract the devastating psychological trauma she suffered. But no amount of medication had been strong enough to fill the black hole that consumed her.

She hated being reliant on her 65-year-old mother, who already had serious health issues of her own. Before the terrorist attack, Dawn had been diagnosed with Parkinson's disease and the stress surrounding her daughter's life-and-death situation had exacerbated her illness, making her tremors more pronounced.

Therese had sometimes observed her mother sleeping in the chair beside her bed, exhausted from the endless days of worry and the long nights without sleep, and felt more guilty and hopeless than ever.

On several occasions, Therese had asked her mum for a mirror so that she could see the extent of her physical injuries for herself. But no mirror had been forthcoming, and after one of the staff suggested she should consider wearing a mask, she had become frightened and decided it might be better not to see what they had not wanted her to see.

In truth, Dawn had been acting on the advice of Therese's hospital-appointed psychologist, who had been advising them not to overwhelm her. She had struggled with the news that her injuries were the result of a terrorist attack, and had been even more despairing since the news about Bronwyn's death.

The therapist did not think it would be helpful for Therese to be confronted with her disfiguring injuries at this early stage because she was not physically or mentally strong enough. She felt Therese would require more intensive therapy before she could deal with the disfiguring scars and destruction of her former identity.

Therese's fight for survival had become such a lonely and isolating rite of passage. She could no longer allow herself to think about her old life, or Bronwyn – or even her children. Just thinking about her two children made her so depressed that the pain in her heart was paralysing. If she was to survive at all, she could only live in the moment and take each day one minute at a time, or she would not make it.

Therese had been encouraged to share her feelings with her psychologist. But her world already felt like an endless stream of burns specialists, orthopedic surgeons, doctors and physiotherapists; having another professional poking around in another part of her scarred body was something she had been struggling to find the energy for. Amidst the darkness, she looked forward to Cath's letters and Rada's visits, which injected a little ray into her otherwise dark days.

It had been almost two months since she had seen Alex and Katie, when she tiptoed out of the house on 6 October to catch the bus to Melbourne Airport. She had left early that morning because she had not wanted to wake them up. But she had told them the previous evening when she kissed them goodnight that she hoped they would be good for their grandma and would bring them loads of presents back from Bali.

It had been agreed that Dawn would stay at Therese's house with the children while she was away, so that she could see them off to school each day and keep them in their normal routine. The following weekend, Dawn would drop them off at their other nana's place in Little River, where Pam would mind them while their dad was in Adelaide on his annual footy break-up.

Before Therese left for the airport, she had slipped a note under the children's pillows, telling them how much she loved them. She promised them she would be back soon, but she had not been home since.

After two months, hearing their little voices on the phone had become too hard and only added to the guilt she felt about the impact this nightmare must be having on their lives.

Therese had been aware of the regular phone conversations her mum had with Alex and Katie in Melbourne, and had overheard her telling them that she was too sick to come to the phone.

Sometimes, when Dawn was massaging Therese's face, she had updated her on their progress at school, and had repeatedly emphasised that they were settled and happy at their father's place, which had been a shot through their mother's heart.

'Maybe you can speak to them next time,' Dawn had cautiously suggested.

But Therese had barely enough energy to open her eyes each day and there were many mornings where all she wanted to do was close her eyes and not wake up. The news of Bronwyn's death had completely broken her, and the guilt she felt over the loss of her friend was matched only by the guilt she felt about her inability to be a mother to her children.

Chapter 15

Amidst this grief, on 22 November 2002, news emerged that Jemaah Islamiyah's alleged 'field commander', Imam Samudra, had been arrested by Indonesian police and was now in custody in Indonesia.

According to the headlines, Samudra, 35, had been arrested with two other suspects on a bus at the Merak ferry terminal on the north-western tip of Java. At the time of his arrest, he had been waiting to board a boat to neighbouring Sumatra.

A senior police official had told international media that Samudra had seemed resigned to his fate. From the reports, it had been unclear whether he would be held in Jakarta or moved to Bali where another alleged terrorist – Amrozi – was being held.

Amrozi's arrest on 5 November 2002 had been considered a major breakthrough in the investigation. Police alleged that he had bought the explosives used in the attack and had driven the van that later exploded outside the Sari Club in the suicide attacks.

His older brother, Ali Ghufron – aka 'Mukhlas', had been arrested in Java a few weeks later, the Indonesian police convinced he had been the extremist group's operational chief in Southeast Asia.

Therese's parents had been following the news on the TV from Concord, but her therapist had not felt she was mentally strong enough to cope with this distressing information.

Chapter 16

A BIRTHDAY
REUNION

Since the news from Bali on Sunday 13 October, Alex and Katie had been living at their father's home in Werribee, where David had been endeavouring to ensure their lives remained as stable and normal as possible.

In the early days after Therese's evacuation back to Australia, David, an accountant, had taken a week's holiday to settle his children in. When that ended, he had taken carer's leave to enable him to establish Alex and Katie in their new routine.

After some discussion with his mum, Pam, David had decided that the children would remain at the Nazareth Catholic Primary School in Grovedale to minimise the disruption to their lives. He believed maintaining his children's friendships and class routines was worth the inconvenience of the 90-minute round trip to Grovedale and back for the daily school run.

Although the more sensitive and introspective Alex appeared to have adapted well to the changes in his circumstances, it had become clear to David that his son had become detached and closed-off since the news about his mother, and needed professional help to deal with the 'accident' he'd been told had put her in the hospital.

David had agreed with his mum's assessment that Alex appeared to have disconnected, probably as a coping mechanism to protect himself from the painful situation and the fears he held for his mum.

Katie's tears and apprehension surrounding the news appeared to have been overtaken by her anxiety that her mum might not survive.

The Australian Government – responding to the trauma and suffering that the Bali bombings had had on the survivors, their families, and the relatives of the dead – had made funding available to ensure people received the help they needed to deal with the ongoing psychological impact on their lives. David had gratefully accepted the offer of help for his children.

In Katie's heightened state of hypervigilance, her first day back at primary school a few days after the news had only confirmed her fears that things might be more serious with Mum than her dad and Nana had been telling them.

Everything about her return to school had felt different. They had been the only children at school that day not wearing uniform – because they had been staying with their dad and their uniforms were still at their own house in Grovedale.

Students had generally found themselves in trouble when they forgot to wear their uniforms. But on their first back it was different. Nobody seemed to mind – not even the principal – and it wasn't normal.

Furthermore, the teachers and the other children's mothers had been so welcoming and so exceptionally pleased to see them that Katie had found that unsettling too. In the mind of an anxious seven-year-old, it was as though everyone knew something that she and Alex hadn't been told, and they appeared to be trying to compensate for the fact that their mum had been hurt.

It was as though everyone was being especially nice because they felt very *sorry* for them, and it was making the little girl very nervous.

Katie quietly observed the teachers introducing themselves to her dad, who had never been involved in the school run before. She had overheard them asking about their mum and telling him they were here for him if he needed any help.

This sudden abundance of generosity and concern had only reinforced her suspicions that whatever had happened to her mum must have been very bad indeed. Perhaps things were worse than she and Alex had been told after all. Perhaps mum really was going to die. Either way, nothing about this attention felt normal, and Katie had become so scared that she had immediately thrown up outside the school gate.

Over the next couple of weeks, the children's new 'normal' had involved their dad driving them back to Werribee with an assortment of tasty homemade casseroles and sponge cakes on the back seat of his car – courtesy of the big-hearted mums in their close-knit school community, who were doing all they could to support them.

Chapter 16

Katie's fears for her mother had increased after the school mothers presented their dad with a beautifully crafted quilt that they had made for Therese. It was a sincerely kind gesture, born out of empathy and love. These kind mums wanted Therese to know that everyone was thinking about her. But Katie didn't see it that way. She had never known anyone to give anybody's else's mum a gift as special and important as this before. It had felt like such a big deal that she was more convinced than ever that her mum was about to die.

Fortunately, by then, counselling had become part of the children's new routine.

Every Saturday morning, David had been driving Alex and Katie into Melbourne to see the child psychologist who had been appointed to help them. At the beginning, David had been part of the sessions too, listening carefully as the counsellor explained to his children that she was providing them with a safe place where they could share their feelings about what had happened to their mum.

The psychologist had also been a great support to David, by helping him to deal appropriately with any questions the children had. She had also begun to prepare them for what they might expect when they saw their mum for the first time.

She emphasised the importance of being honest with the children without overloading them with the sort of information that might frighten them or add to their anxiety. She had encouraged Alex and Katie to talk about their feelings and their fears, and to let their dad or nana know when they were feeling sad or angry or scared. She had impressed upon them it was normal to feel all those emotions after a parent had been hurt or sick in hospital. And she gave them tips to help them control their emotions when they became too overwhelming.

During the sessions, the counsellor had also spoken about the importance of recognising happy feelings. It was okay for them to be happy, even though mum had been hurt and they shouldn't feel bad about it. It was also important that they had fun with their dad and felt happy about being with him too. It was also important to notice other happy things in their lives – such as mum still being here, even though she was in hospital in Sydney.

More importantly, she told them that if they were ever feeling anything other than happy, it was important to tell their dad so that he could help.

The children had not been told that Therese had been blown up in a terrorist attack, but that she had been badly burnt in an explosion. The counsellor thought they might be frightened if they knew the whole story.

She had also explained that when they saw their mother again, she might look different to the way she used to look. But under the bandages she was still their mum and she loved them.

With the counsellor's help, David had been able to allay his daughter's fears that her mother was dying, without lying to her, or giving her unrealistic expectations.

He explained that nobody knew if Mum was going to recover from her injuries. And nobody could tell them that she was going to be fine because she might not. But it was also possible she would get better as everyone hoped she would. Whatever the outcome, regular therapy had been helping to prepare the children so they would be better able to deal with it.

David understood how much they missed their mum and their grandma too. Therese's mother had played a major role in their lives, and they had a very close relationship with their grandma. They had not seen her either since their mother's arrival in Sydney, though they understood that Grandma needed to stay at the hospital until their mother was better. When Mum was well enough, they would all fly to Sydney to see her.

As the children became more comfortable with their therapist, David withdrew from the sessions, satisfied that Katie and Alex were confident enough to talk to her on their own. With the psychologist's help, he had been preparing the children for what they would see when they finally visited their mum, and how they would feel about it.

Katie told the counsellor that she had been missing her mum and grandma and now felt anxious about anyone she loved leaving her, even if they left her to go in a different room, or out to the shops. The psychologist noted that Katie was suffering from separation anxiety, which was completely normal for a child whose mum had gone on holiday and hadn't come back.

The little girl had also told her about the notes her mum had left under their pillow before she went to Bali. They had found them after she'd gone. Katie could not remember everything her mother had written, but she remembered the sign-off-line very clearly. Her mother's note had ended with the words: 'I love you a million trillion times around the world and back again.' Katie said her brother had found a note from her mum under his pillow too, but she wasn't sure what his note had said.

Still, Katie was enjoying her time at her dad's and was spending lots of time at her other nana's place in Little River, where they played with their cousin and did lots of fun things. She just wished she had brought all her Barbies rather than the few she had put in her bag. She would have, if she had known she would be gone for so long.

David had organised for the counselling sessions to take place early on Saturday mornings, which meant they could spend the rest of the day in the city, doing fun things together as a family.

After the sessions with the psychologist, he had taken them to one of the parks in the city, or to the museum or the zoo. They had ridden a tram and taken a trip to the top of the Eureka building where the children had been able to see all the way to the Dandenong Ranges.

Some Saturdays they had enjoyed lunch in one of the cafes at Southbank overlooking the Yarra River or grabbed a burger in McDonald's.

Given the changes in their lives and the absence of their mother, Alex and Katie had adapted well. They had already been accustomed to spending alternate weekends at his place, but it had still been a relief to see them looking settled and happy with their permanent full-time arrangement.

* * *

In Sydney, the nightmare continued for Therese, though every passing day had given her parents more hope that she would prove everyone wrong and pull through.

The doctors had remained non-committal. Her regular physiotherapy – despite being painful – had given her a little mobility and the nurses had started to encourage her out of her bed into a chair. Dawn hoped that the physiotherapy that

Chapter 16

Therese hated so much might soon have her back on her feet where she would have to learn to walk again.

In the meantime, Dawn was planning a birthday party to celebrate the milestone nobody had ever expected Therese would be around to see.

Rada, who had been a regular visitor, said she would travel down from Queensland for the big occasion, while Cath was flying in from Brunei. Therese's dad was coming down from Brisbane. Damien and his wife, Lisa, were travelling up from Melbourne – and the Red Cross had organised flights for David and the children for their reunion with their mother.

'We will all be here to celebrate with you,' said Dawn, desperate to cling to every precious milestone on the long road back to recovery.

Therese had been feeling anxious about this family gathering. Although she desperately wanted to see her children, she did not want them to see her like this.

She was worried that her injuries might frighten them, and was not sure how she would deal with the agony of them leaving again without her.

In many ways, it was easier not to see them at all than deal with the heartache of saying goodbye when all she wanted was to go home and be their mum again.

But Dawn had been desperate to see her grandchildren, and after everything Therese had gone through to be here, this was one birthday they all wanted to celebrate.

Damien and Therese both loved seafood, so Dawn had decided to book a feast of prawns and calamari, along with other assorted party nibbles and two separate birthday cakes. Therese smiled for the first time in months. All their lives she had shared a birthday cake with Damien, who she had joked was Dawn's golden child. In the past, their mum had always bought the cake he had liked best. Having a cake of her own was tangible evidence of how bad things were for Therese.

David attended the children's next counselling session, where the psychologist reminded Alex and Katie that Mum was going to look different, but that she was still the same mum under her bandages.

'Will we be able to hug her?' asked Katie. Her dad wasn't sure. 'Probably not this time,' he said.

The therapist discussed this significant reunion between the children and their father and felt it was important that he was present at this first meeting with their injured mother. He would be on hand to give Alex and Katie additional support or take them for a walk if they became distressed or overwhelmed.

The flights to Sydney, although organised by the Red Cross, were funded by the government. The Australian Government had injected a considerable amount of money into reuniting families with the survivors of the bombings, particularly those who were being treated at major trauma hospitals interstate.

David and the children arrived in Sydney a couple of days before Therese's birthday. He had a few things planned that he hoped might relieve the tension surrounding the reunion with their mum.

They had been to Darling Harbour and caught the ferry from Circular Quay to Taronga Zoo, where the children enjoyed seeing the chimpanzees. Later they all went shopping for a birthday present for Therese. The children chose a special birthday card with '30' on it, which they had both signed.

Chapter 16

Because it had been so long since the children had seen Therese, it had been agreed that the reunion should take place *before* her birthday to break the ice before the big day itself.

They arrived at Concord Hospital on 2 December to find Dawn waiting for them. The reunion between the children and their grandmother was an emotional one and Alex and Katie were as overjoyed to see her as Dawn was to see them.

Therese's mum had been awake all night worrying about their reaction when they finally saw their mother. She remembered how shocked she had been when the bandages came off and she had seen Therese's confronting injuries for the first time. The doctors and psychologist had been concerned too.

Before the meeting, David and the children had been ushered into a private room where Dawn and one of Therese's nurses wanted to talk to them.

'Has the counsellor told you Mum has lots of bandages and looks a bit different to the way she looked before?' their grandma asked them gently.

Alex and Katie nodded. The psychologist and their dad had explained it to them, they said.

There was something else the nurse wanted to speak with David about before they went into the room. Over the past couple of days, Therese had been panicking about the visit, terrified that her appearance might be too distressing for her children. But while she knew this would be hard enough for her and them, she had been adamant that she did not want David to see her in such a vulnerable state.

The nurses had spoken to Dawn about it. This would be the first time Therese had seen anyone other than her immediate family and Cath and Rada.

'This is a really big deal for Therese,' the nurse explained to David. 'We don't want her getting distressed, so it might be better if, on this occasion, she saw the children on their own.'

Although Dawn respected Therese's wishes, she hadn't been comfortable with the request. After everything David had done, it sounded ungracious, and she felt upset for him. Before the meeting, she told the staff how she felt.

'But this isn't about David,' the nurse reminded Dawn. 'This is about Therese and what *she* is able to deal with.'

David was taken aback by the news. For months, he had discussed the reunion with the psychologist. She had agreed that it was important for the children that their father should be there to support them. But after everything Therese had been through, he respected her decision and offered no argument.

'No worries,' he said. 'I'll be outside if you need me.'

He reassured the children they would be fine and watched as the nurse opened the door and led them into the room where Therese lay on the bed.

Katie surveyed the heavily bandaged patient in the full-body pressure suit half propped up against the pillows on the bed. Therese had dressings wrapped around her head, and her face looked very red and sore.

The counsellor had warned them that their mum might look a bit different, but Katie did not recognise this stranger at all. Her mum was skinny and suntanned. She had long brown hair and a pretty face and she chased them and played ball games with them. But this person had no hair and her face was so scarred and raw that she no longer resembled her mum.

Katie clung to her grandma and began to cry. This stranger in bandages looked nothing like her mum and she was so scared she didn't want to go anywhere near her.

But Alex would have known his mum anywhere. He had inherited his mother's quiet reserve and her courage. Without any prompting, he walked straight over to the bed and gently touched Therese's hand over the bandages. Privately, he wanted to hug her but had been too afraid of hurting her.

'Hi, Mum,' he said, smiling at her.

Therese had been overcome with emotion. It was such a relief to see her children after all this time. Yet she felt inexplicably guilty for putting them through this ordeal when they had already been through so much.

'Hi, sweetheart,' she whispered.

He stood helplessly beside her, not sure what to do. He studied the bandages covering her from head to toe.

'I don't think you look as bad as I thought you would,' he whispered, putting on a brave face.

Therese could feel her heart racing in her chest. Alex was so brave, and Katie was so frightened it broke her heart. Trying to hide her own pain, she gave her daughter a few moments and spoke to her.

'Hi, bubby,' she said, calling Katie by the nickname she had given her as a baby.

Katie glanced up through her tears. Only her mum called her 'bubby' she thought, though she was still too scared to approach her.

After a while Katie finally wandered over to the bed, holding tightly to her grandmother's hand. She stood in silence beside her big brother, her eyes taking in the bandages and the tears around the familiar brown eyes.

Without saying a word, she placed her small fingers very gently against the dressings. Did it hurt? she asked. Her mum assured her it didn't.

Therese desperately wanted to scoop them up in her arms and hug them and shower them with kisses. But she could not move. She could not do anything.

On their counsellor's advice, the reunion had been brief.

Therese watched her children following their grandma out of the room with a pain in her heart that felt like labour pains in reverse. Alex and Katie were her entire life and it was agony watching them leaving without her.

Until that moment, she had always hoped she would get better and return home and everything would go back to normal. But she had cried for hours after they left, convinced nothing would ever be normal again.

Before they left, Alex told his mum that Dad was taking them sightseeing tomorrow and might even go to the big aquarium.

'That sounds like fun,' Therese said, feeling horribly conflicted. She was happy that their dad was making this difficult time enjoyable for them – but resented him for doing all the things she should have been doing with her children.

They would be back in two days for her birthday and Dawn hoped things would be easier now that the initial meeting had broken the ice.

On 6 December, Damien arrived early in the ICU early to wish his twin sister a shared happy birthday. Therese had been

sleeping when he came into the unit but had woken to the sound
of his voice whispering in her ear.

'Wake up – I'm still the youngest!'

When Therese opened her eyes he was grinning at her.

Ever since she could remember, the six-minute age difference
had been a standing joke between them. Therese was the first-born
twin at 7.30am, and Damien had followed at 7.36am. On their
birthday every year at precisely 7.30, he had taunted her for being
the old twin and today was a tradition he was not about to break.

'I hear you've got your own cake, old lady,' he joked. Therese
smiled.

'Mum has chosen it for me,' she said, feeling more alert on her
birthday than she'd felt since she arrived here.

Rada and Cath were the next to arrive, their broad smiles
lighting up the burns unit.

'Happy birthday, Therese,' she said, handing her a card and a
small gift.

Among the cards that had arrived that day was a card from
a surprise well-wisher. The birthday card had been sent by the
Australian Prime Minister. Later, in the morning, John Howard
telephoned the hospital and spoke to Therese's mum. 'I hope
Therese has a happy birthday in the circumstances,' he said.
Dawn said afterwards that he had not made the call in his official
capacity, but as a regular father. He genuinely wanted to wish
Therese a happy birthday and understood their pain.

The nurses helped Therese into a high-backed chair with a
cushion. It had taken every ounce of strength she had to get out
of bed and into the chair. But she had been driven by a desire to
make sure her kids could see that she was getting better.

When they arrived with their dad, they appeared more relaxed than they had on the previous visit, and that lifted their mother's spirits.

'David might as well come in too,' Therese told her mum, feeling bad. He had taken the trouble to fly up with the children and as there had been nothing she could do about her appearance, she saw no harm in him coming in to see her too.

The children had had weeks of counselling to prepare them for this moment; however, David was not prepared for the extent and severity of Therese's burns and he had been visibly shocked when he saw her for the first time.

Dawn had warned him that she looked bad, but as he surveyed the bandages and pressure suit that covered Therese's body, it was worse than he ever imagined.

Her parents appeared to be more optimistic about her chances of pulling through, but David wasn't so sure. He observed her mother helping her drink through a straw and felt devastated for her.

How on earth would anyone come back from this? he wondered. Dawn and Chris had warned him that Therese had a long way to go, but from what he could see, this was going to be a very long, hard road.

David watched his children cautiously posing for photographs with their mother in front of her birthday cake. It was not the sort of 30th birthday he had envisaged for his former high school sweetheart, but he felt proud of the way his children dealt with this painful reunion.

Therese watched them leaving, feeling as desolate and broken-hearted as she had suspected she would. To see them so briefly, and lose them all over again, was just another painful reminder of all that she had lost, and she cried for days.

But Damien and his wife, David and the children had not been the only ones travelling down to Melbourne. Dawn had also booked a flight to Victoria to attend the fundraiser for Therese. It was her first trip home since her daughter's life-and-death arrival at Concord three days after the bombings.

Cath and Rada also flew down for the event at the Kardinia Heights Centre in North Geelong, which was being telecast live to Concord where Therese and her father would be watching it on the TV in the burns unit.

It had been decided that Chris would remain in Sydney after the birthday party so that Dawn could attend the fundraiser with Damien and his wife.

As a special treat, Chris had organised Therese's favourite pizza for dinner, which she had eaten in her hospital bed.

Therese and her dad had settled themselves down in front of the TV with their pizza, stunned to see the number of people who had turned out to offer their support. They might not be able to ease her physical suffering, but they could raise enough money to remove some of the financial pressures she might face in the future.

It was one of the one of the most overwhelming and humbling experiences she had ever known, though she had felt bizarrely disconnected from the proceedings, and felt as if she was watching a video about someone else's life, and listening to someone else's story of suffering and endurance being related to the audience.

Was that really her name on the screen, she wondered? Were people really doing this for her?

Therese had always been a private, introverted individual who had been uncomfortable about being in the spotlight. Now, a whole room full of people she had never met suddenly knew her name and her life story.

Sadly, she ended up missing the finale of the fundraiser, because she was throwing up the rich pizza that had been her dad's special treat. It was the first time, apart from a few prawns on her birthday, that she had eaten anything other than hospital food and her stomach had immediately rejected it.

Therese would later discover the generosity of strangers helped to raise more than $20,000 to help her on this impossible journey, and she had no idea how she was going to repay their kindness.

Chapter 17

THE
HOMECOMING

After Therese celebrated the birthday nobody expected her to see, her more stable condition had her specialists tentatively considering her transfer to a rehabilitation hospital closer to home.

Although they remained cautious about possible setbacks because of the ongoing risk of infection in the new skin grafts, they had begun to discuss the possibility of sending Therese back to Melbourne in time for Christmas.

Dawn saw this as another positive milestone in her recovery, but before the doctors could consider sending her back to Melbourne, there were many obstacles that Therese would have to overcome.

The impact of the explosion had affected the pressure in both ears and had left Therese with ongoing ear infections and loss of hearing, which was compounded by other infections from her burns. And the head injury and shockwaves from the bomb blast had caused such trauma to her body that she had forgotten many of the basic life skills that she had learned as a small child and had been having to learn everything again.

She would need help and practice to learn how to feed herself, clean her own teeth, hold a pen or do any of the things that her scrambled memory and physical injuries now prevented her from doing for herself.

Therese had forgotten how to write and had been struggling to sign her signature on the piles of paperwork her father had been bringing into the hospital. Instead of her usual signature, all she had been able to do with her injured hands was make the mark of a small wobbly cross on the dotted line.

Developing all these basic skills was going to take time, but they were all things that the doctors believed could be addressed in rehab with physiotherapy and practice.

On a positive note, the physiotherapy that had originally caused her so much pain had helped her to flex her calcified joints and stretch the skin that had been feeling too tight for her body. She had recently begun to take a few tentative steps around the ward on her injured feet and was learning to become more mobile.

Overcoming these mobility issues, and re-learning all the life skills that she had forgotten in a facility closer to home, were now the new goals in the next stage of Therese's recovery.

The news had been welcomed by the rest of the family, who had become increasingly concerned about Dawn's worsening tremors. A possible transfer to Melbourne offered Therese's mum a glimmer of hope that things might finally be moving in the right direction.

It would also mean that David would be able to bring the children to see their mum at weekends, which would also be good for Therese's morale.

The rocky road back to recovery would be filled with potholes, with further skin grafts to be performed, and years of treatment ahead of Therese, but Dawn hoped that things might slowly be turning the corner providing the doctors could keep on top of the continual infections.

In December, Therese underwent a procedure that involved grafting new skin onto her face, harvested from the foreskin cells of a newborn baby boy. This was just one of the pioneering surgeries that Australian doctors had been perfecting on the burns survivors from the Bali bombings.

These fibroblasts from newborn babies' foreskins held special regenerative properties that had fostered the growth of new skin on Therese's burnt face. The skin remained angry and raw; however, this pioneering treatment – and her mother's healing hands – had contributed to a noticeable improvement in her appearance.

Although Therese's face was still confronting to look at, her injuries could have been mistaken for a serious gravel rash injury that you might expect to see in a motorcyclist who had been dragged along the surface of the road at high speed after a collision.

The next time Therese heard from Cath, she told her that she was now officially a 'dickhead'. She had been in the ICU for so long that, like other long-term patients with chronic illnesses or injuries, she had developed a black humour that was helping to make her impossible battle a little more bearable. Therese's joke had given them both a laugh, even though giggling hurt her.

But for all the things she had to learn to do again, there were many other things from her old life that the doctors had warned her it was unlikely she would never be able to do again. They were not optimistic that she would ever be able to live an independent life, or care for her children on her own, or drive a car, or wear make-up on her face, or return to the nursing career that she had loved.

She would not be able to sit out in the sun, because her sweat glands had melted away and her body's damaged thermoregulatory system meant she no longer had the ability to control her own body temperature.

When she finally returned home, her life would be a battle of ongoing surgeries, physio, treatments and specialist appointments, and she would require nursing support at home to bathe and care for her. She would also need help with the cooking, the shopping and transport. Therese's new normal would be a very different kind of 'normal' to the one she had known before Bali.

Therese listened to this pessimistic forecast, feeling more angry than hopeless.

'Well, fuck you,' she inwardly fumed. 'Just watch me!'

Dawn knew that defiant expression only too well. She had glimpsed it many times during Therese's rebellious teenage years. Telling her stubborn daughter what she could not do was guaranteed to make her want to do it even more. Secretly, Dawn hoped that some of that fighting spirit was still in there somewhere under those bandages.

Over the next couple of weeks, Therese had gone from hobbling to and from the chair in her room to limping around the hospital on her bandaged feet with her morphine drip. The doctors had told her that one of the reasons she appeared to be recovering so well was due to her fitness levels.

In her 'other' life before Bali, Therese was fit and active. She ran 15 kilometres every morning on her treadmill before her working day began, and her body had been in tip-top condition. According to the doctors, this high level of fitness had become her secret weapon in her recovery.

On his frequent visits from Queensland, her dad had been persuading her to walk around the hospital with him, and to venture outside to get some fresh air. With every visit, he coaxed her to walk a little bit further, and she was regaining some strength in her legs and some of the lost muscle tone.

But it was not only her physical injuries that made this step so huge. Therese found the idea of venturing outside into the normal world terrifying – partly because the last time she had done it the unthinkable had happened, but mostly because she could not bear to be seen.

With her father's persistence, she finally plucked up the courage to do it, and it was good to smell the fresh air and watch the people coming and going. She had not been 'people watching' since their holiday in Kuta and it felt good. Because of her inability to control her body temperature, she tended to go first thing in the morning, or later in the day when the temperatures had dropped.

On one of his visits, her father had encouraged her out to his car with the intention of taking her for a drive around Sydney. He had driven the car and parked it close to the hospital entrance, so she would not have so far to walk.

But when Therese reached the car, she had forgotten how to get inside. The realisation that she had forgotten something so simple made her panic, though her dad told her not to worry. He helped her lower herself into the passenger seat, but she had spent the car ride around the city in tears.

For the past couple of weeks, the doctors had been talking about her return to Melbourne, possibly in time for Christmas. But when the fragile skin grafts on her chest showed signs of breaking down again, she had resigned herself to the fact that she would be spending the festive season in hospital.

Amidst the gloom, a gift arrived for Therese that lifted her flagging spirits. It was from one of Cath's young students in Brunei, a little girl called Bronte Scott, who had been moved by her teacher's stories about the incredible Bali burns survivor who was fighting for her life in Sydney.

The seven-year-old had told her family about Therese, and they had gone shopping for a gift that Bronte hoped might bring her some Christmas cheer.

The seven-year-old's mother, Denise had told Cath in an email on 12 December that her daughter had chosen the Christmas angel to let her know that people all over the world were thinking of her.

'I hope she is feeling a bit better and her kids get to spend Christmas with her,' she wrote from Brunei. Denise had posted the gift on her daughter's behalf to her parents in Brisbane where Cath was still on unpaid leave and having for psychological counselling.

Cath had posted the angel on to Concord and hoped Therese would enjoy her gift.

Therese had placed the angel on the cupboard beside her bed in the burns unit, hoping it might bring her some good tidings this Christmas and cast a few heavenly blessings her way. God knows she needed them.

The stories that Cath had told her families in Brunei about her experience in Bali, and the incredible survivors she had met, had touched a note with everyone in her school community.

The students and staff at her school had rallied around and raised a large sum of money for the people in Bali who they had heard were doing it tough this Christmas. One of the school families travelled from Brunei to Bali for their Christmas holidays and presented the delightful manager of the Bounty Hotel with a cheque to help the staff who had been injured in the terrorist attacks, and those who had lost their jobs since the downturn in the tourist economy.

Therese spent a miserable Christmas in Concord with her mum. Despite the staff's attempts to inject some festive spirit into the ward, she just wanted to sleep it all away.

She had not wanted the children to have to come to the hospital that Christmas just because she had to be there. The pain of seeing them was too painful to bear. Therese wanted Alex and Katie to have a normal Christmas with their dad's family just like the rest of their friends. It was easier for them not to come than have to say goodbye again.

Between Christmas and New Year her dad flew down to see her, and they went outside for a walk. But as Therese hobbled after him outside the hospital's main entrance, she tripped against the uneven easement on the footpath and fell heavily onto the concrete.

Her screams had brought the nurses running and she was immediately rushed back into the hospital where scans confirmed what their preliminary examination had told them – that Therese had broken her hip.

'You are going to require surgery on that hip right away,' said one of the doctors, obviously concerned. For although this would be a straightforward operation for most 30-year-olds, for a woman without a full covering of surface skin, and tissue-like grafts that had yet to heal, the risk of complications was enormous.

Therese emerged from theatre surgery with another scar and a heavier heart, in more pain than she had been before. She had hit the concrete so hard that the fall had damaged the paper-thin skin on her hip and other parts of her body. Without full skin coverage, infection soon crept into the wounds and a pick line had to be inserted into her heart to pump antibiotics into her system. The painkillers and morphine had been increased and Therese returned to the burns unit in despair.

New Year 2003 came and went in a blur, and while it was another milestone to cling to for her parents, there had been nothing happy about it; Therese spent it watching the fireworks over Sydney Harbour Bridge on the TV with her dad and listening to the real thing out of the hospital window.

She woke the following morning to a different year, but the same nightmare.

Her broken hip looked set to add at least another six months to her stay in hospital, and possibly more surgery. She would have to learn to walk all over again, undertake even more intensive physiotherapy and occupational therapy, and battle her way through a whole series of new skin grafts to repair the damaged skin tissue.

January brought more unsettling news for Therese when the children's father rang to say he had enrolled Alex and Katie at his own local primary school for the coming year. The news came as an unexpected shock for Therese, who felt another piece of her old life slowly being stripped away.

Although she had now come to realise that the journey ahead of her was going to be a long and arduous one, the move of schools was another abrupt reminder that Alex and Katie had moved on and had left the lives they'd lived with her behind.

In her logical mind, she understood that the long trek up and down the freeway on the daily school run must have been exhausting for David and the children, but she resented him for living the life that had once been hers.

The move of schools meant much more than geographical logistics to Therese. It was another reminder that her life was never going to be the same again.

For David, the move to a new school was purely practical. The kids were as tired of all the travelling as he was of the driving. Being closer to home would free up some time for the children to take part in a few after-school activities, or allow them the chance to play with friends at the end of the school day.

To make life easier, his mum and stepfather decided to rent a house around the corner, so they could share the school pick-up duties and support him with childcare when he needed to work late.

In her heart, Therese knew it made sense, but she was shattered about the development all the same. She resigned herself to the new changes, and decided not to overload her head with anything other than her own struggle for survival.

In late January, she discovered she was being transferred to a rehabilitation facility in Melbourne. The transfer would take place almost immediately, and she had the choice of going to Geelong or one in the city.

Therese realised that rehab in Geelong would be more convenient for her mother and family, but she opted to go to one closer to the Alfred Hospital, where she would resume her treatment.

Therese had been terrified that in Geelong she might find herself being cared for by one of her former nursing colleagues or one of the doctors she had once worked with. She hated the idea of anyone seeing her such a distressing state, and felt that she would be more anonymous in an inner-city hospital where nobody would know her.

Only her serious friends would be inclined to travel to Melbourne to visit her, whereas in Geelong, she would have the ordeal of having to see people when all she wanted was to hide her disfiguring burns.

Tentative arrangements were organised by Concord Hospital for Therese and Dawn to fly down to Melbourne on a regular Qantas flight from Sydney.

'That is not happening,' fumed her dad.

Therese was still heavily bandaged and struggling to walk with her broken hip. She would not cope with the ordeal of sitting on a packed commercial flight full of holidaymakers. As Chris pointed out, January was the main holiday season and it was unlikely that there would be any available seats any way.

'It's not appropriate for someone who has been through the ordeal Therese has been through,' said Chris, demanding an air ambulance.

An air ambulance was booked and a nurse organized to accompany them on the one-hour flight to Melbourne.

Therese was greatly relieved by the decision. She could not begin to imagine how much attention she would attract on an ordinary Qantas flight in her bandages and pressure suit in the height of summer.

She wondered what the other passengers would feel having a mummified 'tourist' with heavily bandaged feet, sitting across the aisle from their kids as they made their way home from their summer holidays.

Before she left Sydney, she received a letter from Cath with a poem bearing a positive message that she hoped would bring her some comfort.

In the letter, faxed to Concord on 14 January, Cath wrote:

Dear Therese,

As this poem says, a friend celebrates your successes – I am celebrating your success of moving into the next stage of your recovery – returning closer to home. Know that although I cannot be there in person, I am with you always in spirit and heart. Have a safe journey.

Rada flew down to witness the momentous occasion and photograph another milestone in Therese's miraculous recovery. On 17 January, Therese was wheeled out of the ICU in combat mode.

She had been told she had to wear a compression suit with a full-face mask for the onward journey, though she had not been wearing a face mask for the past months in hospital.

'No way,' said Therese, digging her heels in and refusing to let the nurses put it on. She would be wearing the full body suit *without* the face mask and that was that!

The news surrounding Therese's imminent release sparked a media frenzy and although she was unaware of it, an army of photographers and cameramen had congregated outside Concord to capture the discharge of the patient doctors had dubbed 'the miracle woman of Bali.'

When one of the nurses mentioned the media posse to Therese, she panicked.

'I don't want a fuss,' she said, looking distressed.

To avoid any attention, the staff wheeled her out through a side exit, and the only photographer to capture her leaving the hospital was Rada - on her own camera.

She was whisked out of Concord Hospital and onto the small air ambulance with her mother, leaving Rada waving to her from the ground below.

'I'll be down to visit you,' Rada promised.

Three long months after leaving Victoria on the flight to Denpasar, Therese peered out of the windows of the air ambulance in time to see the familiar Melbourne city skyline rising from the heat of a sultry summer afternoon.

There had been so many times during the last three months that she'd dreamed about this moment. But it was not the happy homecoming or celebration she had envisaged.

Her thoughts turned to Bronwyn, who had returned to her family in a coffin, and to Aaron and Justin Lee – the brothers from Geelong they had met on the flight to Denpasar – who had lost their lives at the Sari Club with Justin's wife Stacey and their unborn child. If the outward scars of the Bali bombings were visible in the burns and open wounds covering her body, the guilt and sadness were eating Therese alive from the inside out.

Chapter 18

A DIFFERENT PERSON

From the moment Therese was wheeled into her the rehabilitation hospital in inner city Melbourne, she hated everything about it.

The place was as old and tired as its patients, who were mostly elderly and recovering from an assortment of aged-related conditions, from strokes and heart attacks, to hip replacements and falls.

Although Therese qualified for the latter, she had been a nurse who, only a few months ago, had been caring for patients like the ones she was now in rehab with. But the Balmoral Nursing Home where she had worked in Grovedale had been immaculate and nothing like this depressing place.

Even from a cursory look around her new surroundings, she could see it was not the sterile, pristine environment she was used to in Concord; the bathrooms looked as grubby as some of the patients who sat patiently waiting for their meals.

She had not wanted to be cared for in Geelong, but observing what she anticipated would be her new home for at least the next three months, she was already wondering if she'd made the right decision.

Some of her more recent skin grafts had not taken well, and she feared that if the standard of hygiene was as poor as it appeared to be, they would become infected in no time.

In Concord's new burn's unit, she had been allocated a private area which was sectioned off from the rest of the ward and had allowed her more privacy. But here, she was sharing a room with another patient.

Fortunately, the patient in the bed opposite hers was under 30 – though that was all they had in common. The young woman was rehabilitating after cancer surgery and appeared to be convalescing well, so Therese imagined she would be going home soon.

But she hated her depressing surroundings and felt more isolated than ever. If she had felt distressed at the idea of her children visiting her in the ICU, the thought of them coming to see her in this 'aged care' facility was totally demoralising. However, as she would soon discover, the standard of care at the rehab hospital was first class and the staff were professional and caring.

Because there was nowhere in rehab for her to stay, Dawn arranged to stay with a friend in a nearby suburb and came in every day to support her. In Concord, Dawn had made a promise never to leave Therese alone again – and she intended to keep it.

The day after her return to Melbourne, Cath called Dawn to find out if the transfer had gone smoothly. With her usual diplomacy, Therese's mother told her it had all gone well, but that the new rehabilitation hospital was very different to the modern hi-tech burns unit at Concorde.

While Alex and Katie were trying on new uniforms for their new primary school and Therese was getting acquainted with her new surroundings, Cath was preparing to make some changes too.

On 19 January, in another faxed letter from Brunei, Cath revealed that she had just been offered a two-year contract at one of the top 10 international schools in Europe.

Since the bombings she had been reassessing her life and with her contract in Brunei almost at an end, she would be returning to Queensland for a few months on unpaid leave before she started her new teaching job in Germany.

'I felt strongly that if I was meant to be in Germany, then the offer would come … just like I felt very strongly when I received my present job in Brunei,' she wrote.

Cath had become convinced that the reason she had taken the job in Brunei in the first place was because she was supposed to cross paths with Therese in Bali.

In her letter, Cath revealed she had been considering the move to Germany since 2001 after spending time with some friends who taught at the international school in the Bavarian countryside outside Munich.

'I am sure you would love visiting this place,' she told Therese brightly. 'Can you please let Katie know that I will not be her teacher just yet?'

The move had not been an easy decision for Cath, after experiencing the shattering effect of the bombing attacks on so many families. She'd briefly entertained the thought of returning to Queensland to be closer to her own family and closer to Therese and Bronwyn's family, who had now become an important part of her life. But she loved her career too and had decided that a change might be therapeutic for her.

Changing the subject, Cath asked Therese what her new hospital was like and hoped she was powering ahead with her rehab.

'Just think, it won't be too long now before you are back home … what a special day that will be,' she wrote, trying to keep Therese focused on her own future.

Cath mentioned that it was Bronwyn's mother's 50th that day and that she had called her to wish her a happy birthday.

'She was asking about you,' she said.

'She [Jenny] was so pleased to hear that you are now back in Victoria. She would dearly love to come and spend some time with you … this I know is going to be a difficult but special time for you both. She is such an amazing lady, so positive, so understanding and so gentle.'

Cath concluded the letter with a friendship prayer and thanked Therese for being her friend. She said their friendship was a gift she would never take for granted.

Therese was so grateful for having friends like Cath and Rada in her life. They had been her guardian angels in Bali and had continued to support her through the darkest times in Concord. Therese had never met such generous women and their friendship had shown her the kindness in people.

Reading about Bronwyn's mother in the letter made Therese want to cry. She felt so guilty about Bronwyn that it was too painful to think about her, though she crept into her dreams all the time. The thought of seeing Bronwyn's mother brought that guilt to the fore.

How could she even begin to apologise to Bronwyn's mother for being here when her daughter was not? It was hard enough to find the energy to survive each day when the world felt too hard.

At barely 30 years old, the prospect of spending three months in rehab made her more depressed than she had ever felt.

Sadly, the weeks ahead confirmed what Therese had suspected when she first arrived – that the lack of hygiene *was* going to be a problem for someone with serious burns. Her skin grafts, particularly the area on her chest, broke down and she battled new infections that antibiotics were not strong enough to control.

With the help of physio, she had begun to walk again, though her hip was taking time to heal and was hindering her mobility. But the ongoing infections, which she discovered other convalescing burns patients had also been battling, were soon so out of control that her parents were warned she would be lucky to survive them.

The nurses had been dressing Therese's wounds every day, but her world had become so bleak and full of pain that she had been referred to a psychologist to deal with her deepening depression.

She told the counsellor she was so sad it had become paralysing. She also admitted she was on a roller-coaster of emotions that she was finding difficult to control.

These days, she often felt angry and resentful about everything. When her mother told her she had to keep fighting, she felt like screaming out loud.

No-one understood how hard it was. Sometimes she did not think she had the stamina to keep soldiering on, though she did not want to give up either. After all the things she had been told she would never do, she did not want the doctors to be right.

Before one of her skin grafts in Concord, she had passed another critical bomb survivor, Ben Tullipan, in the hospital corridor. She imagined he had been on his way into the operating theatre – probably for more skin grafts like her – or on his way back to the ICU after surgery.

Therese's mum and Ben's mother became friendly during their time at Concord, where both of their adult children had been badly burnt and in comas. Ben's mother had told Dawn that her son lost both of his legs in the bomb blast outside the Sari Club as well as suffering burns.

According to Dawn, they had drawn comfort from each other and regularly discussed their own feelings about the terrorist attacks that had torn their families lives apart.

Therese had never had the opportunity to speak with Ben about his journey. Now she wished she had. He would have understood the challenges better than anyone. Therese often thought about Ben – particularly when the doctors had referred to her as the 'miracle woman of Bali' or described her as the most badly burnt patient they had ever treated.

Their words made her cringe. How could anyone say this, when Ben had lost both his legs and had also suffered 60 per cent full-thickness burns to his body? If anyone was a miracle, he was.

On a few occasions while Therese had been in Concord, she had spoken to Ingrid, the German girl who had been evacuated from Bali with the Australian casualties. They had met for the first time shortly before Therese's fall when she'd been learning to walk again. She and Dawn had bumped into Ingrid and her mum wandering around the corridors. Ingrid's mother had immediately recognised Therese as the burns survivor that Cath had told them about.

The two survivors and their mothers spoke briefly about the impact this terrorist attack had had on them, and all the other innocent people who had been killed. It was a tragedy that had changed so many lives, but Therese and Ingrid had agreed that they did not want to be defined by what had happened to them – they just wanted to get on with their lives.

Just before she left Concord, Therese had seen Ingrid running around the ward, trying to regain some of the fitness she had lost so she could resume her life and move on.

Therese wondered if it was even possible to move on and discussed it at her next counselling session.

The only upside of being in rehabilitation was that David was bringing the children to see her more regularly, though there were occasions when even that had become too upsetting to bear.

Five months had been a long time in Alex and Katie's lives, and while she had never noticed their growth spurts when she'd had them all the time, now when they came to visit, they had changed so much it took her breath away.

They had grown so tall and had become more independent and confident. Listening to them talking about the new friends they had made at their new school, it occurred to Therese that she knew nothing about their lives.

In Grovedale, where everyone knew everyone else, Therese had known all her children's friends, and many of their mothers too. But now she had no idea who their new best friends were, or the names of their teachers – or even the lessons that they liked or didn't like.

In Bali and later in Concord, she had fought for her survival because she believed her children needed her. They were her reason for living and she could not bear the thought of leaving them to grow up without her.

But now she was not sure they needed her at all. They had new lives with their father and were slowly leaving her behind.

Therese's guilt about the destruction of her children's lives continued to gnaw at her. Because of her injuries, they had been forced to leave their home, their primary school, their friends, and the life they had shared, to start all over again.

Sometimes she wondered if it would have been better for Alex and Katie if she had died in Bali. At least they would have been able to mourn for her and move on. Instead, they had to make the trek to this terrible place to see her looking helpless and hopeless among the elderly residents.

But Alex and Katie were happy to see their mum and appeared unfazed by the surroundings and the elderly clientele. Katie was relieved to see her mother looking brighter, though she was taken aback by her appearance, which had changed dramatically since her return to Melbourne.

Therese had recently been prescribed steroids, and one of the side effects of the medication had been considerable weight gain, which had left her burnt face bloated. The long straight hair that had been burnt off during the explosion had begun to grow again and Katie had been shocked to see that it had grown back curly. This overweight woman with a round puffy face and short curly hair was not the skinny petite mum who had once chased her around the park, and Katie no longer recognised her.

* * *

Therese had been in rehab for around three months when her friend Michelle Larkins came to see her. The trained nurse was as shocked as David had been by the extent of her friend's injuries – and concerned about the level of pain she was in. She looked far worse than Michelle had ever imagined, and seeing her again had unearthed all her own feelings of guilt about the job which had saved her from the holiday from hell.

Now, as she studied Therese's burnt face and her bandages, she felt bad all over again. She felt relieved that she had been spared this kind of suffering and hated herself for feeling so grateful that she had been spared. Michelle understood something of the guilt that she imagined Therese must be feeling about Bronwyn, and she struggled to know what to say.

'I understand your fall damaged the new skin, and some of the grafts had to be done again,' said Michelle, who had nursed patients with serious burns, though not the 'wartime' injuries that she had heard the doctors saying the Bali victims had suffered. She did not know anyone who had nursed a patient who had been blown up by a bomb before.

Although Therese had been dreading anyone seeing her like this, when Michelle arrived at the rehab hospital, she was relieved and happy to see her.

For weeks, Therese had been complaining about a foul-smelling discharge that had been coming out of her ears. She had been prescribed a course of strong antibiotics for the infection, but it had been getting worse and the pain was relentless. Therese asked her friend if she would mind taking a look.

Michelle studied the pus and fluid leaking from her friend's ears and recoiled. It smelled rank.

'This is bad,' she said, visibly alarmed. 'You need to go straight to the nearest A and E.'

Dawn immediately relayed this to one of the doctors and Therese was transported to the nearby Alfred Hospital, where she was admitted under the care of the Director of the burns unit, Heather Cleland.

'You have a very nasty infection, Therese,' said the doctor, ordering CT scans to determine the cause of the infection. The scans revealed an advanced infection of the mastoid bone, which was potentially life-threatening.

The mastoid is located directly behind the ear and forms part of the temporal bone of the skull. It is a fragile structure filled with tiny air cells made of bone, resembling honeycomb. These cells protect the delicate structures of the ear and regulate ear pressure as well as protecting the temporal bone during trauma. An infection of the mastoid can cause serious complications including hearing loss, blood clots, meningitis and a brain abscess.

Cleland was concerned that the mastoiditis might invade the lining of Therese's brain, which could kill her. She was immediately put on intravenous antibiotics.

Upon closer examination of the patient, the specialist also became concerned about the breakdown of Therese's skin grafts, particularly the large area on her chest that was now an infected open wound. The antibiotics would hopefully get rid of that infection too, and allow them to perform a new skin graft that would give her full surface coverage.

'How long will I be here?' asked Therese. The doctor was cautious.

'Let's see how it goes.'

Therese slumped back against the pillows, relieved to be out of the rehab hospital and back in a safe and sterile environment.

The following day, the Alfred Hospital's social worker came to speak to Dawn about the accommodation they offered to the relatives of long-term patients.

'We have units over the road at a motel – we'll get you settled in there right away,' she said.

If all went well, Therese might be allowed to stay at the unit too, and attend the hospital as an outpatient. But for now, the doctors needed to get her burn wounds and her mastoid infection under control.

Within days, Therese was back in theatre; the surgeons removed samples from the thin strip of skin around her wrist that had been protected from the flames by the cheap shell bracelet she had been wearing that night at Paddy's bar.

When the infection in her wounds was finally under control, the cells they had cultivated from this tiny area of healthy skin tissue were grafted onto her chest and used to close the open wounds on her back. This time, the procedure was successful.

One of the nurses caring for Therese was a young fresh-faced graduate who had the same compassionate personality as Rada and Cath.

She helped Therese to figure out how to use the adapted cutlery that would allow her to feed herself and reclaim some of her lost independence. She also helped her shower and tended to her dressings. The pain that had been off the scale at the rehab hospital was reassessed and her new pain management plan was making the excruciating process of having her dressings changed more bearable.

At rehab hospital there had not been a single day that Therese had not sobbed in the shower from the pain. But now that her pain medication was under control, life was more tolerable, although she still needed the nurse to help her shower and change her dressings.

Over the next few weeks, Therese returned to surgery for an operation on the mastoid. This involved irrigating the honeycomb structure to flush out the stubborn bacterial infection that had probably been festering since her eardrums had burst in the explosion. They also pumped antibiotics directly into the tiny air cells in the mastoid.

Therese had been feeling much better when two AFP officers arrived at the Alfred Hospital with something for her.

They produced a sealed polythene crime scene bag containing her purse, which she had slipped into her bag before they left the Bounty Hotel for their final dinner in Kuta. She had last seen the bag at Paddy's bar.

Therese's hands were still bandaged, so they handed the bag to Dawn, who opened it. To their amazement, the purse was intact apart from a fine film of dust.

When Dawn opened the purse, it smelled strongly of smoke. But all Therese's money and credit cards were untouched and did not have a mark on them. She wondered how her purse had survived the destruction when she had been so badly hurt.

The strong smell of smoke must have tapped into her sensory memory because that night Therese had dreamed about Bronwyn and the holiday in Bali.

Therese remembered so little about the blast except being thrown high into the air and smashing her head. She vaguely recalled the choking heat and the flames around the bar where the alcohol had ignited. She remembered the popping sounds of the bottles of booze and flames leaping from her body. And she recalled the Indonesian man who had passed by on his way to the dance floor and Eminem blasting as she left Bronwyn dancing to go to the bar. But apart from that, she remembered very little of the explosion.

Occasionally, Therese had flashbacks of Cath in her yellow polo short pouring cold bottled water over her sizzling body, and Rada talking about her life in Tewantin. Sometimes she heard herself screaming for her children on the tarmac at Denpasar. She even remembered the Balinese nurse begging the doctors to take her on the plane out of Bali, and the army doctor cutting into her arms and legs without anaesthetic.

After the AFP officers' visit, these images surfaced again in her dreams, and she remembered some of the things her conscious waking mind had not been ready to deal with.

After the police visit, Therese had felt Bronwyn's presence beside her hospital bed – just as she had on the tarmac at Denpasar. She could not see her, or hear her voice, but she knew that Bronwyn was there. Then the night nurse turned the lights on, and her friend was gone

A week or so after her mastoid operation, Therese was at the Alfred waiting to see the ear nose and throat specialist when she noticed a strapping young man waiting in the corridor. He also appeared to have an appointment with the ENT doctors and was chatting to some of the nursing staff.

They looked at one another with a strange kind of knowing that Therese could not explain. This man was also wearing pressure bandages and was obviously a burns survivor. Had he been in the Bali bombing too? she wondered. Later, one of the nurses had told her that the patient was football star Jason McCartney. He had also been injured in Bali.

Therese realised that McCartney was the burns survivor her mum had read about in the newspapers, who must have been standing a few feet away from her when the bomb went off in Paddy's bar.

McCartney and his friend had been chatting to another guy from Perth when the bomb exploded. He had suffered serious burns to his arms, legs and hands, and a life-threatening shrapnel wound to his back. He later told his father that the impact of the explosion against his back had been so horrific that he thought he had been shot.

He escaped from the carnage with his friend, but despite his own injuries had risked his life by returning into the burning building to help rescue other survivors. McCartney and his friend had then raced back to their hotel without realising they had been seriously injured and required urgent medical attention.

Later, during the evacuation, the 28-year-old footballer surrendered his seat on the first plane out of Bali to another survivor who he considered was in worse shape than himself.

By the time McCartney was finally evacuated, his fiancée Nerissa van der Heyden and his brother Brendon were already waiting to meet him at the Royal Darwin Hospital. Later, he had been transferred on an air force Hercules to Essendon Airport in Melbourne, and then rushed to the Alfred Hospital.

Although his friend was fortunate enough to escape with minor burns, McCartney had suffered second-degree burns to over 50 per cent of his body. He underwent emergency surgery to remove the shrapnel from his back and clean the debris out of his burns. He had briefly died on the operating table but had been revived and spent a week in an induced coma.

He endured countless skin grafts and battled many of the infections that Therese was still fighting. He had also developed a potentially lethal case of blood poisoning.

But despite the challenges, by the time Therese saw McCartney, he had achieved his goal of marrying his fiancée in the fairytale wedding they had planned. McCartney was now in training to fulfil his next goal of returning to AFL.

McCartney had recently spent three days in Bali with his new wife. He felt he needed to face his demons and put the tragedy in its place before he could return to football and move on with his life.

When Therese told her mum about the encounter, Dawn told her that Jason McCartney had only been in Bali two days when the bombers struck.

Therese had been disappointed that she had not been introduced to him. He would have *understood.*

Nicole McClean had certainly understood. This Bali survivor had visited Therese on a couple of occasions at the Alfred and related to her struggle.

Nicole had been the young woman survivor who owed her life to her friend Natalie Goold. McClean, also 23, had subsequently had her lower right arm amputated and had suffered burns too. Goold's quick thinking on 12 October 2002 had saved her life.

On another occasion, Nicole had come to visit Therese with some other Bali survivors – including burns casualty Peter Hughes, whose blistered face had appeared on Australian TV screens in the early news reports, unaware how seriously hurt he was at the time.

Hughes had been a regular patient at the burns unit in Perth, had undergone the range of skin grafts that Therese was still going through, and also suffered from post-traumatic stress. But he had since befriended McCartney and, like the footballer, was working his way through it.

At the time, Therese was not sure if someone from the burns unit had arranged the visit, or if one of the other burns survivors had mentioned she was still in hospital.

But the person behind the visit turned out to be McCartney, who was preparing to make his own trip back to the Alfred to offer her some support of his own.

Shortly before Easter, one of the nurses told her that there was someone to see her, and the mystery visitor was Jason McCartney, who was as warm and friendly in person as he had appeared to be when she had seen him outside the specialist's rooms.

McCartney asked Therese how she was faring, and explained he had been in a coma too and had also experienced problems with ongoing infections and fragile skin grafts. He told her he was back training again, and that he was now married. Therese was so shocked by her unexpected visitor that she would later struggle to recall the rest of the conversation.

Before he left, the footballer handed Therese two tickets to his comeback game for North Melbourne, which was due to take place in June.

'I hope you'll be able to make it,' he said.

He left the Alfred that afternoon in awe of Therese's courage. He thought that his own injuries were bad enough, but her burns had been even more severe. As some of the other survivors were constantly saying when things were tough, there was always someone doing it harder.

Therese was determined to go to the game. This strapping young athlete had almost lost his life too. He was still wearing pressure bandages when he came to visit, and she, of all people, understood the strength and stamina it had taken for him to even consider returning to the game he loved.

Their shared experience and the nightmare they had survived forged a special bond between survivors like themselves, and she found it so encouraging to know she was not going through this alone.

Jason McCartney became a beacon of hope to everyone who had been injured in the terrorist attack in Bali, and his comeback game gave Therese something to look forward to.

It had been decided that Damien would take Therese to the game at the Telstra Dome in Docklands on 6 June 2003 – her first outing since the terrorist attack.

Despite her excitement, Therese was nervous about attending the event because she had not been in a crowd since the bombing at Paddy's bar, and the thought of being among so many people made her highly anxious.

Her hip had healed well enough for her to be able to walk from the car park to her seat in the stadium. She would not have missed this moment for the world.

More than 43,200 supporters packed out the stadium for the Queen's Birthday game between the North Melbourne Kangaroos and Richmond – the two Victorian teams in the top eight – who were heading into a round dedicated to the 202 people who had lost their lives in the Bali bombings

The roar of the crowd resounded around Docklands as McCartney ran onto the oval with his teammates, wearing the numbers '88' and '202' on the front of his long-sleeved blue and white guernsey. These numbers represented the total number of victims who had died in Bali and the 88 Australians who had lost their lives.

Many supporters in the crowd held up signs saying 'Bali 88/22' while other Australian victims were remembered in a video that was displayed on giant screens around the stadium ahead of the game.

Also attending the event were representatives of the five Australian Rules football clubs who had lost players in the attacks. Other AFL survivors were also there to support McCartney, including former Melbourne player Steven Febey and emerging Demon's player Steven Armstrong, who had suffered shrapnel wounds in the bombings.

McCartney came on as a substitute at full-forward to a resounding cheer from both sides. He was still wearing compression garments and protective gloves over his injuries. In the fourth quarter he kicked a goal that put the Kangaroos ahead by nine points.

North Melbourne won the game by three points. It was a fairytale ending to a horror story that survivors like Therese Fox would always remember as a bright light in a dark chapter of her life.

After the game, the footballer who had become such an inspiration for so many announced his retirement in an emotional post-match interview, telling the crowd that it was time to hang up his boots and move on.

'It's been a tough time but that's enough for me,' he told the cheering crowd. He was happy to be leaving on a high note.

The photograph of McCartney triumphantly leaving the field on the shoulders of his teammates would go down in history as one of the most inspirational moments in Australian sports.

Therese had tears in her eyes that night as she listened to McCartney's emotional retirement speech. The cameras flashed across the other Bali survivors in the crowd who were there to witness this historic sporting moment and had settled on Therese's burnt face.

Later, she had been besieged by media wanting her thoughts on the game, and she had told them that the footballer was an inspiration who had given her hope that there was a life to be had after Bali – and that the terrorists had not beaten them.

Therese came home on a high that night. Soon it would be time for her to move on too. It was a terrifying thought, but if McCartney could achieve what he had just accomplished, it gave her new hope that she might reclaim her own life too.

Chapter 18

A major step in Therese's recovery had been her recent move from her hospital bed to the motel unit across the road where she was now staying with her mum.

She still had to wear the full body pressure suit over her dressings and remained reliant on morphine to control her pain. But the nurses had been coming over every other day to shower and change her dressings and keep an eye on her latest skin grafts, which, though fragile, were slowly beginning to heal.

It had given Therese such a lift to finally be out of the hospital, though she still needed her mother's help to do most things, including brushing her hair, putting on the kettle and going to the bathroom.

She had been taking each day one minute at a time and had been working towards reclaiming her independence.

It had begun by learning to feed herself again with her specially adapted cutlery, but she was getting there.

Alex and Katie were impressed with their mum's new surroundings, which they thought was more like holiday accommodation and better than the hospital setting they had visited her in. They liked being able to watch cartoons on the TV, and lounge back on the small sofa. It was like being at home and they would be able to come and see her more frequently here.

Therese had been staying at the unit for a few days when she first noticed the mirror over the sink in the bathroom. The last time she had looked at herself in a mirror had been in Kuta on their final night. She remembered brushing her long brown hair and touching up her lipstick before she and Bronwyn headed out for their farewell dinner.

Until now, she had not had an opportunity to examine her injuries because she had not been able to undress herself. But the chance presented itself one morning after her shower when the nurse ducked into the other room to get fresh dressings.

As she left, Therese caught sight of her raw face and shoulders in the mirror and was shocked to see the stranger looking back at her.

With tears in her eyes, she studied the bright red patches on her face from her latest skin grafts. Gone was the long trademark dark hair that had been her crowning glory. Her new hair growth was still short and patchy. Her face had become so bloated from the steroids that she no longer recognised herself.

In her shock, the towel slipped onto the floor, exposing her injured arms and torso. When she turned around, she could see the gravel-rash redness covering her back. Her entire body had the appearance of a raw patchwork of angry red scars.

Therese now understood why the counsellor at Concord Hospital had advised her parents not to let her have a mirror. The stranger in the bathroom mirror was not the same skinny sun-tanned mum who had run on the treadmill and kept herself in shape.

The bombs had not just destroyed her body, they had annihilated her entire identity, and she no longer knew who she was. In her old life, she had been defined as a full-time working mother and a proficient capable nurse.

Looking at herself in the mirror, she now saw her life in two distinct and separate parts: the 'before' Bali, when life had been normal and purposeful, and after – her life since the terrorist attack, when she felt irrelevant and redundant.

Chapter 18

The lines that defined the two lives had been etched in the embers of Paddy's bar; the young mother who left Melbourne on that ill-fated holiday had died on 12 October with her friend.

The horrifically burnt stranger who had come home in her place was not that carefree young woman anymore and would never be that person again.

It was ironic, but her mother's worst fears had been realised after all. Another woman's daughter *had* been lying under those bandages, and the adopted daughter she had loved her whole life lay buried beneath the ash in Paddy's Irish Bar, never to be seen again.

Chapter 19

GOING HOME

In June 2003, while Therese was struggling with the loss of her identity, one of the terrorists involved in the attack was preparing to stand trial in Bali for his role in the bomb blasts.

Amrozi was dubbed the smiling assassin by the world's media because of the obvious glee he had shown after his arrest over the destruction he had helped to cause.

The former mechanic from West Java was the first of more than 30 suspects being held in Indonesia to be tried under its new anti-terrorism laws.

Security in Bali had been tightened for his arraignment amidst concerns about another terrorist attack on the court. Among the charges before the court were allegations that he had purchased the materials for the bombs and had committed a terrorist act of great suffering – crimes that would see him facing the death penalty.

The ABC reported that a large crowd had gathered outside the court including ambassadors and diplomats, several Australian victims and their families, the widows of local Balinese men who had lost their lives, and a large contingent of international media who had turned out in force to cover the high-profile case.

ABC reporter Mark Bowling reported that Amrozi had arrived at the court in an armoured police truck and after smiling again for the waiting cameras, had entered the court giving a thumbs-up sign. The prosecution was about to begin the process of running through the charges which had been estimated to last the entire day.

Dawn, observing Therese's shaken expression, had immediately turned the TV off. 'Great suffering' did not come close to describing the agony he and his co-accused had caused to her daughter and many others. He had shown no remorse and she could not bear to see his smiling face or watch the trial and his grandstanding.

It was hard enough watching Therese struggling through each day and she had no stomach for this. But seeing Amrozi's smirking face all over the news had left Therese furious – not just for herself, but for Bronwyn's family and all the other survivors and families whose lives he had helped to destroy.

But some of the survivors, including the now retired footballer Jason McCartney had returned to Bali to face down the terrorist alleged to have played such a leading role in the carnage.

McCartney's earlier trip to Bali in March had allowed him to confront his demons, so that when the AFP contacted him to inform him that he was being called back to Denpasar to give evidence in Amrozi's trial, he was more than ready.

The former footballer, his friend Peter Hughes, and another Australian survivor – Stuart Anstee from Tasmania – had been asked to give victim impact statements to the Indonesian court, to offer some insight into the suffering the carnage had caused to the innocent victims.

They would not just be speaking about their own ordeals but would be a voice for the 202 victims who had lost their lives, and all the other survivors whose lives had been forever changed following the attacks in Kuta on 12 October 2002.

On 16 June 2003, the day before he was due to give evidence, McCartney told the *Sydney Morning Herald* that despite the battle to recover from the terrible injuries inflicted by the bombers, the trio's return to Bali showed they had not been beaten.

He spoke about the joy and happiness his comeback game had given to all the survivors and said it proved that although the bombs had burnt their skin and flesh, they had not taken their hearts and souls away.

The newspaper reported that while McCartney had been exploring a new career in television, Anstee had resigned from his work in environmental science and had been retracing his steps in Bali, before moving to a new life in Perth. Meanwhile, Hughes had sold his construction business in Perth and was now planning a new career as an inspirational public speaker.

The following day, the trio looked Amrozi in the eye as they gave harrowing accounts of their experiences on the night of the bombings.

Anstee told the court how he had been partying with five of his friends at the Sari Club when the car bomb ripped through the popular tourist haunt.

Three of his friends had been killed in the explosion, which had knocked him unconscious.

'When I woke up, I noticed blood spurting from my neck and my leg and my left arm. I saw many dead bodies inside and outside the Sari Club.'

He told the court that Australia was angry with the people who had committed this terrible crime.

Glaring at Amrozi, Jason McCartney showed the court the scars from the burns he had suffered during the attack on Paddy's bar.

'The ugly visions are still there,' he said. 'I don't know how long it will take for them to go away.'

McCartney revealed he had been receiving counselling and had been afraid of returning to Bali.

At the trial the court had heard that the bombings had been part of a plan to wage war on the United States. Amrozi's brother, Ali Imron had told police after his arrest that Bali had been chosen as the target for the bombings because many white people would be there including visitors from America and its allies.

Their older brother, Ali Ghufron Mukhlas - 43, was also charged with plotting, organising and funding the bombings. The Muslim preacher was also accused of being the operational head of the al-Qaeda-linked Jemaah Islamiyah, though the indictment against him did not mention the group by name.

The prosecution alleged that Mukhlas met Osama bin Laden in Afghanistan in 1987 during his three-year stint there fighting Soviet forces. The Islamic extremist had been responsible for radicalizing his two younger brothers.

But Mukhlas had denied his role in the blasts, which under Indonesia's recently introduced anti-terrorist laws carried the death penalty if the case against him was proved. It later emerged that his younger brother, Ali Imron, had helped to make the main bomb that destroyed the Sari Club, and that Amrozi, had bought the chemicals for the bombs and had purchased the minivan used in the attack.

But Therese had vowed not to watch the trial, or spend any more energy dwelling on the motivations behind the attacks. It was hard enough living with the scars, and whatever the verdict, she hoped Amrozi and his cohorts rotted in hell for the destruction they had caused.

Therese had just celebrated Mother's Day, and the children had been to visit their mum at the unit, which her own mum had filled with balloons and fresh flowers.

Dawn had proudly watched her daughter struggling to tie a ribbon into Katie's hair with her injured fingers – a simple task that a year ago she would have performed blindfolded in seconds.

She had not dared to offer her help. Therese had made it clear that she needed to do this herself. She was trying to be a mum again, and her own mother had been resisting the urge to help to respect her wishes.

After dozens of gruelling operations, it was another miracle milestone in a battle for survival that continued to defy all odds.

Therese had been settling into the unit when Michelle came to visit her again. At the time, her mother was brushing her hair, which had slowly begun to grow again.

The texture of her hair had changed, and it was thinner and patchier from all the anaesthetics she had undergone for her repeated surgeries, and from the steroids. Steroids are often given to burns victims to put on weight, as most lose weight and muscle mass. Steroids also increase lost muscle mass.

Unfortunately, a common side effect of steroid treatments is that it increases metabolism and the way the body deposits fat. An increased appetite causes weight gain – and in Therese's situation, where she was also too disabled to exercise, the weight gain had been considerable. She had also been put on a high dose of antihistamines and vitamins to prevent itching and irritation, which had come with the growth of new skin.

Michelle watched her now unrecognisable friend struggling to hold a cup with her severely injured hands and felt like crying for her.

Therese had been such a proficient and capable nurse. She had a reserved and gentle way about her and was kind and compassionate with the patients. This must be such a painful struggle, and Michelle's heart went out to her and to her mother, who Therese described as her 'rock'.

Almost reading her mind, Therese told her she could not wait until she could brush her hair again.

'I am going to be so grateful for being able to do all the little things that people take for granted … that I took for granted,' she told Michelle.

Her friend felt choked. 'These things take time,' she said sadly.

Therese was in less pain these days than she had been at the rehabilitation hospital, but she was still on morphine for the pain.

Dawn followed Michelle outside to say goodbye.

'Thank you so much for coming – and for your phone calls,' she said. 'They brighten up her day – you brighten up her day.'

Michelle went home with a heavy heart. She wished she could do more. She still felt so guilty about Therese and Bronwyn, and these visits to the city always seemed to resurrect the grief she felt over the death of her brother.

All the way back to Geelong she thought about him and the agonising deaths his fire crew must have suffered when the fire storm swept across their truck during the bushfire at Lynton. A memorial for the fallen volunteers had since been erected in West Park, Geelong West, and another at Lynton in Victoria where they had died.

Michelle visited the memorial in Geelong regularly, and every visit to Therese unearthed the grief she still held for her brother.

But, despite everything, Therese had survived, and as Michelle had already known, her gentle exterior belied her strength and determination. As she had repeatedly told Dawn, her daughter was made of tough stuff and would come back from this stronger than ever. Her love for her children would see her through.

The move to the motel unit, and the marked improvement in her health, meant that she had seen David more regularly over the past weeks when he brought the children to see her. And while she still resented him for a situation that had not been of his making, she admired the way he had embraced the change in his own circumstances and was proud of the fantastic job he was doing with their children.

Before Bali, things had been awkward between the separated parents, and they had struggled to speak to one another on occasions. But the events in Bali had given them both a very different perspective on life, and different priorities. These days they could hold a reasonable conversation without feeling annoyed with one another, and David often stayed with the children and helped Therese with things she needed to give her mum a break.

Chapter 19

Over the past few weeks, the hospital had been encouraging Therese to return to her home in Wingarra Drive, Grovedale, as a practice run for her final discharge, which they hoped would be before the end of the year.

Although she was excited about going home, she was also terrified of not being able to cope when she finally returned to her life. The weekend stayovers were designed to build her confidence and prepare her for her final discharge from hospital.

Her first visit home took place during her final weeks at the rehabilitation hospital and was a very painful and surreal experience.

Returning to her family home for the first time in seven months left her feeling very anxious, and she waited apprehensively on the doorstep while her mother opened the front door and led her inside.

It was like stepping back in time. Everything looked exactly as she had left it on that Sunday morning in October, and yet everything had changed.

She had wandered apprehensively into her children's bedrooms, which looked as they always had, except that some of Katie's favourite Barbie dolls had gone to her father's, and so had Alex's much-loved games and toys.

Therese looked inside their wardrobes, which had since been emptied, though she doubted the clothes that had been hanging there a year ago would even fit them now. The rest of the place looked the same, but nothing was the same.

The children came down later and were happy to see their mother home again, and even happier to spend the night in their own beds. Dawn and Damien stayed over too, to give Therese some support on her first night at home – but she felt like a fish out of water.

Still, the visit to her family home had taken the edge off and the next visit would be easier. Unfortunately, on the second stayover, Therese developed a sudden attack of gastro and, to the children's alarm, had to be rushed back to hospital. Their father met them on the freeway as they passed on their way to the city, and took the kids back home with him.

The incident was upsetting for Alex, who had become very alarmed over his mum's sudden deterioration. On another occasion, Therese developed an infection and the same thing happened again.

* * *

In September, another development prompted Therese's return to Grovedale, and it came from left field. She received a letter from the producers of the Channel Nine show *Backyard Blitz* created by celebrity gardener Don Burke, who had been following her progress in hospital.

The network had heard about the 'Miracle Woman of Bali' and wanted to do something to make her return home from hospital extra special. It would air on the first anniversary of the Bali bombings, and would remind viewers that the road to recovery was far from over and that the scars of the terrorist attacks for the most badly burnt survivor would take many years to heal.

At the time, only Dawn had been aware of the surprise garden makeover, to preserve the big 'reveal' when the work was finally complete. Therese had a small backyard at the rental property where she had lived before the terrorist attacks and the producers were planning to create a beautiful courtyard garden that would provide her with a sanctuary where she could sit after her return home.

A film crew arrived at the hospital to interview her about her fight to defy the odds, and film her daily struggle to reclaim her life after Bali. But Therese realised something more was going on, and her mother finally showed her the letter telling her what the filming was about.

At Wingarra Drive, the landscaping was already underway to create the courtyard garden that would welcome her back from hospital. But the producers needed to film the big 'reveal' ahead of the show going to air on the first anniversary of the Bali bombings in October.

Rada, who had been flying down to Melbourne to visit Therese in hospital and Bronwyn's family in Geelong, had also been invited to take part in the filming. Sadly, she had booked an overseas trip and had not been able to come.

In September, Dawn drove Therese down the freeway to Geelong to collect the children from their father's place and take them all home for the filming. But first they called at Dawn's house to find something to wear for the show's grand finale. Therese had struggled to find anything that fitted her, and found some loose-fitting clothes she would be comfortable in.

Although she had known about the surprise, she was stunned with the amazing transformation and all the colourful pot plants and screening foliage that created her a private place to heal.

To her amazement, the presenter, TV celebrity Jamie Durie, also presented her with a brand new blue Holden Cruze, and handed her a cheque to cover her rent for a year while she continued her recovery at home.

As Katie watched the cameras and the action capturing the family's' reaction to the amazing magic that had transformed their ordinary little suburban backyard into a spectacular oasis, she experienced the same anxiety that had made her throw up on her first day back at primary school after Bali.

She had never known anyone who had had a TV crew in their backyard before. It was such a big deal that it was another reminder that their ordinary normal lives were not ordinary or normal anymore.

Therese was very grateful for the kind gesture and hoped that the little blue Cruze sitting in her garage would be the incentive she needed to prove the doctors wrong and drive again as soon as she could.

The kindness and generosity of strangers never failed to astound her, although she hated being the centre of attention and being in a situation where she was grateful for help. Still, it had taken the pressure off, knowing the financial burden had been lifted and all she had to do now was focus on getting better.

'What do you think?' asked her mum, putting on the kettle.

It had all been so overwhelming Therese had not known what to think, so she sat in her new outside courtyard, trying not to think anything at all. It was too hard.

With any luck, she might be home by October, and they would watch the show in her loungeroom with the kids on her own TV, said Dawn, sipping her tea.

It was something that, in the early days, Therese had dreamed about. But being close to the hospital had become her safety blanket and now that her discharge was approaching, she felt absolutely petrified.

For the past nine months she had not permitted herself to think about the future and had stopped setting goals. If she was to survive, she had to let things take their course and go with the flow.

The future had become so frightening that she had been seeing her psychologist more frequently to manage the anxiety and terror she felt whenever anyone mentioned going home.

During her counselling sessions, Therese had confided that she was feeling frightened about everything. She was afraid about returning home – and terrified that the doctors in Concord might be right and that she would not be able to take care of herself or her children independently.

She was frightened that the next infection might be the one that finally killed her – and even more petrified of being alive.

Therese's anxiety, like her worsening depression, had been spiralling since she had seen herself in the mirror. Her psychologist increased her antidepressant medication. She had been counselling her more often to address the physical trauma caused by her injuries and the psychological trauma associated with the loss of her identity.

In the early days, Therese always imagined that she would miraculously recover from her burns and be home in time for Christmas, which may have been the case if she had not fallen and broken her hip.

Over the past few days it had become more real as her mother made trips up and down the freeway in her car, emptying their motel unit of clothes and other belongings. When they finally left, at least there would be room in the car for all Therese's dressings.

On Sunday 6 October 2003 – exactly one year to the day that Therese had crept out of her house to begin her dream holiday in Bali – they finally closed the door to their motel unit and headed over the Westgate Bridge towards Geelong.

Therese sat quietly in the passenger seat feeling very anxious as Dawn drove out of the city towards the Princes Freeway.

It had not been the big homecoming or celebration she had imagined it would be. Her home was the same, but the single mum and the two children who had lived here had moved on and their lives would never be the same. They had only been home a few minutes when her brother arrived. But Therese decided to spend her first night at her mother's house where she felt more secure and less anxious.

Although Therese was apprehensive, her mother was relieved to finally be home. Driving up and down for the past few weeks to empty the unit had been tiring, and living on adrenaline for a year and supporting Therese through the seemingly endless list of operations and infections had taken its toll on Dawn's health, which was now deteriorating.

Therese had already decided it was time for her mum to return to her own home and wanted to reclaim some of her own independence – even though it was a prospect that terrified her.

She wanted her mum to have her own life back, so she could spend time with her friends and catch her breath, instead of living on her nerves and caring for her.

There would be a team of professionals coming into the house to help with the cleaning, shopping and errands, and the nurse would be in every other day to shower her and change her dressings. It was time to cut the umbilical cord and learn to do things for herself. Therese imagined the separation would be as hard for her mother as it would be for her.

But being in her own surroundings again would be easier for the children and more convenient for their dad, who had been negotiating the city traffic most weekends to drive them to the unit near the Alfred Hospital that had been their home for the past three months.

It was agreed between the two parents that Alex and Katie would complete the school year at Werribee and return home to live with Therese in December.

In the New Year, they would resume their education at their former primary school in Geelong. The kids seemed happy enough with the arrangement, and understood that each Friday after school, their Aunt Lisa would drive their mother up the freeway to collect them from their dad's for the weekend.

But living in her old house on her own created a new anxiety in Therese. Their once busy family home felt so quiet and empty without Alex and Katie that it no longer felt like hers anymore.

Therese knew she could not care for the children the way their father could. It was hard enough getting through each day on her own with lots of help. But the house felt so lonely that she became more depressed than ever.

Dosed up on a cocktail of painkillers, sleeping tables, steroids, antibiotics and morphine, she just wanted to sleep and shut the world out. Her mum was still calling around most days, and Damien and his wife were also dropping in more frequently than they had. Even that did not feel normal. Nothing did.

On Friday afternoons after picking the children up, Therese perked up a little, though the thought of having to send them back again on Sunday night left her desolate.

Therese's inability to do even the simplest things for them only increased the sense of failure. Sometimes she wondered if she had the strength to be their mum, let alone the strength for these heartbreaking goodbyes, knowing it was going to be another week until she saw them again.

The irony of the complete role reversals had not been lost on her. Therese had once been the parent who had cared for the children full time, and their dad had been the weekend parent. Now it was the other way around and she hated it. It was another reminder of everything she had lost.

Katie, observing her mother struggling to feed herself, worried that her mum might not be able to look after them when they finally returned home. She felt so bad for her mum, but she was scared about what would happen to them if mum couldn't cope with being mum anymore.

* * *

On the anniversary of the Bali bombings, *Backyard Blitz* finally aired. It was an emotional episode that reminded everyone of the heartache and suffering that the terrorist attack had caused to so many Australian lives – particularly this miracle woman who had not been expected to survive. The episode had been watched by millions and was one of the highest rating *Backyard Blitz* shows of the year.

When Alex and Katie went to school on Monday, all the children were talking about it.

'We saw you on television with your mum,' said their classmates. Did that make them famous? Katie wasn't sure. She hadn't wanted to be famous, let alone appear on TV. And she hated being noticed. She just wanted to be normal like everyone else.

In Melbourne, Rodney Cocks' mother had also watched the show and had immediately emailed her son to tell him she had seen the burns survivor he had told her about on the TV. Cocks, who was now working with the UN's de-mining unit in Baghdad, was stunned to hear the news.

After seeing Therese and Bronwyn's names listed among the fatalities on one of the hospital notice boards in Denpasar the day after the bombings, he had returned to his peacekeeping duties believing she was dead.

'Are you sure it was Therese Fox?' he asked his mother, in his next phone call home.

'It was definitely her,' said his mum, emphatically.

Cocks immediately obtained contact details for Therese and emailed her. He was overjoyed that after everything she had been through, she was alive and on the road to recovery. He promised that on his next trip home he would visit her.

On the first anniversary of the Bali bombings, Therese and her friend Michelle attended a special memorial service at St Mary's Cathedral in Geelong to remember those who had lost their lives in the Bali bombings.

Jess was at the service with Bronwyn's friend, Oriana, as were the friends and relatives of the Lee brothers and Stacey's family, the Thornburghs. Time had not healed anyone's pain.

Bronwyn's mother had made a heartbreaking pilgrimage back to Bali with her eldest son, Anthony, to visit the site of the terrorist attack that had claimed her daughter's life. It was a painful visit, but she felt she needed to complete the trip she had felt too distressed to make in the aftermath of the bombings.

Although Ross, Libby and Michael had been to Bali, the rest of the family had never been there before. Jenny and her son had accepted the Prime Minister's official invitation to the survivors and the families of those who had lost their lives to attend a cleansing ceremony to honor the 202 people who had died and the 325 people who had been injured.

For Jenny, it was a rite of passage she felt compelled to go through. They had no idea what to expect, but it became clear from the now deserted streets of Kuta, and the empty beaches, that the Prime Minister's predictions about the terrorist attack devastating its tourist economy had been correct.

The ceremony took place in an open-air theatre near the ocean – a short distance from the site of the terrorist attack in Kuta. It was a coming together that reflected the cultures and religions of those who had died.

Christian hymns were interspersed with traditional Balinese music as their families remembered the people they had loved. The names of the victims who had died were read out one by one, and prayers were offered by Christian and Muslim clerics. There was also a prayer from the leader of Bali's Hindu community, who asked for the families to find the strength to move on.

The Australian Prime Minister, John Howard, told the gathered crowd that the tragedy had brought the Indonesian and Australian people closer together. And he thanked Indonesian officials for the police work that resulted in the alleged perpetrators being arrested for the attack.

'Australia will never forget the 12th October 2002. But it has taught us a number of things about ourselves. It has taught us about our strengths … about the need to co-operate with others in the ongoing fight against the terrible deeds – and the terrible hatred that caused so much pain and so much misery a year ago,' he said.

Australia's unofficial anthem, 'Waltzing Matilda', was played to honour the victims, and wreaths were laid at the site of the bombings.

It was a quiet and peaceful visit for Bronwyn's mum, who was touched by the compassion of the local people who had stopped them in the street to express their deep regret about the bombings and to apologise for their tragic loss.

Unfortunately, Jenny Hobbs' pilgrimage to the place where Bronwyn had lost her life was so traumatic that it triggered a series of debilitating panic attacks. When she spotted a white van driving by, she recalled the headlines describing the white Mitsubishi van carrying the bomb that had ripped through the Sari Club, and she fell apart. They decided to cut their visit short and return to Australia.

A whole year had passed, and the guilt that Therese felt over Bronwyn's death continued to consume her. She never imagined that time would ever heal the grief in her broken heart and found it very painful to face her friend's family, who looked as broken as she felt.

She had not been able to watch the memorial service, which had been all over the news. The pain she felt that day was unbearable.

During the days leading up the anniversary, there were several instances when Therese strongly felt Bronwyn's presence around her – particularly at night when she felt her slipping into bed beside her.

Therese sensed that her friend had returned to comfort her – to let her know she was not on her own. But Therese wasn't reassured by this presence and became unsettled by it.

Not long after the anniversary Rodney Cocks rang. He was home on leave and wanted to come to Grovedale to visit her.

Therese was thrilled, but very nervous. Her recollection of the dreadful events that followed the bombings was sketchy. But she desperately wanted to meet the stranger who had played such an important part in saving her life and thank him in person.

When Cocks arrived on her doorstep he was younger than she thought he would be, though she remembered his voice rather than his face.

'I didn't think you would make it,' he admitted

Therese smiled. Nobody did.

* * *

In November, Therese was admitted to the John of God private hospital in Geelong for more surgery on her calcified elbow.

To her relief, she was just another patient arriving for day surgery. This time the operation was a success and the surgeons were able to remove the new bone which had grown over her elbow joint, restoring the mobility to her arm.

Therese would need the same operation on the other elbow in the future, but the one that had been causing her the most pain had finally been fixed.

The surgeons told her that in six weeks, when the cast came off, she would be able to move her arm freely and do more of the things that would make her feel more like herself.

She wanted to tie the ribbon in Katie's ponytail again and make the kids' school lunches and do all the other mundane things she had once grumbled about. After everything she had been through, she would never take anything for granted again.

Therese was still in her cast when she and Dawn made a trip to the shops, where they watched the Christmas trees going up in the windows of the bigger stores.

After their miserable Christmas at Concord without the children the previous year, seeing the cheerful lights and tinsel in the shops really lifted Dawn's spirits. This year, she wanted a big celebration with all the family together again.

It would be good to welcome the children home with a traditional Christmas lunch in their own home, and they would all pitch in with the cooking and the children.

As far as Dawn was concerned, this was another milestone in her daughter's miraculous recovery that she had never expected to see, and she was determined to celebrate. If the horrors of Bali had taught Dawn anything, it was that life can change in a heartbeat and that it was important to cherish what you had while you had it.

Therese lay on the sofa lost in thought while the children decorated the Christmas tree. Her love for them – and her mother's love for her – had been the only reason she was still around to see another Christmas.

Her determination to see Alex and Katie grow up had kept her going on even the darkest days when all she wanted to do was close her eyes and never wake up. Despite all the challenges she had fought and overcome, the only gift she had wanted this Christmas was to have her children back. But now they were home she was terrified that she did not know how to be their mother.

Therese had insisted on doing her own Christmas shopping, dosed up on morphine. She ordered the kids the bunk beds they had been pestering her for and intended to surprise them with a new outdoor pool in time for the summer holidays. She only wished she had been able to join them in it, as she once did, but her bandages and pressure suit meant it would be a long time before she could do this. And even then, she was not sure she would be able to deal with people seeing her scars.

For the past couple of weeks, the ongoing pain in her hip had been making it difficult to sleep at night, and she had found it easier sleeping on the sofa than getting in and out of bed and disturbing everyone.

She had also noticed more shrapnel working its way out of her skin, which the doctors had warned her might continue for years. She would still have to return to the Alfred for follow-up appointments, so that the doctors could monitor her healing burns and check on her hearing, which had been damaged in the blast.

Therese's hip might also require further surgery in the future, and the GP had warned that unless the pain settled down, she might even be looking at a hip replacement. Prosthetic hips only had a short life span of around 10 years – and two hip replacements were the maximum – so, it was possible that by the age of 50 she might not be able to walk.

But after all she had been through, Therese was not going to let her hip stop her going to Carols by Candlelight or attending Christmas Mass with her children.

Her biggest problem during her recent outings had not been the pain, or her mobility, but fending off the unwanted attention of strangers who now appeared to view her as public property.

After her garden makeover on *Backyard Blitz* a few weeks earlier, Therese was easily recognisable in her small community in her bandages and pressure suit. She had always been intensely private and reserved and this sudden 'celebrity' status was making her want to run and hide.

'I know you – you're the burns woman off the TV,' said a middle-aged Christmas shopper, approaching her in a cafe where she was resting her aching feet while her mum ordered coffee.

Therese had nodded politely, not sure how to respond.

'You're incredible,' said the woman, beaming at her in admiration.

The woman's friend came over to join them, the unwanted attention provoking more stares in the crowded cafe.

'It's amazing what you have had to overcome,' added the friend. 'I don't think I could have done what you have done.'

Therese cringed. These kind people were only trying to be supportive and empathetic. But all the attention felt very unsettling for a young mum who was trying to blend into the crowd.

She did not want to be ungrateful, but she resented feeling like public property. When well-wishers approached her to say she was amazing for overcoming such terrible injuries, all she could think about was Ben Tullipan, and Nicole McClean – who had lost limbs as well as suffering burns – or Jason McCartney, whose legendary comeback game had inspired an entire nation.

Being told she was 'amazing' when it meant life or death also caused her to reflect on her mother's role in her recovery. Therese recalled how Dawn had sat by her hospital bed for a whole year, religiously massaging Sorbolene into her face until it resembled porcelain. She had stayed with her until it was time to come home, just as she said she would.

Her poor mother had done all a mum could possibly do – and she had done it out of unconditional love. Therese had no idea how her mother had done it, and these compliments – though well intended – left her feeling like a complete fraud.

But while Therese wanted to set everyone straight, she didn't want to be ungracious or mean spirited because she was thankful for her community's support and knew people meant well. She had gratefully accepted their comments, but hated the 'miracle' survivor tag which seemed to define her existence.

After the latest upsetting encounter, she felt so frustrated that when they arrived home, she climbed out of her mother's car determined to do something to change the narrative.

Therese would not be defined by her burns or the calamity that had befallen her. She desperately needed to do something to shake off the spectre of Bali and allow her to feel normal again.

She grabbed the keys to the new Holden Cruze that had been sitting in the garage since September and opened the double doors.

'What are you doing?' asked Dawn, hurrying after her.

'What does it look like I'm doing?' she snapped. 'I'm going for a drive, of course.'

Therese shuffled into the driver's seat and gingerly reversed her new car out of the drive and onto the street, observing her mother through the rear vision window.

Dawn was sobbing and smiling through her tears. Therese took off in the car with her arm cast, wishing the doctors at Concord could see her now.

Her mum was still weeping when Therese returned and pulled up on the drive, triumphant.

'Hmmmm … remind me now … didn't somebody tell me I would never drive again?' she called through the open car window.

For the first time in a long time, Dawn laughed out loud.

No-one who knew Therese would ever dream of telling her 'never'. The word was a challenge for someone as stubborn as her daughter. 'Never' was such a big word and Therese's strong will was even bigger.

Telling her that she would never achieve things only made her determined to do them. Thanks to the doctors, she now had a second chance. Perhaps their list of 'never agains' were just the incentive Therese needed to prove everyone wrong.

Dawn followed her daughter back into the house feeling immensely proud of her. It was another important step towards reclaiming the life that those evil people had tried to destroy with their bombs.

The Prime Minister had been right, she thought. They had not broken the Australian spirit – and they would not destroy her stubborn daughter.

Chapter 20

MOVING ON

The new year brought new challenges for Therese. The summer of 2004 was particularly hot and dry, which posed a new problem for a survivor without sweat glands. Until her melted glands regenerated, Therese lacked the ability to regulate her own body temperature and keep herself cool.

She had been sweltering in her pressure suit and was constantly hot and uncomfortable. The new layer of surface skin that covered her body had become angry and irritated in the heat, and she could no longer hop under a cold shower as she used to do when the mercury climbed.

Instead, she had to wait for the nurse who arrived every second day to help her shower and change her dressings. That January, she spent many days sweltering under the air conditioner in her lounge, desperately trying to keep herself cool and comfortable.

Therese was not the only one who had not been feeling like herself lately. Since Christmas, her mum had also appeared to be out of sorts. The stress of the past 15 months was etched in her sunken face and her tremors had been progressively worsening. These days, Dawn struggled to hold a cup of tea without spilling it, and her daughter had become worried about her.

Dawn had spent so long living on adrenaline that it had put years on her. Seeing what this atrocity had done to her made Therese feel terrible and added another layer to the guilt she had been carrying since the attack.

Like Therese's children, her mother was one of the invisible casualties of the Bali bombings – a secondary victim of a terrible crime that should never have happened. Therese often felt they had all been inadvertently caught in a war that was not of their making.

She felt furious with the terrorists responsible for all the destruction and wanted them to be punished. But she did not want them executed, which she understood was what some of the other survivors and grieving family members had been calling for.

Death was too easy for the evil bastards, who had been convicted the previous October for their roles in the bombings and sentenced to death by firing squad.

Therese would have preferred to see them getting life sentences, so they would spend the rest of their days rotting in an Indonesian jail, suffering like their victims – like she still was.

Although Therese had been improving since her elbow operation, each day was an uphill struggle. She was still on antidepressants and struggling with the extra weight she had piled on from the steroids.

Over the past year, her weight had ballooned from a petite 60 kilograms to 124 kilograms, which put extra stress on her injured hip and stretched the new skin, which now felt tight and painful.

The extra kilos had further compounded the depression she felt over the loss of her former identity because she no longer recognised herself. It was hard enough being burnt and horribly scarred without being obese too.

Even Therese's feet were now twice their size, and although they had begun to heal, she could no longer fit into any of her old shoes, let alone any of the fabulous sandals she had bought in Bali. The injuries to her feet and her hip problem prevented her from wearing the shoes she had always worn, and she was now shuffling around in comfy runners or Ugg boots.

Every time she caught sight of the treadmill, it was another reminder of all that she had lost. The fitness equipment was now as redundant as she was, so she advertised it and sold it.

On *Backyard Blitz*, and in some media reports during the trials of the ringleaders of the bomb blasts, there had been a strong focus on the physical scars suffered by the survivors.

But since her return to 'normality', Therese had been struggling more with the psychological trauma surrounding the destruction of her former identity than the physical limitations of her injuries.

In late January 2004, Alex and Katie began the new year back at their former primary school in Grovedale, where they were excited to see their friends again.

Therese waved them off, grateful that she had a team around her to help with the school drop-offs and pick-ups that she was still struggling to manage.

Until the cast on her elbow came off, she still struggled to do all the things she used to do. Her hair was growing back now, and she longed for the day she could brush it herself.

Alex and Katie's first day back at school was exciting and their former friends and teachers gathered around to welcome them back. Everyone had seen them on the TV with their mum and the other children now seemed to think the family was famous.

Katie felt her heart sink. She was as uncomfortable about this newfound celebrity as her mum and suspected they were only in the public spotlight because awful things had happened to them. Life had not gone back to normal and she doubted it ever would.

She watched her mum struggling in her plaster cast to make the sandwiches for their school lunches and felt bad for her. Mum tried so hard, but sometimes she looked so sad, and that made Katie feel sad too.

Fortunately, their first day back had gone better than she and Alex had expected, and they both slotted back into their new classes feeling as if they had never been away.

When the children returned from school that afternoon, their mother was sleeping on the sofa – exhausted after her shower and having her dressings changed. As much as Katie wanted to help, she was a little kid and felt very guilty for not knowing how to shower her mum – and not wanting to have to.

Her grandma had told her that it was okay to not want to do this. It was a grown-up's job, and the nurse would be coming to help her. Her mum had lots of carers doing things for her. But Katie didn't know anyone else whose mum had to have a nurse to help her shower, or to brush her hair.

It was just another sign that everything about their lives had changed.

* * *

In the first couple of weeks following Therese's discharge from the Alfred Hospital, Dawn drove Therese back to the burns unit for an outpatient check-up. The specialist was pleased to see that the large burn on her back that had earlier broken down was now healing well, as was the rest of her body. She would need to wear her pressure suit for at least another year, but this was a process that was going to take time. Therese had plenty of time.

'You're very lucky that your skin is healing so well,' Dr Cleland had said, repeating what the doctors at Concord had said about her fitness enhancing her body's ability to deal with the trauma and help in her recovery.

At the ENT clinic, the mastoid infection that had threatened her life had finally cleared up, although the hearing in her left ear had suffered permanent damage from the blast. She now had 80 per cent hearing loss in that ear, which had been aggravated by the mastoid infection. Her hearing in the other ear was also impaired. This was common for the survivors of major explosions, explained the doctor.

Leaving the hospital that day, Therese reached an important decision. She did not want these injuries to control the rest of her life. For the past 12 months, her life had revolved around hospitals and specialists, without whose care she would certainly have died. But she had been feeling so powerless lately. She decided that if she wanted to reclaim her life, she had to be responsible for her own recovery. Therese made up her mind that the appointment at the burns unit would be her last and she would be moving on at her own pace.

Therese was fortunate enough to have an excellent family GP who was more than capable of dealing with any medical issues that might arise.

She also found a good psychologist in Geelong who was helping her address the grief she felt over the loss of her old life and her former identity – and the limitations posed by her disfiguring injuries.

Regular therapy also helped her to deal with the recurring flashbacks that seemed to come from nowhere. A loud banging noise or the sudden startling sound of a car backfiring took her straight back to that night in Paddy's bar.

She could see herself rolling in the debris trying to douse the flames, or see Rada's face, and Cath in her yellow top pouring cold water all over her while she screamed on the grass.

The flashbacks were as terrifying as they were debilitating. During her time at the motel near the Alfred Hospital, there had been a police raid at a nearby apartment complex when armed officers from the Special Operations Group had arrested several suspects believed to have committed a robbery.

The sound of the door smashing open and police officers storming into the nearby apartment had caused a flashback of the explosion in Paddy's bar, and Therese's body had shut down in shock. She had been taken to the A and E department and immediately readmitted for post-traumatic shock, then spent days reliving the events her mind had tried to block out.

Therese's conscious memory of events was still sketchy, but these flashbacks were vivid and terrifying. And it wasn't just sounds and sudden noises that sparked the flashbacks – sometimes the smell of burning wood or smoke was enough to take her back there and leaving her gasping for air.

Frightening images of that terrible night crept up on her unexpectedly, and she had been considering having hypnotherapy to fill in the gaps that her therapist believed her mind had blocked out as a mechanism to protect her from her pain.

Her psychologist explained that recognising the triggers and talking them through would help Therese to understand and manage the symptoms so that she could heal. She found it reassuring to know that these flashbacks were common symptoms of post-traumatic stress and that other people who had been through a major trauma experienced them too.

Amidst this emotional turmoil, Bronwyn's sister, Jess, had called around to see how Therese was going. She came with Bronwyn's friend Oriana to bring a DVD of her sister's funeral service for Therese to watch.

Therese was sleeping when she called around and her mother, aware of her highly anxious state, told them it was not a good day.

'She's not coping very well emotionally right now,' said her mum, keeping them on the doorstep.

Jess said she understood and left the DVD for Therese to watch when things were better in her life.

'We just want her to know we are thinking about her,' she said.

Later, when her mother told her about the visit and the DVD, Therese felt guiltier than ever. She could cope with the pain of the burns all over again if she had to. But knowing Bronwyn had died when she had survived was a pain like no other.

For days afterwards, the guilt had eaten her alive. Not only was she feeling guilty about Bronwyn's death, but guilty about the guilt that made it so hard to face her friend's beautiful family. The fact that she found it too hard to see them added another layer to her suffering. She discussed it with her counsellor at her next visit and he advised her to do whatever she needed to do to survive.

* * *

In May, Therese's landlord announced that he was not intending to renew her lease and was planning to renovate the rental property and put it up for sale. It was the nudge that she needed. She decided to look for a new place and close that chapter in her life and move on.

Therese went house-hunting with her mother and found a new property in nearby Church Street, close to the children's primary school.

She was unpacking when she found the Lauren Manning book that Cath had given her on one of her visits to Melbourne before she had left to start her new job in Munich.

Cath had told Therese that she had bought the book in Singapore airport on her way to Bali, recounting Manning's inspirational journey back to recovery after the terrorist attack on the World Trade Center.

'It's an incredible book,' said Cath, hoping it might bring some comfort to Therese to know that another burns survivor had walked in her shoes and understood the suffering. She believed it would make her feel less alone and might give her hope.

Cath said she never imagined when she bought Greg Manning's book about his wife's survival that within hours, she and Rada would be helping people from the new 'ground zero' in Bali. How could she have known then that she would be supporting another young woman of around the same age on a journey that mirrored Lauren Manning's?

Therese had put the book to one side. When she was feeling better, she would read it and perhaps it would help her.

The overwhelming sense of Bronwyn that Therese had felt so keenly in her old house followed her to her new home in Church Street.

Within days of their arrival, she felt the same chill as Bronwyn's spirit slid into bed beside her at night when she was alone. It felt as though her friend had followed her to check on her progress and let her know that things were going to be alright. Therese had felt her more over the past few days when she had been feeling vulnerable.

Therese, who had always been a spiritual person, made an appointment to see a psychic in Geelong. She told the psychic that the presence was now making her anxious and that she had no doubt this was her friend connecting with her again.

It was as real to her as the intuitive sense of danger that had troubled her in Legan Jalan on the afternoon of the bombings.

'Trust your instinct,' advised the psychic. 'Tell your friend that you are okay now and it is time for her to go.'

The next time Therese felt the presence in her bedroom, she did what the psychic had suggested and said it was okay to leave. She hated herself for doing it because it felt as though she was rejecting her friend. It added to the burden of guilt that she had carried with her every day since Bali, and would weigh heavily on her for years to come.

Chapter 21

BONDS
FORGED
FLAMES

From her new school in Germany, Cath kept in touch with Therese to update her about her adventures in Germany and check on her progress since her return home.

Cath's letters were as bright and cheery as her personality and injected a much-needed ray of light into Therese's life – particularly on the bad days when she found herself struggling.

Rada was still in Tewantin and had been keeping in touch through regular phone calls and the occasional visit to Grovedale to visit Therese and the children, or to stay with Bronwyn's family in Geelong.

Before Cath's big move to Germany the previous August, they had both flown down to stay with Therese during one of her weekend releases from the Alfred Hospital. They had helped to clear out her shed and tidy things up for her return, which Dawn had been hoping would be before Christmas.

Rada had also been down to stay at Therese's new place in Church Street too. She had been encouraged to see that she was getting out and about more with her children, who appeared to have made the transition back from their father's home relatively seamlessly.

If one positive thing had come from this catastrophe, it was Therese's friendship with these two generous women whose kindness had restored her faith in humanity. After experiencing the worst that mankind was capable of inflicting, it was rewarding to see the goodness in people.

By mid-2004, Therese was socialising with her children again. She had been catching up with her best friend – another Michelle – who she had known since school, and had enjoyed several playdates at her home with Alex and Katie.

They had also been out for family dinners and enjoyed spending time at the local park or along the bike track. During the recent school holidays, she had taken Alex and Katie to the movies where they had thoroughly enjoyed themselves, though Therese anxiously checked the nearest exits before she was able to settle in her seat.

Since the events in Bali, Therese had become hypervigilant about the potential for danger in every situation. In her old life she never gave these things a thought, but unthinkable events *had* already happened in her life, and they might happen again.

Life was fragile and uncertain, but Therese had never thought about life that way before Bali. Now she could not stop.

On the upside, the operation on her elbow freed up her arm; she no longer needed help and could have a shower whenever she felt like it.

Her wounds were healing so well that the nurse who had been coming in every other day to change her dressings said she no longer needed her help and was making an incredible recovery.

Her full body suit had been replaced with pressure bandages on the upper part of her body only, where the burns on Therese's chest, back and arms had been taking longer to heal.

But towards the end of 2004, the nurses decided she no longer needed those either. Therese had been waiting for this moment for so long, but when it finally arrived, she panicked.

For the past two years, her body suit had been a comforting armour which protected her body from further injury and hid her disfiguring scars. Without her pressure suit and bandages there was nothing for Therese to hide beneath, and she felt vulnerable and exposed. The pressure suit had become as much a part of her new identity as the scars all over her body, and she felt like child being forced to give up the comforting 'blanky' that they needed to feel safe.

The first few days without the pressure bandages left her feeling naked and scared, although it felt strangely liberating without them.

Therese had been so hot and uncomfortable in that suit during the hot summer months at the beginning of the year, and it was a relief to feel the cool breeze on her skin again.

The sweat glands that had melted in the explosion had slowly begun to function again, and her body was now regulating her core temperature on its own. This meant less time under the air conditioner and lower bills. Things were slowly returning to a new kind of normal, but it was nothing like the old one.

Therese still relied on morphine for the pain in her hip but had gradually been weaning herself off it. She had taken herself off the steroid medication altogether and the excess weight that had been a side effect of her treatment had slowly started to fall away.

Being able to do some of the things she had done in her old life had helped her regain some of her old independence, and Therese was having more good days than bad.

The endless skin grafts – and her mother's healing hands – had given her a smooth flawless face. Her features were fuller and unlike the old fine-boned face Therese had been accustomed to seeing, but thanks to her mum's devotion, she had the complexion of a porcelain doll.

On one of her recent trips to the local pharmacy, Therese had found herself wandering up and down the make-up aisles. Before Bali, she would not have gone out of the house without a full face of make-up. But the doctors in Concord had advised her that she would never wear it again, and if by some miracle she ever did, it would have to be make-up customised to conceal disfiguring burns.

Studying her old foundation, Therese wondered if she might look and feel a little more like her old self with some make-up on her face and decided to buy some.

In the privacy of her bathroom, she applied the new foundation with a sponge and brushed some powder blusher over her cheekbones. But when she inspected the results in the mirror, she hated what she saw.

No amount of concealer and contouring had been able to resurrect the old Therese and she cringed at the face looking back at her. She would never be the same pretty fresh-faced young woman she had been before Bali and no amount of make-up was going to fix it.

Her face looked like an ill-fitting mask – nothing like the one in her old family photographs. Therese's life had changed in every way, particularly her physical appearance. Those bastards had done this to her, and she wondered if she would ever be able to look in the mirror and accept the woman she had become.

Therese had never been able to face the holiday snapshots of herself and Bronwyn on their idyllic holiday in Kuta before the bombs.

Now she felt compelled to dig them out and see the carefree faces of the two young friends she grieved for every day.

Looking at the photographs was bittersweet, but it was good to remember that before the terrorists attacked, they had been truly happy. On her next shopping trip to Geelong, Therese bought herself a photo album and slipped the haunting snapshots into its pages. From now on, she would not hide the photographs away, and she would not hide from them either.

Her photographs gave her a glimmer of hope that one day she might smile like she had back then, even if she did not look the same.

Although Therese embraced her newfound independence, her mother was struggling with it. Dawn had always been very involved in her adopted children's lives, and they had been the centre of hers.

After the collapse of her five-year relationship with the children's father, Therese had returned to her mum's with Alex.

She had already been pregnant with Katie by then and after her birth, had brought her newborn daughter home to her mother's too.

Apart from when Therese had stayed briefly with her father in Queensland when her children were small, Dawn had always been around. The children had missed their grandma so much in Queensland that it had been one of the reasons Therese had decided to return to Victoria, where her mother had continued to play a major role in all their lives.

Without her mum's love and support, and her own determination to see her children grow up, Therese had no doubt she would never have made it.

When she had hit rock bottom, her parents had been there to lift her up and she was grateful for their love and support. But if she was to be a parent to her children again, she needed her mother to allow her the space to do it.

Living around the corner from each another was making the separation difficult. Since Therese's return from Bali, her mother had become overly protective and had been cosseting her ever since. Therese realised that if she was to be an independent parent again, she needed to set a few boundaries to ensure she and Dawn lived their separate lives, instead of clinging to one another.

Dawn struggled with Therese's withdrawal and felt hurt over what she perceived to be a major rejection. After sitting beside her hospital bed for a year, she had found a new purpose as a crutch for Therese to lean on during her recovery. But Therese appeared to be putting up a wall and her mum felt there was no longer a place for her in her daughter's life, and she was floundering.

The new boundaries that Therese erected for her own survival became a growing source of tension between mother and daughter. The more Therese pulled away, the more her mother clung to her, causing frustration and resentment on both sides.

* * *

Therese and Dawn weren't the only ones who struggled to find a new purpose in their lives following the terrorist attacks in Bali.

Since Bronwyn's death, Jenny – a critical care nurse – had been so overcome with grief that she had taken time off work to deal with her loss.

Like Therese, she had also been wracked with guilt and overwhelming sadness. She blamed herself for not driving Bronwyn to the airport to say goodbye – and for not taking the time to say all the things she should have said to her while she had the chance.

Jenny had found it distressing that people failed to grasp the torment of those uncertain weeks before Bronwyn was formally identified.

Even her own GP had shown no insight into her suffering and had recommended an immediate return to work, at a time when she had been waiting for a knock on the door to tell her that her daughter had indeed been one of the fatalities of the terrorist attack.

When hundreds of Australian families were holding funerals and memorials for their loved ones, Jenny could not imagine going back to work in a place where other people's lives were hanging in the balance, while waiting for the police to turn up to tell her that her daughter was dead.

She was not sleeping and could not concentrate on anything let alone care for people whose lives were in her hands. She trusted her own instinct and ignored the GP's advice. Instead she took the 10 months sick leave she had accrued.

By the time it ended, Jenny had been offered a job in coronary care at the Geelong University Hospital. Her intuition told her that she was still not ready, and this was proved correct when she suffered a panic attack while resuscitating a patient.

'I'm not coping,' she told the doctor she had been referred to speak to. But he didn't pay attention either.

'It's like riding a bike,' he said dismissively. 'You just get back on and keep riding.'

Jenny continued to struggle on, but when she developed an anxiety-related rash, she realised it was time to listen to her heart, and handed in her resignation.

Bronwyn's death caused her to reassess her entire life. In 2004, she opened a new business in Geelong with her eldest son, Anthony, and younger son, Jason, who were bakers. She called her new bakery-café Bron's Café after her beloved daughter.

Jenny had put a great deal of research into her new venture and on one of Rada's visits to Geelong, they had toured the local café's and bakeries to sample the different cakes and pastries so she could come up with a wish list for the boys to bake.

Rada supported Jenny's new initiative and was one of the first customers to enjoy a complimentary specialty coffee. It was called 'gorgeous girl', the nickname Jenny had given to Bronwyn.

'It's delicious,' said Rada, sipping her coffee in honour of the young woman she had never managed to meet in her lifetime.

The venture gave the grieving mum a new purpose and while the boys baked the goodies, Jenny ran the café. Her days were longer and her week fuller, but she was no longer dealing with life and death or having panic attacks.

Shortly after the business had opened, Jess called around to visit Therese at her new home, with a friend. Her mum sent some cakes and pastries for Therese and the children, and Jess had told her all about the new family business.

It was a painful meeting for Jess and Therese, who had both been grappling with guilt: Therese for surviving when Jess' sister had not, and Jess because she had been spared the nightmare because she had not been able to save the money in time for the holiday.

Jess and her mum still felt horribly guilty about Therese's injuries, because they felt certain the idea for the last drink and photo in Paddy's bar would have been Bronwyn's idea. Tragically, it had been a decision that had cost Jess' sister her life and was one her friend now had to live with. Jess, like her mum, felt terrible about it.

'I'm so sorry,' she apologised, in tears.

'No – *I'm* sorry,' said Therese.

She had watched the girls go, hating herself all over again. If the physical scars were a legacy of that terrible night, so was the enduring guilt she felt whenever she saw Bronwyn's family.

Her mother had met with Bronwyn's mother on a few occasions when she came to visit them at the Alfred. On one of those occasions, Dawn had told her that she had been grateful that her daughter's face had not been burnt beyond repair, though the rest of her body had.

Jenny had felt a lump in her throat, thinking of the small things that mothers cling to when they are grieving. She was grateful that her daughter had died quickly and that her body had been returned to them.

Some families had not been as fortunate and were grateful for the clump of Balinese earth they had been given because they had no body to bury.

Therese had been so ill at the time that she only vaguely remembered Jenny coming to see her. Bronwyn's family were such beautiful people, just as Bronwyn had been, and the shame Therese felt after their visits was excruciating.

She had told her psychologist about it at her next counselling session, where she explained her guilt was making her avoid situations she could not handle.

'Jess said she was sorry – but why should she feel bad? She hasn't done anything wrong. This wasn't her fault, or Bronwyn's,' she said, answering her own rhetorical question.

The therapist listened sympathetically.

'And neither have you,' he pointed out. The people who perpetrated this dreadful crime were the ones responsible for this.

Therese had reflected on their discussion all the way home.

She had recently seen old TV footage of Amrozi, one of the three terrorists now awaiting execution in Indonesia after being convicted of plotting and helping in the terrorist attacks. It was patently clear from the smirk on his face that he was not feeling guilty about anything at all.

After his arrest on 5 November 2002, he was pictured smiling and waving for the cameras. He was surrounded by laughing senior Indonesian police officials, and had pointed at Western journalists and said in Bahasa that they were the sort of people he wanted to kill.

His contempt for the authorities and obvious lack of remorse for the suffering he had caused prompted outrage from the survivors and families of his victims. But even this absence of contrition, and his sneering at Western media, had done nothing to alleviate the guilt that weighed so heavily on Therese, and she imagined nothing ever would.

Two years on, Therese often thought about Damien's ominous premonition of danger. She had been so flippant about his concerns regarding the threat of terrorism and yet he had been right.

After the suffering inflicted by al-Qaeda on innocent Americans on 9/11 the world had *not* been a safe place – and yet she had somehow imagined herself to be invincible and immune from the danger. These terrible things happened to other people, in other countries, not to ordinary Aussies on their holidays.

But it *had* happened – and it had happened to her and Bronwyn, and hundreds of other people. And it could happen again. This was the reason why she now felt compelled to check the nearest exits wherever she went. It was why she felt so frightened and anxious in the football crowd at Docklands during Jason McCartney's comeback game. It was why she would never feel safe ever again.

Later that night, Therese dug out the Lauren Manning book *Love, Greg and Lauren* that Cath had given her. Once she began to read it, she wasn't able to put the book down. She was amazed to discover that their stories were so similar. Manning had also been a mother with young children when the terrorist attack on the twin towers brought her whole world crashing down.

She had also survived with disfiguring burns and had battled for her survival. Therese understood Manning's pain, and yet the US mother appeared to have come out the other side stronger.

After reading the book, Therese sent Manning an email, telling her how her husband's book had inspired her and given her hope for her own future. She did not know anyone else – apart from the Bali survivors she had met – who had been injured in a terrorist attack, and the story had made her feel less alone on her journey.

It would be a few months before Lauren Manning finally replied. She thanked Therese for reaching out and wished her well for the future. She also asked for her address so that she could send her a copy of her second book, which had not been available in Australia. A second book! thought Therese. It was inspiring to know that Manning had a sequel to her incredible survival story. It gave her the hope that it might be possible for her to write a few new chapters in her own life.

Chapter 22

A NEW
THREAT

While the spectre of the Bali bombings continued to cast a shadow over Therese's life, a new sense of urgency was slowly beginning to emerge. After reading Manning's story, she was even more determined that she could not allow the tragedy to overtake the life she was yet to live.

If Bronwyn's passion for embracing every minute had taught her anything, it was that you only had one shot at life and it was important to pack as much as you could into it, because things could change in a heartbeat.

After witnessing the many lives that were shattered in that 20 fatal seconds in Bali, Cath was prompted by this same sense of urgency to reassess her own life.

In 2005, as her two-year contract in Munich came to an end, she settled on a new adventure and accepted a teaching position at another international school in Beijing. She told Therese all about it in her next letter.

The same urgency had led to Jenny leaving her nursing position and opening *Bron's Café*, and was set to inspire her son, Philip, to follow in his eldest sister's footsteps by following his own dreams of a 12-month working holiday in the UK.

The tragic events in Bali in 2002 changed everyone's perspective and priorities, and Phil decided he needed time out from his career in logistics to pursue a new adventure.

Before Bronwyn's trip to Bali, he had always believed he had time on his side, and that his dreams could wait for a while. Now that she was gone, time had become more pressing and he wanted to squeeze as much into his own life as he could, and experience new things, just as Bronwyn had.

Before her death, it had been his sister's cherished dream to become an embalmer and she had completed a course that would take her a step closer to her new career.

Although her mother had considered working with the dead to be a maudlin career path, Bronwyn had taken a different, more uplifting view. Being entrusted to make people look their best for their journey to the afterlife – wherever that might be – was an honour, and a gift she wanted to give to grieving families.

Sadly, time had run out for his sister, and Phil decided that he needed to pursue dreams of his own.

In early 2005, he packed his bags and headed to London, hoping the change would give him the space he needed to reflect on the loss of his sister and figure out what he wanted for his own life.

Chapter 22

But Phil had only been in England a few months when another suicide attack sent shockwaves around the world. On 7 July 2005, news emerged from the UK about a series of bombings which had just taken place during the morning rush-hour commute on London's crowded transit network.

The bombings on London's Underground had appeared on the Australian national news early in the evening where it had been revealed that three separate explosions had just occurred on the Tube – leaving an undetermined number of people dead and hundreds more injured. The victims had all been heading into workplaces across central London.

Jenny Hobbs was at Jess' house in Melbourne when the news broke. They watched in disbelief as images of bleeding commuters staggered from the Underground, where terrorists had activated a carefully coordinated bomb attack on three of the busiest commuter lines into the city. Phil was working in London at the time, and his mother immediately began to panic.

'Oh my God, it cannot be happening to us again,' said Jenny, stricken.

What were the chances of losing another child in a different suicide attack less than three years apart? Jenny was beside herself as Jess tried to call her older brother. When Philip's phone rang out, she felt sick too. He should have been on his way to work by now. Where could he be?

Jess recalled her telephone calls to Bali when she had tried to find her sister after the bombings in Kuta. It had been a nightmare. At the time they had still imagined that Bronwyn would have been helping the injured and had been too busy to call home. Now, they knew that unimaginable things did not just happen to everyone else. Horrific things happened to people you loved. Jess was desperate to speak with her brother.

They knew from their regular phone calls with Phil that he travelled on the Tube to work in London every day, and were terrified that he might be caught up in this new atrocity.

According to the news reports from England, four suicide bombers carrying rucksacks filled with explosives had travelled on the Tube to King Cross Station, where they had separated, and then boarded different trains. Two of the bombers had travelled on the Circle Line – one heading east and the other taking a southbound train.

Another suicide bomber was on a train travelling along the Piccadilly Line. Twenty minutes later the trio simultaneously detonated their bombs, leaving an indeterminate number of people dead and hundreds more seriously injured.

The fourth terrorist had left the underground at Hackney and boarded a crowded double bus into the centre of London. An hour later he had detonated a 4.5-kilogram bomb on the upper level of the bus, killing 13 people and injuring over 100 more. Investigators later confirmed that 50 people had died in the attacks and 800 people had been maimed and injured.

Although Al-Qaeda's Deputy Leader Ayman Al-Zawahiri later claimed partial responsibility for the bombings, the British authorities were not convinced that the feared terrorist organisation had been behind the attacks.

They took the view that the suicide bombers were ordinary homegrown terrorists who had been radicalised by extreme Islamic indoctrination.

Chapter 22

Jenny and Jess spent a frantic two hours waiting by the phone before Phil finally called from London to say he was okay. He had left the London Underground at Shepherd's Bush just before the suicide bombers struck.

'I heard a loud noise and when I turned around, smoke was coming from the underground,' he said, describing the chaotic scenes he had witnessed. Shepherd's Bush is less than 6 miles from Tavistock Square where the bus exploded.

He said the whole of London was on high alert and people were anxious that this might be the start of another terror campaign.

Jenny lay awake all night, thinking about all the families like theirs who had been plunged into their worst nightmare. And for what?

Cath also watched the news from London as she packed up her life in Munich. She knew from her regular calls to Bronwyn's mum that Phil was in London and was glad when she rang and heard that he was okay.

For the UK, it did not end there. Fourteen days after the attack, Islamist extremists launched a follow-up attack, and this time Shepherd's Bush was one of the three Underground stations targeted. The explosions occurred on trains on three different lines. One at the Oval Underground Station on the Northern Line, another at the Warren Street Station on the Victoria Line, and the third at Shepherd's Bush Station on the Hammersmith and City Line – the route Phil took each day.

Fortunately, only the detonator caps fired and the bombs themselves did not go off, which investigators attributed to the low quality of hydrogen peroxide in the devices. The explosions had been small – with the power of a large firework, and the only injury reported had been from someone with an asthma attack. But the new attacks sparked a major evacuation of the underground system and caused chaos and panic across London.

Therese was watching the news on the TV at home and found it so upsetting she had had to turn it off.

Anything could happen to anyone, anywhere – and at any time. But this could not stop people going about their business and living their lives, or the terrorists would win. All the same, she would not be travelling anywhere ever again. It was too dangerous.

The third anniversary of the Bali bombings were just a few weeks away, and Therese had been trying not to think about it. She still struggled with post-traumatic stress and guilt, so every anniversary served as a haunting reminder that life, like death, was nothing more than a random lottery where some survive and others don't.

It was a philosophy shared by Rodney Cocks, the soldier who had led Therese to safety when she had been dying in the street outside Paddy's bar in October 2002.

Therese had survived because she had gone to the bar to get a last drink, leaving Bronwyn on the dance floor where the suicide bomber struck.

Cocks had survived because he had headed out to do some last-minute internet banking. But the Bali bombings were not Cocks' only lucky escape.

Ten months after the tragedy in Bali, on 19 August 2003, Cocks narrowly escaped another terrorist attack at the UN headquarters in Baghdad where he was working in the UN's de-mining team.

At the time that the suicide bomber struck, Cocks had left his desk to get a telephone number from a colleague in another part of the building. Seconds after he left, the bomb went off, decimating the offices where he had previously been working. Cocks lost 22 friends and colleagues in the attack.

In a satellite interview broadcast from Baghdad, he would later tell *A Current Affair* presenter Ray Martin that he could not fathom how he had managed to dodge a bullet twice in a year. He joked that they should share a lottery ticket and see if the 'three times lucky' adage was true!

Whether it was fate or good fortune that he had been spared again, Cocks would never know. But lady luck continued to smile on him when he later completed a successful tour of Afghanistan as a UN security adviser in war-torn Kandahar.

In 2005, he was named Victorian of the Year for his humanitarian service in East Timor, Iraq and Afghanistan, and for his selfless actions in rescuing and helping people in Baghdad and in Bali.

Therese had later bought his book, *Bali to Baghdad and Beyond*, unable to believe how random it had all been. She owed her life to so many, but if Cocks and his English mate Nick had not rescued her from the destruction in Legian Jalan and delivered her into the safe hands of Cath Byrne and Rada van der Werff, who had lobbied for her evacuation, she may well have been one of the fatalities.

Had it been purely a random chance that she had survived while others had not? Or had it simply not been her time? Therese had often asked 'why me?'

These days she reframed the question and asked herself 'why not me?' It was a question many of the survivors asked themselves in 2005 as they prepared for the third anniversary of the bombings in Bali that had changed so many lives.

* * *

On 1 October 2005, as the survivors and the families of the victims prepared for another pilgrimage back to Bali the fundamentalist terrorist organisation responsible for its destruction was preparing to unleash another attack on Western tourists in Kuta.

Eleven days before the anniversary, and just 48 hours before the start of the Muslim holy month of Ramadan, Jemaah Islamiyah launched another series of suicide bombings that bore all the same terrifying hallmarks as the attack in 2002.

At 6.50pm on 1 October, Indonesian authorities received reports of two simultaneous explosions in Jimbaran Beach – one at a crowded food court and the other close to the Four Seasons Hotel. Ten minutes later, a third blast ripped through a restaurant in the Kuta Square shopping mall.

The three attacks had all been strategically planned, and again the terrorists had targeted locations popular among Western tourists. The blasts were timed to coincide with the Australian school holidays when around 7500 Australian visitors were anticipated to be in Bali, whose tourist industry had been struggling to recover since the 2002 bombings in Kuta.

Over the past 12 months, tourists had begun to return to the holiday island, despite the ongoing warning from Australia's Department of Foreign Affairs and Trade (DFAT) advising its citizens to avoid all non-essential travel to Indonesia. Two weeks before the new attacks, DFAT had issued another warning, advising Australians against visiting places where Westerners were known to congregate. The same warning had been reiterated by the US Trade Department to its own citizens.

The US warning followed the discovery of an unassembled bomb on the fourth floor of the Kuta Paradiso Hotel and came after intelligence reported that the violent extremist organisation was planning another bomb attack in Indonesia or the Philippines. Unfortunately, intelligence sources had been unable to uncover specific details that would have prevented the bombings in which 20 people were killed and over 100 were injured.

Evidence from the bomb sites revealed that at least three suicide bombers had been involved in the attacks and had either carried the explosives into the locations or had planted them in the restaurants in advance.

The casualties would have been higher but for the quick thinking of the Indonesian security forces, who shut down Bali's entire mobile network after the first explosions to prevent further bombs being activated by mobile devices. Later, the authorities discovered three more undetonated bombs which had failed to go off in the busy tourist areas.

The Chief Commissioner of the AFP, Mick Keelty, told media that while the 2002 bombings were chemical blasts, the latest bombs had been filled with pellets and ball bearings and most of the injuries were caused by shrapnel from the explosions including broken glass.

Four Australians and 15 Indonesians were among the dead. Nineteen of the 120 casualties were Australian and were evacuated to Darwin aboard an RAAF 3-130 Hercules. An earlier attack on the Australian Embassy in Jakarta had led Australian political figureheads to the conclusion that Australians were the true target of the terrorist strikes.

For Therese, the latest suicide attacks confirmed her belief that the world was a dangerous place and validated her decision never to go to Bali again. Even on her home soil, she still struggled being in any kind of a crowd as it gave her flashbacks of that Saturday night in October 2002 when the world stood still.

Instead, she spent the third anniversary at home in a private moment of reflection, and she and Michelle quietly raised a glass to the friend who had been an innocent casualty of the sort of hatred that was still flourishing around the world.

Both mothers remained dogged by the survivor guilt that many of the returning survivors had described to the media – Michelle for the job that had kept her at home with her children – and Therese for being fortunate enough to return to Alex and Katie.

Chapter 23

NEVER SAY
NEVER

The suicide attacks in Bali in 2005 were not enough to deter the Balinese people from holding their annual remembrance service to honour the lives that were lost on 12 October 2002.

And the threat of terrorism didn't discourage the families of the victims – or the survivors of the terrorist attacks – from making the annual pilgrimage back to Kuta to remember the people they loved who had died there.

In 2004 a permanent memorial had been erected on the original site of Paddy's bar. It was built from carved stone and bore a plaque with the names and nationalities of all the victims, flanked by their national flags.

Over the 10 years that followed the tragedy, nine-day cleansing ceremonies were held there, and wreaths placed in honour of the victims. There had been prayers, Balinese music, dancing and parades.

By the tenth anniversary of the Bali bombings, the 'Kuta Karnival' had grown into a major tourist event in a country where the people refused to bow to the threat of terrorism.

In 2012, the bar where Therese had been so horribly injured was thriving again – albeit under a different banner in a different location further along the road from the Bali Bombing Memorial.

The memorial, which is known to many as a 'sacred place', is located between the two detonation points where the suicide bombers set off the deadly explosions which ripped through the original Paddy's Irish Bar and the Sari Club – which in 2022 is still a deserted car park.

Therese Fox had never seen the memorial. And she vowed she never would.

In October 2012, Rada Van Der Werff joined the Hobbs family and other Australian families of the victims and survivors for the tenth memorial service, which was held at the Garuda Wisnu Kencana Cultural Park in Jimbaran, Bali

Among the Australian and Indonesian dignitaries at the services were the Australian Prime Minister, Julia Gillard, and former Prime Minister John Howard. Each read a reflection that remembered the 202 innocent people who had been injured or killed in what Mr Howard had once described as a brutal act of mass murder.

Grieving father Danny Hanley from Western Australia – who had lost his daughters, Renae and Simone, in the bombing at the Sari Club – delivered a reading on behalf of the families of the victims – and the hundreds more living with the scars of that fateful night.

Chapter 23

But not all the victims lived to see that anniversary.

Therese's mother, Dawn, and more recently her father, Chris, were among what Therese describes as the 'invisible casualties' of the terrorist attacks in October 2002 – the ones whose lives had also ended prematurely because of the suffering inflicted in Kuta.

Tragically, Dawn Fox had passed away on 13 November 2008 – four days after the perpetrators of the atrocity – Amrozi, his brother, Ali Ghufron (Mukhlas), and its mastermind, Imam Samudra – were executed by separate firing squads on the Indonesian prison island of Nusakambangan off the coast of Central Java.

Amrozi and Mukhlas's younger brother, Ali Imron, received a life sentence. He was the only member of the Bali bombers to show any remorse for the crimes that had killed and injured so many people. In court, he shed tears and apologized for what he had done.

But his brothers and their accomplices showed no contrition. After his conviction, Amrozi gave a thumbs-up sign and said he was happy to die a martyr. Even as the trio were being led to their executions, they had defiantly shouted 'Allah Akhbar,' (God is Great).

Dawn and Therese had not cared one way or the other. Nothing could change what had happened.

Dawn's passing left a massive void in Therese's life, and she had no doubt that the anguish her own suffering had caused to her mother over many years had contributed to the heart condition that eventually led to her premature death.

Therese was convinced that the stress and worry surrounding her fight for survival had taken a heavy toll on her parents.

During Therese's long months in hospital, Dawn had existed on anxiety and adrenaline, which adversely affected her Parkinson's disease and exacerbated her tremors. In more recent years, her mum had been receiving psychological counselling to help her manage the symptoms of her post-traumatic stress, which also put pressure on her heart. Despite being fitted with a pacemaker in 2007, Dawn's health had continued to deteriorate.

On 13 November 2008, Therese called in on her mum, who had been feeling unwell. She called an ambulance, but after being told there would be a long wait at the hospital, she took Dawn home to keep a closer eye on her.

An ambulance was called again the following afternoon after her mum collapsed on her loungeroom floor. Therese watched helplessly as the paramedics tried to revive her. But her mum had already gone.

Dawn Fox had been just 71 years old.

Therese had called Rada in great distress, and Rada caught the next flight to Melbourne to support her. Cath rang from the international school in Beijing where she was now teaching to offer her sincere condolences. Dawn had been Therese's rock, and the friends wondered how she would cope without her.

Dawn was laid to rest at Highton Cemetery outside Geelong – her sudden passing leaving a hole in the hearts of her adopted twins and the grandchildren who adored her. An autopsy later revealed that Dawn died of respiratory problems and a heart condition.

But Therese was convinced that the events in Bali in October 2002 had broken her mother's heart beyond repair.

Chapter 23

In her mind, her parents and her children were the secondary victims of this heinous crime, although their names would never be included in the list of casualties of the Bali bombings.

Therese often wondered if Stacey and Justin Lee's unborn child had ever been counted among the 202 victims whose lives had been snuffed out in the terrorist attack. It broke her heart whenever she thought of them. Their baby was as much a victim of the Bali bombings as his or her, parents had been.

Alex and Katie, who had been very close to their grandmother, were devastated by her death. But their mother was inconsolable. On the night of Dawn's passing, Therese cried so much she was afraid she might never stop.

Therese and Damien had been blessed to have had the unconditional love of this warm and caring woman who had taken them into her heart as tiny babies and loved them until the day she died. They had been Dawn's entire world, and Therese wished she had told her mum more often that she had meant the world to her too.

Therese knew that her mum understood how much she was loved, but her death had been so sudden and so final that there were many things she would never have the chance to say.

Rada stayed with Therese after the funeral to support her. With her help, they cleaned out her mum's home and the remains of a life she had put on hold because her daughter had needed her.

Therese spent weeks after her funeral quietly reflecting on the woman who had spent the latter years of her marriage in the shadow of a controlling, dominating husband who had never been happy in the relationship.

After her parents' separation, her mum had finally blossomed into the person she wanted to be – and now that he was happy, her father had too.

Therese's mum possessed a quiet strength that had flourished with her newfound independence. After her separation, Dawn achieved all the things she had only ever dreamed of in her marriage.

She had learned to swim, taken a mechanic's course, so she could fix her own car, and she had joined a creative writing course. Dawn had taught Therese what it meant to be strong. After her death, Therese realised she had been the glue that held their family together.

When she hit rock bottom, Dawn had been there to pick her up and show her the way out of the darkness. Therese's new face was a legacy of her mother's infinite love, and her life would not be the same without her.

But for her mother's love for her – and Therese's love for her own children – her name might well have been added to the other 202 casualties who had lost their lives in Bali.

Fortunately, her mother had lived long enough to see the perpetrators of the bomb blasts that had caused her such heartache finally brought to justice.

When the media called asking for Therese's reaction to the terrorists' sentences, she told them she had never sought revenge. No punishment would ever change what had happened to her, or to her friend Bronwyn – or any of the other innocent people the terrorists had killed and maimed. She had no room in her recovery for blame, or forgiveness. Her mother had just died, and she felt numb.

Chapter 23

After the original trial and the convictions in 2003, Therese had felt that a life sentence had been the appropriate punishment for the trio. She wanted them to suffer for the rest of their lives, just as she and the other victims had.

But from discussions she'd had with people who worked in the justice system, she feared they posed an even greater threat in prison, where they might be revered for their foul deeds. More than that, she feared that in prison they would have the influence to radicalise other devotees with their extreme fundamentalist Islamic views.

Her fears were not unfounded. A month before her mother's death and his own execution, Amrozi, the 'smiling assassin', issued a chilling warning to the Western world, promising that his friends would avenge their deaths.

His blatant threat confirmed Therese's belief that a death sentence was the only deterrent the courts could serve to discourage other extremist fanatics from doing it all again.

But John Howard had been right, she concluded. These hateful people had not won. Despite the scars and hideous injuries, they had not crushed the Australian spirit and Therese owed it to herself and her mum to live the best life she possibly could.

She had grown tired of being at home on a disability pension. She did not want to be 'disabled' by her injuries – or defined by what had happened to her. She owed it to herself, and to her mum, to move forward and keep proving everyone wrong.

* * *

A year after her mum's death, she applied for a job in an aged care home in Lara. The time was right now, she told herself after the interview. She was right. The nursing home rang to tell her the job was hers.

In 2009, seven long years after the Bali bombings, the woman who was told she would never drive, never wear make-up, never return to nursing and never live independently defied the odds again.

She touched up her make-up, dropped her children off at school, and drove herself to her new workplace to start a new chapter in her working life that would have made her mother proud.

No-one knew Therese, or anything about her inspirational battle to overcome the most impossible odds, and that's how she wanted it.

She slipped her nurse's uniform over her scars and left the 'miracle woman of Bali' behind, ready to redefine herself in her new workplace as a qualified, competent and professional state-enrolled nurse. It gave Therese great satisfaction to know she had been employed for who she was and what she could do – not for what had happened to her. At work, she was just another new face in the tea-room. And she loved it.

Therese returned to full-time nursing with new knowledge that none of her training courses had been able to teach her. It came from her time spent as a hospital patient.

She knew how it felt to be needy and helpless – to be infirm and disabled. As a patient, she had spent so long trapped underneath those bandages that she understood what it meant to lose all sense of who you really are.

The elderly people she now nursed had once been young, capable, active and busy people. They had been parents and teachers, bank managers, police officers and CEOs. They had run farms and businesses and they had raised families.

As far as she was concerned, they were all of those things *and* they were her patients.

Therese had been settling into her new life as a full-time working mother when her father's health began to decline too. Her dad, who was several years younger than her mum, had also grown after the marriage had ended.

Chris Fox had always been a ladies' man, and it had caused her mother great pain during their marriage. After they separated, he'd had a string of failed relationships, and by the time Therese left the Alfred Hospital, he had become involved with yet another younger woman who had children the same age as his grandchildren. Yet, for all his flaws, he was still Therese's dad and she loved him regardless.

Sadly, Chris' smoking and drinking lifestyle had not helped his diagnosis with coronary pulmonary obstructive airways disease, and when his health began to fail in 2011, Therese made constant trips back to Queensland to care for him, the way he had once cared for her.

Sadly, Chris Fox passed away in July 2012, three months before the tenth anniversary of the Bali bombings.

Although Therese found no comfort in memorials, or anniversaries, or plaques or prayers, she sat at home as she always did on 12 October, and raised a glass to her friend.

But Bronwyn's family found comfort in returning to Kuta and made the pilgrimage back to Bali for the tenth anniversary, to say prayers, lay wreaths and remember. Jenny's three boys had all wanted to go, along with Jess and her new husband, Adam, who she had married in May.

Rada also decided to make the journey back, to support Pauline Whitton and Jodi Wallace's mum, the grieving mothers she had met in the days after the terrorist attack when they had flown to Bali to bring their daughters, back.

She lit candles and said prayers for Bronwyn, Charmaine, Jodi and all the other victims - and for her own son, Matthew, who she missed every day.

Time had not healed the wounds for these families, and the executions of the perpetrators had brought them no satisfaction and no peace.

Rada understood their pain. After years of fighting for answers surrounding her own son's death, it had been deemed an accident and not the neglect she had claimed it was. And though she had been awarded compensation, there had been no answers or closure for Rada, only an enduring grief.

Therese did not believe there was any such thing as closure. As far as Therese was concerned it was a term used by those who are fortunate enough never to have walked in their shoes, and trivialised the suffering of victims of violent crimes such as these. For survivors like Therese, there are two lives – the one before, and the other after the event, when nothing is the same again.

For Bronwyn's family, the trip back to Bali was very different to their mother's previous trip before the first anniversary. Ten years later, they found it cathartic visiting the sacred site which marks the spot where Bronwyn and so many others had died.

For Jenny and her family, the tenth anniversary was a time of reflection and acceptance. And a time for moving on. In October 2012, for the first time, they glimpsed the beauty that Bronwyn had seen. It was no longer the cruel country that had taken Jenny's daughter away from her. They loved the place and its peaceful, friendly people, and it was time to let go.

Chapter 23

After visiting the memorial, Jenny had walked down the road, arm in arm with Jess, reflecting.

'We don't need to come back here anymore,' she told Jess. 'I know now that Bronwyn would have been happy here – we can say goodbye.'

But her son Phil was not ready to say goodbye to Bali.

Three days earlier, on 9 October, he had celebrated his 33rd birthday with his brothers and Jess' new husband in a local German sports bar, where a beautiful Balinese girl had caught his attention.

She was celebrating her birthday that day too, and invited the boys to her birthday party. Though his family had thought nothing of the chance encounter, their tenth anniversary visit was about to change all their lives.

By the time they left, Phil had found another reason to come back to Bali.

But Therese, back at home in Grovedale, could not think of a single one.

Chapter 24

UNFINISHED
BUSINESS

The fine vertical scars that thread like string down the insides of Therese Fox's arms and legs are barely visible today among the fading burns which cover her body.

These scars are not the injuries spawned by hatred that were branded onto her skin during the terrorist attack in Kuta in 2002.

They are the surgical scars that were made by army doctors as Therese fought for her life on the Hercules before she was evacuated from Denpasar in October 2002.

Twenty years later, the scars are a legacy of an extraordinary battle for survival – and a haunting reminder of the courage and determination that brought a young Australian mother home to her children.

Today, they stand out among the random patchwork of skin grafts and burns to tell a story that defies belief and shines a light on the power of the human spirit.

Chapter 24

Two years ago, Therese made the decision to embrace her most unsightly scar – one which ran down her left leg from her knee to her ankle – where the explosion at Paddy's bar had scorched through layers of skin and destroyed the muscle.

She chose to turn it into a work of art by having a giant tattoo of pink roses etched over it so that every time she noticed it, her tattoo would be a reminder that she had reclaimed ownership over her badly scarred body and taken control of her life.

Therese's tattoo is an emblem of victory -her message to the world that hatred has not beaten her.

Among the many positive postings applauding Therese's boldness on her Facebook page, she received other private messages asking her why she had chosen to hide a scar which told the story of her life and had become a part of who she was.

She told them this: her scars are *not* who she is but are merely a record of something that once happened to her, in another place and at another time. She does not want to be defined by them or become a prisoner of her past. Her scars are simply evidence of what had been done *to* her 20 years ago. But they are not her.

Twenty years is a lifetime. In 20 years, babies are born and become adults, lovers exchange marriage vows and others call it a day. Those who have passed are mourned by families who loved them; people have swapped countries, changed jobs … Life goes on.

Thanks to the doctors and the generosity of complete strangers, Therese Fox has had the opportunity to experience most of those things.

Her second chance has allowed her to watch her children grow up into kind, compassionate adults. To grieve the deaths of her parents, to buy her first home. In 20 years she has returned to work, found a new job that she loves, and continues to defy the odds every single day by living a productive, independent life.

Therese has seen her daughter, Katie – now 27 – follow her into nursing. She has lived through the global pandemic that has killed millions and sent the world into lockdown.

During two years of lockdowns in Australia, at a time when Victorian hospitals were on 'Code Brown' and all holiday leave had been cancelled for essential health workers, mother and daughter worked long shifts – Katie as a pathology nurse, and Therese in a small country hospital where she is still an aged care nurse.

And during those 20 years, Therese has become a grandmother for the first time.

On 24 April 2015, she celebrated the birth of her first grandchild, Flynn. Therese and her former partner, David, were at the Geelong Hospital with Katie's partner, Tom, to hear new life emerging from the operating theatre where her grandson was delivered by caesarean section.

Her newborn grandson's first cries were a defining moment for Therese, who has embraced a new joy that 20 years ago was impossible for her to imagine she would ever experience again.

At seven, Flynn is now the same age his mother was when Therese left on her ill-fated holiday to Bali. His proud grandmother adores him, and says he has added a new layer of love to her life and has enriched it in ways she never dreamed possible.

Flynn continues to light up Therese's world in the same way her own children do, and she has found new purpose in her new role as his grandmother.

Many things have happened since 12 October 2002, and in that time, I have seen Therese Fox literally rise from the ashes of Bali to fulfil John Howard's prediction that the Australian spirit could not be broken by bombs or crushed by the threat of terrorism.

Before this book went to print, I emailed Mr Howard's office, to ask him if he remembered Therese Fox, and to let him know that 20 years later she was moving on and had asked me to write a book about her extraordinary journey of recovery.

The former Prime Minister's reply was instantaneous. He told me he remembered Therese and that her courage was amazing.

'The courage displayed by Therese Fox after the terrible injuries she suffered in the terrorist attack on Paddy's Irish Bar in Bali is inspirational,' Mr Howard said in his response to me.

'It is an heroic example of the best of the Australian spirit. The unimaginable pain she endured over such a long period was driven by the love she had for her children and others. It should humble us all.'

Mr Howard is right. Therese's story is incredibly humbling. It is why so many of the survivors have agreed to speak to me about her, paying tribute to her astonishing bravery and unshakeable will to survive – thrilled to hear that she refused to let terrorism destroy her.

Sadly, the scars of Bali run deep. Although her injuries have slowly faded over the past two decades, Therese still struggles with the survivor guilt that has dogged her since 2002, and the loss of the people who are missing from her life.

The strain of surviving the blast trauma generated by the suiciding bombing at Paddy's bar has left Therese with impaired hearing and damage to her heart. She still needs an operation on one of the elbows that was calcified in the heat of the inferno, and the psychological trauma of the Bali bombings continues to affect her.

It is the reason she begins her day at 4am – to prepare herself mentally and physically for the hours ahead, which begins with her hospital shift at 7am.

But nursing is a job that she loves as much as the colleagues who have embraced her for who she is today, without needing to know about her past or the road that she has travelled.

In December, the miracle survivor who celebrated her 30th birthday in a body suit and pressure bandages at Concord's ICU is turning 50.

And she wants to embrace this new chapter in her life by doing something she vowed she would never do. She wants to return to Bali to finish what she began all those years ago, in another time when she was someone else.

The decision is a 360-degree turnaround for Therese, who has not travelled overseas since her evacuation from Bali in 2002 on an army plane when she was not expected to survive the journey home.

After everything that happened to her back then, the thought of travelling outside Australia is one that has been too terrifying to contemplate.

'I didn't know how I would cope with it, even if I had found the strength to do it – and I did not want to put my family through that when they have been through enough,' she says.

And yet, before Bali, she had always yearned for adventure. She had wanted to see the world and it had been a dream which originally took flight when she headed off to Bali with her friend Bronwyn all those years ago. It was a dream that, until now, had died there.

But in 2022, as she approached 50, it occurred to her that her life was slowly passing by, and that there were things she wanted to do while she was young and able.

Her long-time friend Michelle Fogarty suggested it was an adventure they should do together. Their children had grown up now, and the only thing stopping Therese – apart from Covid – was herself!

It became another challenge for her to overcome.

Where would they start? they asked themselves.

'Back at the beginning,' said Therese.

In 2022, 12 October marks the twentieth anniversary of the Bali bombings, and Therese has decided to return to Kuta to visit the memorial she has never seen and pay her respects to Bronwyn and the other 201 victims who lost their lives that tragic night.

She wants to complete the holiday that she and Bronwyn never had the chance to finish by visiting Ubud, the mountain resort where they had been intending to stay at a health spa.

And she wants to see the vacant lot where the Sari Club once stood, which in February 2022 its Indonesian owner agreed to sell for the construction of a peace park as a living memorial to the victims who lost their lives twenty years ago. The land under negotiation is smaller than the 700 square metres that the nightclub originally occupied, but designs have been drawn up to create a tropical garden there.

'Bali is unfinished business for me,' explains Therese. 'I am older now, and for me to be able to move on and visit other places in the world, it felt important for me to be able to go back to where it all began and complete the holiday I never had the chance to finish.'

This time, Therese will be making the trip with her two children, her son-in-law and grandson and her best friend, Michelle, and her teenage daughter, Lucy. She hopes it will be a trip that will allow her to confront her demons, lay old ghosts to rest, and remember the friend who did not make it home.

It is a trip that thrills her and terrifies her, but one she feels it is time for her to make.

'Bali affected all our lives in so many ways,' says Therese. 'It affected my entire family – it took my parents' lives too soon.'

She sees its lasting impact on the life of her grown-up daughter, who still suffers from separation anxiety. And she sees it in her son's reluctance to even talk about what happened to her on that ill-fated holiday.

'Alex is now 29 – the same age I was when I went to Bali,' she says.

'And all these years later, he still can't talk about it – it's heartbreaking.'

'It also breaks my heart that Katie still panics when anyone she loves leaves her alone – even if they are only leaving the room for five minutes – or happen to be running late,' explains Therese.

'Who can blame her? I went on a holiday promising I would see them soon, and didn't come back for a whole year!'

For all these reasons, Therese believes it is important that they go together as a family, so that they can make new memories that will allow them all to move on.

Therese intends to visit the Bali Bombing Memorial in Kuta, but she has no plans to stay in the beachside resort where she and Bronwyn once stayed. It is a place that holds too many painful memories for her. Instead, she has booked to stay in Seminyak – where 20 years ago, she and Bronwyn watched the sunset from the beach on what was then, an idyllic dream holiday.

It is a sentiment that her friend Cath Byrne shares, and which Rada van der Werff understands. Bali remained unfinished business for them too, and in the years since they have each made their own separate pilgrimages back to Kuta to revisit the painful memories and give themselves a different experience of the peaceful pretty island, which, in 2002, they did not have the chance to see for themselves.

When Rada returned for the first anniversary she stayed at the Masa Inn but Cath, who visited a few years later, did not. She briefly walked past the hotel but did not venture inside. Instead, she remained on the footpath, staring into the lobby where Therese had first walked into their lives all those years ago.

On their return visits, both women visited Ubud independently to complete the holiday they had not been able to finish in the aftermath of the terrorist attacks. They came away with better memories of a very different Bali than the one they had seen after the bombings.

Cath had been working in Germany on the first anniversary when Rada made the journey back for the memorial service and an emotional reunion with Pauline Whitton, whose daughter, Charmaine, had lost her life in the Sari Club.

There had been many faces at the service that Rada remembered from those distressing meetings at the Hard

Rock Café in the dark days after the bombings. It had been a sorrowful time for everyone.

In 2012 when Rada returned to Bali for the tenth memorial service, Pauline Whitton was there again, and this time they stayed in Nusa Dua. Time had marched on, but it had not healed the pain for parents like Pauline, who had lost children they had loved.

For Rada, the trip had been cathartic. The experience and insight she had gained from her voluntary work supporting the shattered families in the aftermath of the Bali bombings had led her into a new role in disaster relief.

During the Australian summer of 2010-2011 the compassionate mother had helped to support families through the Queensland floods and had become an outreach worker for the Red Cross -supporting families during times of disaster, hardship and emergency.

In the years ahead, Rada's philanthropic work would see her undertaking voluntary work with a refugee support group in Brisbane, as a visitor to the Pinkenba Immigration Transit Accommodation facility supporting refugee families in Australia.

Cath's trip back to Bali had also been peaceful and healing. She loved the scenery and its people and caught up with Danielle, their generous French host who had opened her home to them. Philippe had since moved to French Polynesia, but Danielle and Cath had enjoyed a quiet meal where they reflected on the heartache they had seen and the people they had met.

She had visited the site where Paddy's Irish Bar and the Sari Club had once stood. Standing outside, Cath could still picture the scenes that Rodney Cocks had witnessed when he rescued Therese from the 'Gates to Hell'. It would be years before she could banish the images of the charred outstretched hands in the back of the van leaving the kill zone for the morgue.

Before Cath left Bali, she called in at the Prima Medika Private Hospital to reunite with the doctors who had helped to save Therese's life. They posed for more photographs for Cath to share with a patient they had never expected to survive. They had been very happy to know that she had.

Cath left Bali with such positive memories that she later returned a second time, intending to buy an investment property on another part of the island. In the end, she bought a villa in Tuscany with her brother.

After her own visit to Bali for the tenth anniversary in 2012, Jenny Hobbs also had unfinished business in Bali, though she did not know it at the time.

In August 2016, her son, Phil, married the Balinese girl he had met on the tenth anniversary visit. They exchanged vows in a small low-key ceremony in Bali, surrounded by their families - and again in Australia with the rest of their family and friends.

But Jess, who was pregnant with her second child at the time, was forced to cut her trip to Bali short because her doctors in Victoria were concerned about the Zika virus, which was rampant in Indonesia in 2016.

By 2017, Jess had given her mother two beautiful granddaughter, Adele and Odette and her brother, Jason, had given her two grandchildren and would soon give her another. Three years later, Jenny was a grandmother again when Phil and his wife, Acok, welcomed a son, Noah.

Now, the couple who met on their birthdays on 9 October 2012 are expecting another child on the very same day. Their baby daughter is due on 9 October 2022 – three days before the anniversary of Bronwyn's death.

'I truly believe that Acok and the children are Bronwyn's gift to us – to help our family to heal,' says Jenny.

'Through Bronwyn's death, I have a beautiful Balinese daughter-in-law, a little grandson and by the twentieth anniversary, I will have a granddaughter too.

'It makes you look at the silver lining, as Bronwyn always did. Because if this had never happened, we would never have travelled to Bali and Phil and Acok would not have met – and I would not have all these wonderful things in my life.'

Theirs is not the only family to have found joy among the ashes of Bali. Justin and Aaron Lee's brother Randall later married Sari Club survivor, Jessica O'Grady, who he met in the aftermath of the bombings that claimed his two brothers and his pregnant sister-in-law. He had not been with them on their holiday in 2002 because he had been saving his money to go to South America. But out of the loss, he has found love.

'Bali changed everything for so many people,' says Therese.

'And it wasn't all bad. It has made me a better person – a stronger person. I don't wish any more that it hadn't happened – and I don't ask myself "why me?" as I used to. What happened in 2002 has made me who I am today.

'I can look at myself in the mirror now and not hate what I see, although the survivor guilt remains and there hasn't been a day since that I have not thought about Bronwyn and wondered how I made it out and she didn't.'

It is a question so many others continue to ask themselves. If Rodney Cocks had not left Paddy's to do his banking, he might have been injured with his friends, or not made it out at all. He is now married with children and running his own business.

Why did Carren Smith survive, when her friends Charmaine Whitton and Jodi Wallace perished? Why did Brendan Barry survive the car blast in the 'kill zone' outside the Sari Club when his friend Jodie Carns, 35, did not?

What would have happened if the injured Australian casualty at the Sanglah General Hospital had not noticed the sheet moving on Ben Tullipan's face and alerted the doctors?

And why did Michelle Larkins' job spare her the same fate as her friends, so she had been able to raise her family and become the proud grandmother of a brood of grandchildren?

Tragically, these are the sorts of questions that Therese believes you would drive yourself crazy asking.

'You have to stop asking why, or it would destroy you,' she says.

It is the reason why, 20 years on, there is no room in Therese's life to think about the people responsible for the heinous events that destroyed so many lives.

* * *

Therese refused to watch the trials that went on for years, and the appeals that followed. She had not wanted to know about the executions, she had been too busy trying to survive.

'Whether the terrorists lived or died would not change anything or undo what had been done. And while I don't agree with the death penalty, I felt the sentence was the only punishment that would stop the terrorists from being revered in prison and from indoctrinating others with their hatred,' she says.

It is a sentiment shared by Bronwyn's mother Jenny.

'My children and I came to the decision that we didn't need to fill our thoughts with negativity but needed to support each other to recover in the best way we could,' she says.

'If Bronwyn could see us, I wanted her to see that we weren't broken and would look after each other.'

Jenny recalls how, many years ago, she heard a story about a woman who had forgiven her daughter's killer. Although she could not understand the philosophy behind it then, after Bronwyn's death she understood.

'These people had already taken one child, but they were not going to dictate our lives going forward. I didn't want us to live the rest of our lives carrying hatred and revenge. And while I can't say I forgive the organisers of the bombings, I wanted them to be put where they could never spread their hateful ways to anyone else,' she says.

'But their deaths brought no sense of justice or closure to me ... they were just more lives taken. I felt guilty about these thoughts – I felt I was letting Bron down and all the others who had been killed or wounded.'

However, Therese and Jenny had also been concerned that the alternative – a term of imprisonment – could mean the terrorists having their sentences reduced once the public spotlight had faded.

This is what happened in the case of Abu Bakar Bashir, the Islamic extremist who was found guilty of conspiracy over the Bali bombings, a charge he consistently denied. He was jailed in 2005 but his conviction was later overturned on appeal.

But while anti-terrorist experts said there was no evidence that Bashir, 82, played an operational role in the attacks – or had been involved in seeking funding for them – as the spiritual head of the organisation he had been in a position to stop the bombings and had not done so.

In 2006, Bashir was released from an Indonesian prison after having his sentence shortened, a decision that the then Prime Minister, John Howard, said Australians found very disappointing.

Bashir had been jailed again in 2011, for 15 years, after being convicted of supporting militant training camps in the Indonesian province of Aceh. He was released in January 2021 for good behaviour after serving 10 years of his sentence.

Other key suspects have escaped justice after being killed by Indonesian police before they could be arrested. These included Malaysian bomb expert, Dr Azahari bin Husin, the author of the JL bomb manual.

Azahari, 48, was killed when police raided his hideout in Malang, East Java in 2005. Believed to be the intellectual mastermind behind the Bali bombings, Azahari had a Phd in maths and engineering from Reading University in the UK. He was nicknamed Demolition Man by devotees of the splinter terrorist cell and is alleged to have assembled the Bali bombs.

And fellow bomb-maker Noordin Mohammad Top, was also killed in a police raid in 2009. The Malaysian-born terrorist was one of four extremists killed by Indonesian police during a swoop a militant hideout near Solo in Central Java. Top had been on the run for seven years and was Indonesia's most wanted Islamist militant extremist.

Six months later, Dulmatin – the most wanted terrorist in Southeast Asia – was killed by Indonesian police during a raid at an internet café in Jakarta. The US States' Rewards for Justice Program had placed a 10million US dollar bounty on his head. Dulmatin was wanted for helping to organize the Bali bombings and a string of other terrorist attacks across Indonesia.

In January 2022, another Islamic extremist, Aris Sumarsono, 58 (also known as Zulkarnaen), appeared at the East Jakarta District Court after eluding capture for 18 years. He was jailed for 15 years after being convicted of harbouring some of the other suspects in the Bali bombings, including one of the bomb-makers.

Meanwhile JI's military figurehead, Riduan Isamuddin (Hambali) – once described by President George W Bush as one of the world's 'most lethal terrorists' – remains in Guantanamo Bay, Cuba, awaiting trial.

* * *

Twenty years on, Therese refuses to think about the perpetrators who caused her and so many other survivors and victims' families such suffering.

She has come full circle and it is time for her to move on.

And she has found some comfort during the writing of this book. It is only recently that she learned that her friend didn't suffer and was not left alone to die in the ashes at Paddy's bar that night. Now she knows that Bronwyn died instantly.

'For the past 20 years I have lived with the thought that Bronwyn had been left alone in the rubble, suffering. And that she had been left there for ages without being identified. I know now that was not the case and that is very comforting to me,' she says.

This year, as her fiftieth birthday approaches, Therese is bracing herself for the pilgrimage that is her rite of passage to a new future. She intends to be there with her children, to light a candle for her friend and remember the good times they had in Bali.

'I'm getting older now, and who knows what the future holds? But I don't want to get to the end of my life with regrets. I don't want to look back and wish I had done things when it's too late.

'I'm lucky to be here and it is important to me to make every minute count. And it needs to start in Bali, so I can finally close that chapter of my life and start a new one.'

31 May 2022

ACKNOWLEDGEMENTS

Therese Fox acknowledgements

I have many people to thank for supporting me on this painful journey, particularly my two children, Alex and Katie who grew up with the spectre of Bali and adjusted to the disruption and heartache without complaint. Without your love I would not be here today.

It broke my heart to read about the anguish you suffered when I was fighting for my life in Concord Hospital. The Bali bombings changed all our lives, but you gave me a reason to keep on living when life felt too hard. Being around to watch you grow up has been worth all the suffering.

To my beautiful grandson, Flynn, who has enriched my life in so many ways and reminds me daily to count my blessings and make the most of this second chance I have been given.

Thanks too to my former partner, David Dorling, for providing a stable and normalising influence on Alex and Katie's lives and doing everything in your power to initiate the ongoing relationship between us when times were tough. You did a fantastic job - and I will always be grateful to you.

I want to thank my best friend, Michelle Fogarty, for always being there for me and for supporting me on my return to Bali for the twentieth anniversary in October. Your friendship means everything to me.

Thankyou also to all the friends and supporters in my local community of Geelong and Grovedale, who rallied around me - raising money and supporting my family to make the road we travelled at little easier to bear.

I especially want to thank my two special guardian angels - Rada Van Der Werff and Cath Byrne – who saved my life in the dark hours after the bombings and have supported my recovery ever since.

You showed me the best of humanity after I had been unfortunate to have glimpsed the worst in mankind. If one good thing came out of that awful night on 12th October 2002, it was you. I will be forever grateful for having you in my life and cannot thank you enough for your contribution to this book.

A very big thankyou to Bronwyn's beautiful family for sharing your own heartbreaking journey. Out of the Ashes was always intended to be a story of two young women, and this book is as much Bronwyn's and your family's story as it is mine. Thank you for helping me to tell it so that we could give a voice to Bronwyn and all the other survivors who did not make it home.

And last, but not least a big thank you to journalist and author Megan Norris – for all the hours you spent researching and writing. It is a book that has brought tears to my eyes and will be my legacy to my family in the years ahead. I trusted you to take care of me and tell my painful story sensitively and honestly, and you have.

Through your research I have learned many new things about my journey that I did not know before. For almost twenty years

I lived with the fear and guilt that Bronwyn had died alone and suffering. I cannot tell you what a comfort it has been to discover that this was not true. Thank you.

Megan Norris acknowledgements.

My sincere thanks to Therese for entrusting me with this remarkable story of survival, and for her unshakeable belief that I would do it justice. It is an honour to be asked to write such an inspirational book. It was my hope when I began that I might be able to offer some insight into the destruction caused by this deliberately targeted act of terrorism and generate understanding about the lasting impact it has had on the lives of ordinary people, their families and their communities.

I hope this book is one you will be proud of in years to come.

A big thankyou to Katie for giving her time so graciously and re-living a very painful chapter in her childhood. And to Alex, who despite finding it very difficult to revisit that part of his life, has told me enough over the years to allow a clear understanding of the deep trauma that violent crimes like these have on extended family – particularly young children.

A heartfelt thank you to Bronwyn's lovely mum, Jenny Hobbs, her daughter, Jess Barnard, and Jenny's sister, Elizabeth (Libby) Rogers, for sharing their tragic loss and the enduring impact that this malevolent act of terrorism had on their family's lives.

Your contribution to Therese's story has been invaluable. It has given Bronwyn a voice and helped to ensure that the enduring loss that families like yours live with every day is understood and acknowledged.

Acknowledgemnets

Therese gave me a clear directive when we embarked on this project that this book should not be her story alone – but the story of her beautiful friend who tragically, never made it home. You gave your time so generously and this story is as much Bronwyn's as Therese's and the book is richer for it.

Our sincere appreciation to Therese's good friends – Cath Byrne and Rada van der Werff whose generosity and patience knows no bounds. To Cath for driving to the Gold Coast to spend an impossibly hot day sharing her journals, photographs and recollections of those terrible hours with Therese after the bombings.

Thanks also to Rada who welcomed me into her home and trusted me with her precious photo albums and the diary entries which capture a tragic chapter in Australian contemporary history. Without Cath and Rada's meticulous records of Therese's astonishing story of survival and Bronwyn's family's journey through loss and grief, Out of the Ashes would not be the book that it is.

Your patience through the gruelling fact-checking and editing process has been endless, and your contribution invaluable. Your stories are part of the bigger story of Therese's journey back from hell.

Thankyou Michelle Larkins – one of the three musketeers – for so generously reflecting on the friend you lost and the other whose battle to survive broke your heart.

Thanks also to Katie and Alex's dad, David, for shedding valuable insight into the shattering impact that dreadful events such as these have on the lives of young children. Their reaction to the news of their mother's injuries and the psychological support they required during her time in hospital, has generated a new understanding about the impact of trauma on young children.

Therese and I would both like to thank those survivors who took the trouble to speak with me about their own experiences during and after the Bali bombings -particularly burns survivors, Jason McCartney, Melinda Kemp and Carren Smith who shared their own stories with me.

A big shout out to former UN soldier Rodney Cocks for graciously filling in some of the gaps in Therese's story and helping me piece together the missing pieces of a jigsaw puzzle she was too injured to recall.

My appreciation to Heather Cleland, Director of the Burns Unit at Melbourne's Alfred Hospital for helping me understand the complex injuries that the Bali burns survivors battled, and for translating complicated medical lingo into simple language.

Thankyou too, to Denny Neave and the fabulous team at Big Sky Publishing for embracing this inspirational book and for believing that Therese's story was one that needed to be told.

My love and thanks to my husband Steve, for his eternal patience as I spent holiday weekends and countless late nights typing on my laptop on my rattly old ironing board. Although my brief for this book reduced you to tears, it has such an uplifting ending that I hope this is one you will read.

Thanks to all my friends who have supported me, particularly my good friend and fellow Big Sky author, Emily Webb, and our mutual friend - broadcast journalist and author - Justin Smith. You both believed in this book. Thankyou.

To Kim Ring, the bossiest friend and best motivator I know

for ringing me every day to check my word count and reminding me to stay focussed.

And finally, Therese and I want to express our sincerest gratitude to former Australian Prime Minister, the Hon John Howard, who was kind enough to respond to my email about this book, and generously share his own thoughts on Therese Fox's amazing story of survival.

Mr Howard supported Therese and her family during a very dark chapter in their lives - not just as the leader of this great nation - but as a concerned and compassionate Australian. He has magnanimously sent her words of support again after hearing about this book. Our sincerest thanks and appreciation.

SOURCE NOTES

I n the twenty years since the ugly spectre of terrorism first cast its dark shadow on Australia's consciousness, hundreds of articles and dozens of books have been written on the Bali bombings.

Some of them are investigative literary offerings, others are the inspirational first-hand accounts of those who either survived the atrocity or witnessed it unfolding.

But it has taken two decades of surgeries, skin grafts and physical and psychological healing for Australian burns survivor, Therese Fox to feel strong enough to revisit that dark chapter of her life to tell the extraordinary story surrounding her journey back to recovery.

I first met Therese Fox on a crisp Melbourne afternoon in May 2003 – seven months after the terrorist attacks which left Australia contemplating its own place in the world and its belief that it was a safe and lucky country.

The meeting had taken place on Mother's Day - a milestone that Therese's family had not expected her to survive to see – and she had been spending it with her two children, Alex, 9 and Katie, 7, and her own mother, Dawn.

At the time, Therese was staying in a motel unit over the road from the Alfred Hospital where she was still being treated for her burns, long after the other Bali survivors had been discharged.

When we met, she had still been wearing her full pressure body suit and bandages and was battling with her badly burnt hands to tie a ribbon in Katie's hair. Her late mother, Dawn, offered to do the simple task for her, but Therese had been adamant that this was something she wanted to do for herself.

After being to hell and back, it was her chance to feel like a mum again - and another step towards reclaiming a life that had been stolen from her. She told me then, that all she wanted to do was embrace the mundane chores that other mother's take for granted and frequently grizzle about.

Despite the cheeriness of the brightly coloured balloons and bouquets of fresh flowers, there was a prevailing air of grief in the room that afternoon and it followed me out to the car where I spent a few moments reflecting on the most injured person I had ever interviewed.

In my career, I have written countless stories on survivors of freak accidents and natural disasters like bush fires, tsunami's and floods. I have written even more about deliberate acts of malicious targeted violence where women and children have been set on fire or deliberately disfigured and maimed.

But until I met Therese, I had never interviewed anyone who had been blown up by a bomb before.

Afterwards, I pondered on what Therese had told me: that she would never lead an independent life again, or care for her children, or return to her work as a nurse, or drive a car. And I wondered what the future held for her.

It was a meeting that Therese was so ill and morphine-affected that she only vaguely recalls it. But for me, it was one I will never forget.

In the years since, our paths have crossed many times. I covered her first Christmas at home after Bali, various anniversaries of the bombings, and her return to a new kind of normal where she has embraced her second chance and raised her family.

Therese Fox has a ferocious strength and determination that belies her reserved and quiet exterior.

As her mother once told me, she is a force to be reckoned with and while she detests the tag – she truly is a miracle. So it has been a great privilege for me to have been entrusted with the task of telling her story – which is one of great courage, inspiration and ultimately hope.

In writing this book, I have revisited many of the stories that I have had the pleasure to write about Therese over the years. I have dug out some of my old shorthand notes which record past discussions with Therese and her late mum, and the brief conversations I have had with her twin brother, Damien and her children, Alex and Katie. My old stories are a haunting reminder of just how far she has come in twenty years, and how painful the road to recovery has been.

At a time when Covid restrictions have impeded travel, I have supplemented these notes with hours of telephone interviews with Therese and her family, and with her former partner David. I have also relied on lengthy zoom interviews with Bronwyn's family and had numerous discussions with Therese's friend, Michelle Larkins, and a number of other burns survivors including Jason McCartney, Carren Smith and Melinda Kemp as well as burns expert, Heather

Cleland and former soldier, Rodney Cocks, who rescued Therese from the carnage in Legian Jalan on 12 October 2002.

Rodney has also written a book called Bali to Baghdad and beyond, published by Penguin Books, which describes his own experience of suicide bombers and his encounter with Therese on that fateful night in 2002. It is a great read.

Fortunately, because we live in Queensland, I have had the wonderful opportunity of conducting lengthy face to face interviews with Cath Byrne and Rada van der Werff, as well as following them up with phone interviews.

Their meticulous record keeping and journal entries and photographs capture a tragic moment in Australian contemporary history – and the inspirational journey of a remarkable woman who continues to amaze everyone.

Out of the Ashes is based on these insightful interviews and journal entries and has been supported with existing material as shared by Therese's mum. I have also gleaned some very helpful information on the critical situation in the BIMC and at Prima Medika Private Hospital from emails sent on Therese's behalf to these hospitals, and on emails between Cath and Therese during her recovery.

Incredibly, so many stories and journeys intertwine with Therese's story and I have attempted to reflect this as I wrote. They are all valuable pieces of a bigger, richer jigsaw puzzle which slot into one another as the different players in the story crossed Therese's path.

Apart from the detailed first-hand accounts I have been given, I have relied on a wealth of research material as I delved into the activities of the terrorists responsible for the bombings to paint a clear picture of what they were doing both before, and after the attacks.

I have also relied on media reports and government archives to create a picture of the dangerous climate that prevailed in south-east Asia in the years leading up to the attacks.

This tragic moment in Australia's modern history was very well covered at the time, and in the years afterwards and for this reason I have had a multitude of valuable online sources and media reports at my disposal. I have also followed up lines of inquiry with various Australian hospitals and the Australia Defence Forces to obtain a clearer picture and have trawled their websites.

Among the online media reports that cover the bombings, its aftermath, the victims and survivor stories and the various anniversaries that followed, I have gleaned a great deal of invaluable information from the following:

Melbourne Herald Sun journalist, Keith Moor's revealing and comprehensive reconstruction of the terrorist plot which was extremely helpful for painting a background to the attacks on Kuta in chapter 2: -https://www.heraldsun.com.au/news/law-order/insight-editor-keith-moor-reconstructs-the-story-behind-the-2002-bali-bombing/news-story

Journalist, Patrick Carlyon's tenth anniversary story which ran in the Australian on 11 October 2012 entitled; *Bali Memorial: Sacred place of ghosts and eternal spirit.* https://www.news.com.au/national/kutas-pulse-barely-slowed-for-tribute/news-story/

The Daily Telegraph's special features report, Saturday 19 October 2002 – *Nineteen Million Mates* by Zoe Taylor and Graham Farr; Terror on Our Doorstep – Simple Cross bears the love and loss of so many families by Michelle Cazzulino and Peter Lalor

Daily Telegraph 19 October 2002 *Gaurdian Angels who wouldn't leave Lynley.*

The Sunday Telegraph, 20 October 2002 *Tears of a Nation* special coverage features by staff writers.

The Sydney Morning Herald's Bali Remembered special photo-feature – *Australia's roll call of young lives lost* – by various staffers.

The Sun-Herald 20 October 2002, *Australians Together,* coverage of the National Day of Morning including multiple features by staff writers.

Sydney Morning Herald 13 October 2002 -*Seven Australians Identified among the dead*

Kate Lamb's comprehensive coverage entitled Remembering the bombing victims on its 10th anniversary on October 12 2012 https://www.voanews.com/a/bali-bombing-victims-remembered-on-10th-anniversary-of-attack

In exploring the background to Indonesia's and Australia's response to the Bali bombings I found these links very informative, particularly the activation of the aeromedical evacuation. See the following:

How we handled a crisis that shook the nation. https://www.nma.gov.au/defining-moments/resources/bali-bombings this illustrates the round the clock response from the AFP see http://www5.austlii.edu.au/au/journals/AUFPPlatypus/2002/31.pdf

Another helpful article about the alliance formed between the Australian and Indonesian governments in the days following the Bali bombings can be found here:

Operation alliance – 70 years Indonesia-Australia https://
www.70yearsindonesiaaustralia.com/cooperation-between-
australia-and-indonesia/operation-alliance and on https://
en.wikipedia.org/wiki/History_of_terrorism

www.afr.com/politics/youve oct 17 2002

Other valuable AFP articles can be found on the following:
https://www.afp.gov.au/countering/terrorism/Australian/
Federal/police

https://www.afp.gov.au under the banner, *Lessons learned from
Bali,* the Australian Federal Police.

In order to create a picture of Concord's response to the
courage shown by the survivors, I came across a very illuminating
feature in the Nursing Review in December 2002 penned by
Concord Hospital's chief ICU nurse consultant, Glenda Glynn.
Entitled Bali Bombings – From the frontline of the ICU, this is a
well written and empathetic article written from the point of
view of the seasoned medical staff who found themselves dealing
with the sort of combat injuries that civilian doctors and nurses
had never seen before.

Glynn's feature gave me some insight into the way the staff
viewed the bravery of their patients.

In researching Australia's reaction to the terrorist attacks in
Bali, I have referred to John Howard's impassioned and powerful
speech to the Australian Parliament which he made two days after
the bombings. It is one of the best, most sincere political speeches
I have ever read and it can be found in the Prime Minister's
parliamentary transcript 12915. It not only offers tremendous
into the country's reaction to the terrorist attack on its own back
doorstep, but the outrage which the nation's leader shared with

his citizens. https://parlinfo.aph.gov.au/parlInfo/download/ media/pressrel/K7IH6/upload_binary/k7ih61.pdf;fileType=app lication%2Fpdf#search=%22media/pressrel/K7IH6%22

In the absence of medical reports that, twenty years later, Therese has struggled to access, I have relied on the expert medical overview of Director of the Alfred Hospital's Burns Unit, Heather Cleland who explained to me in general ley person's speak, the nature of the injuries that the Bali bomb survivors were battling.

I have also relied on some helpful reports from the Darwin Hospital and Concord's burns unit and have gleaned particularly useful information from interviews that the Director of Concord's Burns Unit – Dr Peter Haertsch, gave to Grant Holloway of CNN news in the days after the bombings. His interview can be found on: https://edition.cnn.com/2002/world/asiapcf/10/16/australia/bali/hospitals

Another very helpful article appeared in The Medical Journal of Australia in November 2003, under the title *The Bali Bombings: Civilian Aeromedical evacuation October 2003 authored by* Minh D Tran, Alan Garner, Ion Morrision, Peter Sharley, William M Griggs - see https://www.mja.com.au/journal/2003/179/7/bali-bombing-civilian-aeromedical-evacuation

Another insightful and comprehensive article on the Royal Darwin Hospital's impressive response to the mass casualties arriving in Australia after the bombings was penned by its own medical experts and is a fantastic overview of the efficient activation of their emergency crisis management plan: See: *The Royal Darwin Hospital* response by Didier P. Palmer, Dianne Stephens, Dale A Fisher, Brian Spain, David J Read and Len Notaras. https://pubmed.ncbi.nlm.nih.gov/1

In looking at the human face of the tragedy, I trawled through an inordinate number of survivor stories in both the national, international and local media. Some of the local coverage was amongst the best and covered the journeys of survivors like Carren Smith.

One particularly revealing story on Carren appeared on the tenth anniversary of the Bali bombings in the local leader newspaper. https://www.theleader.com.au/story/388802/courageous-fight-for-survival-after-bali-bombings/

I also found an excellent interview with Carren by the ABC's Richard Fidler. See

https://www.abc.net.au/radio/programs/conversations/bali-bombings-survivor-carren-smith-shares-her-poignant-story/

There was a wealth of information and coverage on footballer Jason McCartney who inspired an entire nation with his courage and has done a great deal of work in supporting the survivors of the Bali bombings, and the Alfred Hospital's burns unit where he is highly regarded.

See https://www.heraldsun.com.au/sport/afl/kangaroo-jason-mccartney-makes-remarkable-return-to-afl-after-surviving-bali-bombing/news-story/ and https://www.healthyman.com.au/jason-mccartneys-amazing-comeback-after-the-tragedy-of-the-bali-bombing/

Watching Jason McCartney's historic and inspirational comeback game again after all these years still brought tears to my eyes. See Channel Nine's coverage https://wwos.nine.com.au/afl/jason-mccartney-story-of-recovery-from-bali-bombings-afl-comback

And I found two particularly interesting media reports on survivor, Ben Tullipan's inspirational journey. https://tullipan.com.au/about/

https://www.illawarramercury.com.au/story/5990601/why-bomb-survivor-ben-didnt-care-he-would-lose-both-legs/

I have also relied on the extensive media coverage of the funerals of Bali bomb victims, Aaron and Justin Lee, and Justin's pregnant wife, Stacey, who lost their lives in the inferno at the Sari Club. The stories are heartbreaking and shed new light on the wider impact of the tragedy on the small community where the Lee's and Therese lived.

The Age 28th October 2002. *Brothers, a wife, and an unborn child mourned.*

The SMH October 28 2002. *Tributes Paid through the tears*

Mark Drummond in Kuta. *You've Really got to admit they are here in the morgue. October 17 2002*

In exploring the arrests of the terrorists and various trials I found the following information helpful.

ABC The World Today Bali bombing trial begins https://www.abc.net.au/worldtoday/cont/2003

AFP 6 October 2003 Al-Qaeda financed Bali' claims Hambali report' http://www.smh.com/au.articles/2003/10/06 the Sydney Morning Herald

ABC News 13th December 2020, Indonesia arrests militant linked to Bali Bombing (bomb maker arrest) https://www.abc.net.au/news/2020-12-13/indonesia-arrests-militant-linked-to-2002-bali-bombings/12978822

CNN.com/world. Al Qaeda admits Bali blasts on web 8th November, 2002 http://edition.cnn.com/2002/WORLD/asiapcf/southeast/11/07/bali.bombings.qaeda

The Guardian World News 22 November 2002 by John Aglionby in relation to the arrest of one of the Bali bombing masterminds was also very revealing. https:www.theguardian. com/world/2002/nov/22/Indonesia

The Sydney Morning Herald 9 November 2008 Bali bombers Executed by Tom Allard and Ben Doherty. https://www.smh. com.au/world/bali-bombers-executed-2008

The Sydney Morning Herald Smiling Assassin Interview a 'circus': police chief. 14 November 2002https://www.smh.com. au/national/familys-future-swept-away-2002

https://www.reuters.com/news/picture/indonesia-to-execute-bali-bombers-in-ear-idUSTRE49N1N720081024/6518399

April 29 2021. Suspected Bali Bomber finally goes on trial by Emma Connors and Natalia Santi https://www.afr.com/police/ foreign-affairs/suspected -bali-bomber-finally-goes-on-trial

The Guardian 30 April 2003 *First Bali bomb suspect charged.* Staff and agencies

Geelong Advertiser October 11 2017 Bali bombing 2002 survivor will remember those who died on 15 year anniversary. By Olivia Shyin

Bali Survivor's tell tale heart SMH 11th October 2012 by Rania Spooner

Another useful cutting came from the Sydney Morning Herald 16 June 2003 - *Bali survivors set to face Amrozi* -which describes the witness statements given by McCartney, Peter Hughes and Stuart Anstee in the trial of Amrozi in Denpasar.

Other useful features about the arrests and trials of the various suspects linked to the Bali bombings include Max Walden's story on ABC News 8 January 2021 *Indonesia is releasing alleged Bali bombing mastermind Abu Bakar Bashir.*

Also on ABC News 15 February 2022 Indonesian correspondent, Anne Barker reported on the deal to secure the vacant Sari Club land for a new peace park in memory of the survivors and victims. See *Deal brokered to secure land for Bali bombings peace park for $4.4million but uncertainty remains over funding.*

Another story which was valuable in helping me to understand the reaction of the survivors to the bid to overthrow the death sentence of Amrozi, Mukhlas and Sumarman, appeared in the Daily Telegraph on 3 October 2007. It covers an interview with a number of survivors and reports on their reaction. https://www.dailytelegraph.com.au/news/nsw/bali-survivors-hope-jail-stands/news-story/0d2e13075489493cb4320d509174fee0

Suspected Bali bomber finally goes on trial by Emma Connors and Natalia Santi august 29 2021. www.afr.com/policy/foreign-affairs/suspected-bali-bombeer-finally-goes-on-trial

ABC News 21 December 2021 Indonesian Prosecution Delay Sentencing Demand for top Bali bomb suspect Zulkarnaen see https://www.abc.net.au/news/2021-12-29/sentencing-delayed-for-bali-bombing-suspect-zulkarnaen/100730914

I also explored a wealth of material relating to the London Bombings, which Bronwyn's brother, Phil was caught up in. But the best coverage came from the BBC News which gives a comprehensive snapshot of what happened that day. See BBC News 8 January 2021 https://www.bbc.com/news/world-asia-55583154

418

ABOUT THE AUTHOR

Megan Norris is a journalist and award-winning author whose portfolio includes covering some of Australia's most infamous crimes. In 2017 Megan won the Davitt Award from Sisters in Crime Australia for best non-fiction.

Megan is a regular contributor to *Australian Women's Weekly* and has appeared on Foxtel's *Crimes That Shook Australia,* Channel Seven's *Sunday Night* and *Today Tonight* as well as Ten's *The Project.*

She is a regular guest on the podcast *True Crime Australia*, and has been featured on *The Stalking* podcast and the ABC's *Nightlife* show. Her true-crime stories have been syndicated world-wide.

Megan lives on the Gold Coast with her husband, Steve, their grandson, Nathan, and his dog, Larry.

For more great titles visit
www.bigskypublishing.com.au